Descending Like A Dove

Adventures in Decolonizing Evangelical Christianity

TOMMY AIREY

Kardia Kaiomenē
Ypsi, MI

For the tens of thousands of longtime, low-income Detroiters whose water has been shut-off by the city...

...and for all those who have joined them in the struggle for clean and affordable water.

CONTENTS

PREFACE

Flashback. I'm in the same suburban Southern California high school gym where, back in the early 90's, I played basketball for a team that went all the way to the state final four. This afternoon in early 2003 though, a large crowd of students and teachers gather for lunchtime entertainment. I'm debating my teaching colleague Dr. Jim Corbett. The topic: Should U.S. military forces invade Iraq?

A few days prior, students asked me if I would represent the "pro-war" side. They knew who I was: An Evangelical Christian with an athletic Republican swagger. I parroted Bush Administration talking points on Saddam Hussein and al Qaeda and "weapons of mass destruction." I lobbed in some Bible verses for good measure.

Fifteen years, trillions of dollars and hundreds of thousands of civilian deaths later, it is painfully clear that I was on the wrong side of the debate. This morning, as I stare out the window at freshly fallen snow, I struggle to recognize who that young man was back then. In the winter of 2002-03, I was on the verge of a total theological and political overhaul. I was just about to start connecting the dots in ways that would slowly, drastically change my life.

I am deeply grateful that this book project has demanded some serious life review. I had repressed so much of my pre-2003-Iraq-debate perspective. Possessed by a caffeinated eagerness to explore more critical and compassionate ways of being, I just moved on. I was deeply ashamed and embarrassed of my old ways. Cruising down Amnesia Boulevard was a lot easier than four-wheeling through the agony of re-examining late-stage-adolescent me in the mirror.

Fifty years ago today, Rev. Dr. Martin Luther King Jr. was murdered. He was thirty-nine. On the same date a year earlier, he preached a sermon called "A Time to Break Silence."

He called for an end to the brutal war in Vietnam which was hijacking precious resources from poor and oppressed people at home "like some demonic destructive suction tube." In stark contrast, my old pastors preached that world peace was unattainable until Jesus returned in glory. Outside of some basic charity, there was no use trying to make the world a better place. Besides, it might delay the Rapture.

Dr. King intimately connected Christian faith to the transformation of socio-economic and political structures. From his leadership in the bus boycott in Montgomery to standing in solidarity with sanitation workers in Memphis, King consistently operated out of a biblical worldview that he called "the interrelated structure of reality." Everything is held together in a web of mutuality. Everyone is a child of God and intimately related to each other. No matter what. And yet, so much of the American Dream is built on exploiting and displacing people over *there* so that the fortunate few can experience comfort right *here*. It would take some time for my suburban Evangelical mind to comprehend what Dr. King called "a radical revolution of values." My Damascus Road wasn't one big moment. It was a process years in the making.

I had been introduced to King's life and teaching in the mid-90's in Bill Tuttle's class at the University of Kansas. Way back then, I was attending Campus Crusade Bible study on Wednesdays, drinking a 12-pack of beer on Fridays and going to an all-white Evangelical church on Sundays. My spiritual life was a complete circus. And way back then, not surprisingly, I struggled to make the simple connection that Dr. King was a Christian and that his perspective on Jesus was completely different than what my white Evangelical mentors and heroes were pitching.

At some point though, in that blessed window of opportunity between 9/11 and Hurricane Katrina, as drones and status updates and subprime mortgages burst into our world, Rev. Dr. Martin Luther King Jr. started coming through loud and clear. I got the message. Slowly. It fermented through friends and books and students and travel. This miraculous process pounded my heart with the real, subversive love of Jesus—a life-affirming force that strategized around what King described as "understanding, creative, redemptive goodwill" for all. Meanwhile, as American armed forces invaded Muslim-majority countries, the economy grew, and gas prices fell.

The more the interrelated structure of reality colored my spiritual imagination, the more I became disenchanted with Evangelical Christianity. I eventually followed Jesus right out of the movement. As I studied the Gospels more intently, I discovered that Jesus never turned his back on how power operated behind the scenes. He didn't look the other way or remain silent. The love that worked through him was not just kind and interpersonal. It also involved truth-telling and structural analysis. He called out the hypocrisy of pastors and priests. He lamented that the big house of worship was a "den of thieves," built by extracting precious resources from the land and then defrauding poor workers.

It became clearer and clearer to me that King was the key to understanding Jesus in contemporary American society. A half-century after his assassination, millions of precious Black and Brown children of God, as King lamented in his last Christmas sermon, are still "perishing on a lonely island of poverty in the midst of a vast ocean of material prosperity."

If he ministered in America today, Jesus, too, would negate the nostalgic Nativity scenes on the way through *his* Christmas sermon. Born under a census, killed on a cross, Jesus' entire life was a time to break silence over the economic and social realities of empire. A hundred generations later, these realities remain with us, most of it justified theologically by white Evangelicals.

I am convinced that authentic Christianity is not a belief system or an ideology. It is a *consciousness*—critical, contemplative and compassionate. It soaks all the way through our minds, hearts and bodies, both personally and politically. It seeks "peace on earth," but never mistakes nonviolence for passivity or indifference or inaction. What King called "the revolutionary spirit" remains fully awake to the dehumanizing tendencies embedded in our lives.

Grace grants us the permission to confess our complicities, to come out of hiding, to courageously admit "me too." Love challenges us to let the voice of the voiceless speak to our own blindness, to respect the inherent value and dignity of everyone and everything, to compassionately proclaim "you too."

Currently, one-third of the nation's population strives to "Make America Great Again." Eighty-one percent of white Evangelicals voted themselves on to that island. These troubling trends ought to surprise no one. They unflinchingly follow the long historic script of old time American religion. For the rest of us, the challenge is to embody what is "great" as defined by Jesus: a ruthless commitment to humility, service and compassion. This is the kind of citizenry required to fulfill King's dream "to make America what it ought to be."

The mystery of Jesus' message is that when we cross borders and boundaries and bureaucracies to serve "the other," we discover that she is actually the one schooled in the secrets of heaven. We discover that she possesses massive doses of what King called "the key that unlocks the door which leads to ultimate reality." Love. All-embracing. Unconditional. There's only one thing left to do—drop the familiar and commit our time, energy and resources to finding her. And then follow. This downward mobility is the only way up. It really boils down to this: only she knows the way to peace on earth.

April 4, 2018
Ypsilanti, Michigan

Introduction

"I would like to take what I call a 'realistic position'..."
Martin Luther King Jr.
April 27, 1965, UCLA

1

A Long Way

In April of 1965, Rev. Dr. Martin Luther King Jr. galvanized a jam-packed quad of college students on the campus of UCLA. He was scripting his classic stump speech. Before the recently crowned Nobel Peace laureate summarized the philosophy of nonviolent resistance and detailed the challenges to racial injustice going forward, King kick-started the afternoon on a hopeful note, "We have come a long, long way in the struggle to make justice and freedom a reality in our nation." However, more than a dozen times during the speech, he countered with a clear-eyed cadence, "We still have a long, long way to go."

King animated what he called a "realistic position." He emphasized that it would take more than just a change of heart and charity for justice to become a reality in America. He knew well that both inner piety *and* better policy are required to relieve the pain and suffering of the masses. "It may be true the law cannot make a man love me," he proclaimed, "but it can restrain him from lynching me." King was beckoning young Baby Boomers to embrace a brand of faith and conscience that cultivated a "divine discontent" with evil in all its personal and political manifestations.[1]

On the cusp of the passage of voting rights legislation, Rev. Dr. Martin Luther King Jr. was in Los Angeles recruiting college students to join him in the Jim Crow South that summer to register Black men and women in 120 counties. He challenged the mostly white students to become "involved participants instead of detached spectators."

In attendance that day was a young UCLA student who, though inspired by King's message, chose to stay in Southern California for the summer. He was a good and kind man who cared deeply about doing *something* to end the oppression he was learning about. But like many good and kind people that summer, he stayed silent about what many dismissed as "political issues." King called them "the things that mattered most." That young man was my dad, Dennis Airey.

Fast forward to the mid-1980s, when the U.S. government officially made Martin Luther King Jr. Day a federal holiday while I was attending a private Christian elementary school in Orange County, California. After our daily prayer and Bible readings in class, my teacher (whom I loved) would rhythmically proclaim, "God said it. I believe it. And that settles it."

End of conversation.

I remember the rush of certainty and triumph that would flood my heart and mind when a popular male teacher would pass us in the hallways with his patented greeting: "Good morning, young Republicans." Fifteen years after Rev. Dr. Martin Luther King Jr. was crucified in America, Jesus Christ was Lord and Ronald Reagan was President.

For two decades, I claimed this uniquely American faith, devoted to an almighty GOD and His aggressive GOP— always male, always capitalized, always in control. I was all in—church, Bible study, worship music, Christian bumper stickers on my car and Jesus fish ring on my finger. I never missed my daily devotional quiet times and weekly men's accountability small group.

As I grew into adulthood, though, I started hearing other voices, most clearly that of King whose life and teaching had been beckoning me since my days as a History major at the University of Kansas. I was being called into a journey of transformation, guided down a long winding prophetic path out of my suburban Evangelical Christian comfort zone. I heard the beckoning of the old Hebrew prophet:

> And when you turn to the right or you turn to the left, you will hear a word behind you saying, 'This is the way, walk in it" (Isaiah 30:21).

I simply couldn't silence the whispers prodding me to something more, to stop clinging to comfort and convenience and to stand in solidarity with poor and marginalized people. There was a Spirit wooing me toward a lifestyle more congruent with the courageous sacrifice, self-donating love and humble service of the Jesus of the Gospels.

I also couldn't shake the clear-eyed assessment of the late Abraham Joshua Heschel who prophesied, "The whole future of America depends on the impact and influence of Dr. King."[2] Heschel was a popular Jewish rabbi and Bible scholar who marched with King in Selma and other stops along the way. His proclamation about King and the future of America shimmered deeply within me, a key to my own exodus out of the Evangelicalism of my youth and a big part of what this book is about.

*   *   *

I'm still a follower of Jesus. I may have flown the coop, but I'm still part of the zoo. A hundred generations into the Christian experiment, the good news is that Christianity is a *contested* concept. Today, there are more than twenty thousand Christian denominations offering differing versions of the Way. The fact that there is *not* one thing called Christianity allows me to breathe easy. There are only Christianities. Plural. This has always been the case. In every era, there is a dominant, powerful, mainstream brand of the faith and a handful of alternatives, either neglected or persecuted, under-resourced or underappreciated, barely surviving on the margins of society.[3]

To take up the challenge of following Jesus does not mean that I am on the same team as Christian leaders and communities with beliefs, ideas and practices that I find embarrassing, repugnant or unfathomable. The tradition is at its very best when the intramural competition is at its fiercest. Options offer opportunity and summon accountability.

Monopolies are bad for faith too.

Some of my fellow post-Evangelical friends have discovered other Christian routes that are *sacramental*, whether Catholic or Eastern Orthodox, or *denominational*, like Presbyterian, Episcopalian or Anglican. Others have *dropped out* of the tradition altogether, staking out atheist or agnostic options. There are also those who are most comfortable with being "none of the above," the fastest growing faith category in the United States today.[4]

Because I remain thoroughly compelled and inspired by the life and teachings of Jesus, I have been relieved to discover that there has *always* been a minority report committed to an inclusive, prophetic scripting of his way—an alternative to an establishment narrative that prioritizes personal piety and a guarantee of how to stay out of hell when you die. As King wrote,

> Only a 'dry as dust' religion prompts a minister to extol the glories of Heaven while ignoring the social conditions that cause men an earthly hell.[5]

This "prophetic strand"[6] of the Christian tradition has included communities, some well-known and others unheard of, who have consistently spoken truth to power, who have sworn off violence, who have pledged solidarity with the suffering and oppressed of society, who have cherished voices of the indigenous, women, queer folk and those of other races, ethnicities, religions and creeds.

This tradition includes imperfect and unpolished communities who, like the first followers of Jesus, "acknowledged themselves to be strangers and aliens on earth" (Hebrews 11:13). Many of these have had funny, unusual and unexpected names like the desert mothers and fathers, Franciscans, Benedictines, Waldensians, Anabaptists, Quakers, the Fellowship of Reconciliation, the Southern

Christian Leadership Conference, Maryknoll sisters, Catholic Workers, the Plowshares Movement, the Brown Ecclesial Network, Christian Peacemaker Teams, ReconciliAsian and Carnival de Resistance.

Who would have known that, on the day before Easter 1983, about the same time I was asking Jesus into my heart in suburban Southern California, a peace-mongering band of Christians was sneaking on to the Wurtsmith Air Force Base in Michigan to spray paint "Christ is Risen! Disarm!" at the foot of sixteen B-52s loaded with nuclear weapons? They handed out leaflets proclaiming hope in a conspiring divinity "hidden at the heart of things, breaking in to break out, on behalf of human life."[7]

This is just one manifestation of an alternative movement of Jesus followers that has won my heart over in recent years. Some dare to call it "radical," deriving from the Latin word for *roots*—digging deeper to both eradicate evil and harvest what is radiant. This is a faith that excavates the witness of John the Baptist, calling disciples to pick up "the axe laid at the root of the trees" (Matthew 3:10a). A call to clear the old overgrown brush in our souls and in the world around us. On a fad diet of wild honey and clothed in camel skin, the ancient prophet was blunt, "Every tree therefore that does not bear good fruit is cut down and thrown into the fire" (Matthew 3:10b).

Radical discipleship, though, goes beyond deconstructing. It is a prophetic and personal call to keep digging until a more authentic faith is discovered—one that grapples with the impact and influence of Dr. King. It is a faith that faces what he called "the giant triplets of evil:" *racism, militarism and materialism.*[8] In the American context, these are the key elements of what the Apostle Paul called "principalities and powers" (Romans 8:28; Colossians 2:13-15).[9]

More recently, writer and critical theorist bell hooks has fleshed out the "intersectionality"[10] of King's giant triplets as *imperialist white supremacist capitalist patriarchy.*[11] These often-unacknowledged forces weave below the surface—the subconscious roots of our pain and suffering. They reinforce each other to create new categories of suffering. Working together, they turn the nation-state into an idol, give white and male bodies supremacy and value profit over people.

I call this mainstream American mentality *the colonial script,* a web of de-humanizing cultural beliefs and assumptions that has been shaping Americans from the womb to the tomb for the past five hundred years. The colonial script not only justified the land-theft and near-genocide of the original inhabitants of "the Americas." It promoted it. Then, it orchestrated the kidnapping and enslavement of African peoples to serve every thirst and fantasy of those with European heritage.

However, this wasn't just "back then." It is "right now," too. Our minds and hearts continue to be colonized by destructive ideologies that teach us to dismiss certain humans and to commoditize everything non-human. It is the air we breathe, "common sense" and "normal behavior" to just about everyone.

I confess that the colonial script has become "second nature" to me. As an athletic straight white male, my social connections have always come easy. From early in life, I learned how to seek and find approval from those with power by performing to meet their expectations. Getting straight A's in this curriculum, though, has had dehumanizing consequences.

In her wonderful book *Emergent Strategy,* adrienne maree brown lists many of the "anti-nurturing" ways we've been socialized into:

> We learn to disrespect indigenous and direct ties to land.

We learn to be quiet, polite, indirect and submissive, not to disturb the status quo.

We learn to deny our longings and our skills, and to do work that occupies our hours without inspiring our greatness.

We learn to manipulate each other and sell things to each other, rather than learning to collaborate and evolve together.

We learn that the natural world is to be manicured, controlled or pillaged to support our consumerist lives.[12]

This speaks to the deep spiritual crisis I began to struggle through in my late twenties. In order to be free, I needed a *theo-sectionality*, a compelling life strategy that could engage with the forces that were weighing down my soul. In my ongoing process of becoming free, the colonial script must be unlearned so that I can more intimately know what it means to be fully human. What it means to get saved.

Many have deconstructed Evangelicalism. Few have decolonized it. My ongoing liberation and healing has required the hard and holy work of unwinding the white supremacy, capitalism, patriarchy and imperialism wrapped around my Evangelical mindset. As the Swiss psychiatrist Carl Jung once wrote, "Until you make the unconscious conscious, it will direct your life and you will call it fate." I am in the *process* of picking up the axe and digging up the roots. It is slow-going. The focus is on progress, not perfection.

Decolonization is not about calling out and pointing fingers. It is about taking the log out of my own eye so that I can start to see clearly (Matthew 7:1-5). It is an intentional process of reconstruction, one that moves beyond simply resisting what I have become jaded with. Decolonization is a way of life committed to recovering from the old colonial mindset built into most varieties of American Christianity for the past five hundred years.[13]

Spirituality, I have been slow to discover, is more than just bursting old wine skins. It is the challenging, ongoing task of finding new containers that can hold what is powerful, delicious, vibrant and intoxicating. If the colonial script is not replaced by another Way, then it stubbornly remains my default. No matter how much I deny it.

2

There Is Another Word

This book is written for an audience of readers and dialogue partners who have spent significant time in relationship with Evangelical Christianity and, at the very least, have had mixed emotions about it—and, at worst, have found it embarrassing, obnoxious, awkward, destructive and/or arrogant. It is for all those yearning for a spirituality that is compelling, accessible, sustainable, grace-giving, brutally honest, practical and transformative.

I'm not looking to convert anyone away from Evangelicalism, but instead to woo and beckon the already-jaded post-Evangelical masses who are stuck in foreclosure, with seemingly nowhere else to go with God and religion. I hope this speaks to those who find themselves spiritually homeless.

I do not write for those content with their commitments or certain they have all the right answers. The poet Mary Oliver has convinced me that this is a no-win situation:

Let me keep my distance, always, from those
who think they have the answers.

Introduction

> Let me keep company always with those who say
> "Look!" and laugh in astonishment, and bow their
> heads.[14]

This conversation is for those who refuse to give up their search for compelling answers, who desperately yearn for something more, but aren't quite sure where to find it. I hope the subject matter in the chapters ahead sparks the imaginations of those who long to live outside the box that stubbornly insists on the same old conservative and liberal options.

This book is part-memoir, part-manifesto. It is the story of my exodus out of Evangelical Christianity and my decade-plus wilderness journey discovering a different way of following Jesus. Most of this book focuses on what this alternative way looks like in real-time. Although I flavor it with current scholarship, research, data and experience, it is my hope that readers without formal theological training will be able to understand it, digest it and resonate with it.

More than anything, this work represents my humble quest to ransom a kidnapped tradition. I simply want to roll away the stone from the tomb of Christian language with meanings mired in assumptions and preconceived notions—faith, Bible, Christ, Lord, gospel, repentance, salvation, forgiveness, justification, heaven and hell, prayer, fellowship, church and plenty more.

These concepts have become triggering to many. One friend calls his Evangelical experience "spiritual mind rape." Another friend testified that his spiritual liberation finally arrived the day he realized that only his own self-loathing and fear were keeping him in the fold. Yet another friend confessed that he has PTSD from years of reading the New Testament letters of Paul in Evangelical Bible studies.

Many Black Americans over the past few centuries, in fact, have refused to read *anything* from the Apostle Paul.

They've held him in "righteous contempt."[15] I don't blame them. On Sundays, slave masters became pastors. They preached to the enslaved, quoting Paul freely and fiercely, "Slaves, obey your masters in all things" (Colossians 3:22). This scandal is just one example of the painful history of abusing Christian Scripture, interpreting it through what Bible scholar Walter Brueggemann calls "the zone of imagination," a lens skewed by powerful vested interests, deep fears, unresolved hurts, turning it into a voice over for family expectations, peer pressure, economic opportunity and social ideology.[16]

The Bible, like all sacred texts, contains powerful elements that have been manipulated to construct weapons of mass destruction to serve selfish agendas. Throughout American history, Black communities have been decimated by the atomic abuse of the Bible. Yet, astonishingly, over the past five centuries, many Black folks have chosen to stay in the Christian tradition.

The legendary theologian and civil rights leader Howard Thurman explained this seeming paradox by taking it to the roots of his own Black faith. The enslaved Christians, he wrote, "undertook the redemption of a religion that their master had profaned in [their] midst."[17] They didn't cast off Christianity. They composed it.

Frederick Douglass, who escaped from slavery, committed himself to the prophetic vocation of denouncing both slavery and the mainstream version of American Christianity that justified it. Douglass became a Christian as a teenager and, in the process, learned to differentiate his faith from "the corrupt, slaveholding, women-whipping, cradle-plundering, partial and hypocritical Christianity of this land." The difference between the Christianity of Douglass' brutal slave master and "the pure, peaceable, and impartial Christianity of Christ" was massive. So much so that, according to Douglass, "to receive the one as good, pure, and holy, is of necessity to reject the other as bad, corrupt, and wicked."[18]

Enslaved peoples worshipped the liberator God of Exodus who was fiercely committed to freeing the Israelites by any means necessary, but became known to them as merciful, gracious, slow to anger and "keeping Steadfast Love for a thousand generations" (that's Hebrew for "forever").[19] Thurman knew this redemptive slave religion intimately. He lost his father to pneumonia when he was seven and was trained up in the faith by his grandmother who grew up enslaved in Florida.

Contemporary Black theologian Kelly Brown-Douglas explains that when the earliest slaves listened to the reading of the Bible, they heard the voice of The Great High God—the free, sovereign divinity they knew well from their African heritage. This was the creator God who was far greater than humans and all "the lesser gods" in the universe (Isaiah 55:6-9; Psalm 82; 1 Kings 22:19-23). As it turns out, the thoughts and ways of the enslaver's god were identical to the thoughts and ways of the enslavers themselves![20]

In other words, the slaveholders spoke of *a lesser god*, created in their own image. The same could be said for much of what unfortunately passes as the voice of the divine today. Bible verses are quoted from memory to justify the giant triplets of evil. The thoughts and ways of the gods of the American mainstream are identical to the thoughts and ways of the colonial script! For centuries now, the Christian children of lesser gods have read the Bible through a zone of imagination that highlights men, whiteness, the profit motive and the myth of redemptive violence.

I am compelled by the historic Black church's courageous commitment to redeem the religion of the enslavers. To rescue the God of Steadfast Love. For five hundred years, this overlooked tradition has refused to throw out the Bible with the bath water.

I also concur with my friend Jennifer Henry, the executive director of KAIROS Canada, who was asked why she is still a Christian, "an ancient tradition full of contradictions."

She replied,

> I still believe that all the horror we experience—racism, genocide, torture, misogyny—is not the last word. There *is* another Word and it's our responsibility for that Word to find its voice in the world.[21]

This, Jennifer says, is what *resurrection* is all about for those who dare to reclaim the Way of Jesus. To rise up is to learn how to read the Bible by "looking in two directions at once"— scanning back to the original Roman colonial context and, at the same time, homing in on our own American colonial context. This de-colonial swiveling back-and-forth serves as *compost*, a surprising source for new growth and resurrected life.[22] The good news is that the divinity defined by Steadfast Love is committed to recycling everything.

*   *   *

Rev. Dr. Martin Luther King Jr.'s recruiting trip to UCLA in 1965 has become a historical landmark for my own spiritual journey. My dad was twenty-three at the time—eight years before I was born. Dad didn't follow King to the South that summer because he had to work to pay for grad school and his VW Bug. He also started dating my mom.

Like most white folks of his generation, my dad didn't march with King. When he first broke the news to me, I was disappointed. That was before I came to an understanding of the intergenerational nature of Reality. "The arc of the moral universe is long," King would often tell audiences, "but it bends toward justice."[23] Dad's life was a giant step in the right direction. His own father immigrated from England when he was eight and became a staunch supporter of George Wallace in adulthood.

A few months before King sat in a jail cell in

Birmingham, Wallace, the governor of Alabama, proclaimed in his inaugural Presidential campaign speech, "Segregation now, segregation tomorrow, segregation forever." A few months before King stood in front of the Lincoln Memorial to deliver his famous "I Have a Dream" speech, Wallace stood in front of the doors of the University of Alabama administration building to prevent Black students from entering.[24]

Dad's sisters have told me that old Grandpa Val used to come home from a long day at work, drink beer and watch football. He would constantly berate players and call them the N-word. I never heard my dad utter anything overtly racist. Ever. I have seared in my mind the day we were watching Jim Plunkett on TV together and Dad turned down the volume to offer up the Mexican-American NFL quarterback as his prime role model. Plunkett had humble roots, growing up in East San Jose, working jobs at gas stations, delivering newspapers, bagging groceries, and working in orchards to help pay the bills. Plunkett, for Dad, was a real athlete. He had class, dignity, kindness and work ethic. He was pretty impressive on the field too.

Long after death, our ancestors are still with us, and the challenge, according to psychotherapist Francis Weller, is to "live our lives as carriers of their unfinished stories."[25] Dad responded to Grandpa Val's open hostility and superiority toward people of color with a posture of learning, openness and the safety of silence. Even though he stayed home during the summer of '65, Dad pushed our story a little further along, opening up space for me to seek out a more transformative faith that both challenges and empowers.

Words from poet Rainer Maria Rilke resonate deeply as I press on in this intergenerational process of transformation:

> Sometimes a man stands up during supper
> and walks outdoors, and keeps on walking,
> because of a church that stands somewhere in the East.

And his children say blessings on him as if he were
dead.

And another man, who remains inside his own house,
stays there, inside the dishes and in the glasses,
so that his children have to go far out into the world
toward that same church, which he forgot.[26]

Dad's life was stable, consistent and routine. He worked hard
and coached our little league teams. He was kind and curious.
At his funeral, the pastor called him "an amazing, unassuming
man." Spot on. I am deeply grateful for the many ways he
impacted me. He lived in the same house ("inside the dishes
and the glasses") in the suburban Southern California town I
grew up in for the last 45 years of his life.

Dad was raised outside Seattle. He pole-vaulted south
to Oregon State and UCLA and then settled into south Orange
County, where I was born and where I grew into childhood,
adolescence and early adulthood. For eighteen years, I was a
teacher and coach at the large public high school that my wife
and I graduated from. Slowly but surely, though, we started
hearing a call beckoning us to leave for "a church that stands
somewhere in the East." In 2014, we moved to Detroit. The call
continues, prodding us "far out into the world."

Our eastward journey beckoned us to face into the long
process of being "redeemed from the empty way of life handed
down to you from your ancestors" (1 Peter 1:18). I know I am
actively participating in an unfinished, intergenerational story
of white men—from my Great-Grandpa Tom immigrating to
the States and settling on freshly-stolen indigenous land to
Grandpa Val's vilification of people of color to my dad's quiet
commitment to neutrality to my own hurrying and hobbling
toward solidarity with all those Jesus calls "the least of these."

King's words are truer than ever: "We have come a long
way in the struggle to make justice and freedom a reality in

this country, but we still have a long way to go." This long journey of redemption is marked by what Detroit-based community organizer Monica Lewis-Patrick describes as "having the courage to connect the dots and to tell the truth."

This, I believe, is what my reconversion to Jesus is in a nutshell. *Connect the dots.* Seeking to understand all the ways that work, relationships, finances and faith are built on oppressive social, economic and political realities. *Tell the truth.* Keeping it congruent with intentional practices of confession. In this spiritual journey, massive amounts of grace are required.

Connecting the dots and telling the truth is a hard, slow process. It is at the core of what Jesus meant when he told his disciples, all in the same breath, to deny themselves and "take up the cross" and follow him and to renounce all their possessions (Luke 14). There are real consequences to this path. It is the one I'm committed to pursuing in all its imperfection.

Descending Like A Dove is organized into ten main sections, but divided into forty-four smaller chapters to make the journey of descent more digestible. The book begins by narrating the *genesis* of my own relationship with Evangelicalism and my eventual *exodus* from its captivity (Sections I and II). I dedicate the remainder of the book to my discovery of people of faith and conscience rooted in compassion, inclusivity and truth-telling.

My unfinished journey of descent continues to challenge me to extend my spiritual vision to "the other side," far beyond family, friends and neighbors, all the way to the *margins* (Section III). It prods me continuously to take the imperial context seriously, connecting the death and "lordship" of Jesus and Paul's notion of "justification by faith" with a resistance of and recovery from the American *mainstream* (Section IV).

This lifestyle of descent is committed to a theology of *disobedience* from everything that is dehumanizing (Section V) and equates *faith* with being in solidarity with the oppressed and marginalized (Section VI).

Descending prods me to *listen*, first and foremost, to the voices of women of color (Section VII) and offers a litmus test of authentic discipleship—the will and skill to *speak* out against every manifestation of evil (Section VIII).

Descending commits to a disciplined spiritual practice in order to *stand* firm while so many drown in the fierce cultural currents caused by the colonial script (Section IX).

Descending *rises* above the oppression of the colonial script, tapping into the power and presence of those who have courageously gone before us (Section X).

Descending Like a Dove details my personal discovery of a deeply political faith. It also bears witness that every brand of Christian faith is undeniably political. Those who pledge neutrality, who refuse to rock the boat, are simply signing on to the status quo. Bad news for billions living on this planet.

3
The Way Forward

During the first year I started writing this book, falcons mysteriously appeared on three occasions. The first visitation came while Lindsay and I were living in California's Ojai Valley for a few months, just a short Emmaus road journey up the bike path from the headquarters of Bartimaeus Cooperative Ministries. Late one afternoon, we were power-walking back home after a hot, dusty run up Shelf Road to our favorite valley vista. A rather large lizard shimmied across the road in front of us. When we looked up, the predator-in-flight was heading right for us, ten feet away, preparing for landing. And lunch. The lizard, though, miraculously made it to safety under a jeep perfectly parallel parked to protect her.

A few months later on the Huron River in Michigan, the

falcon returned. He was making daily rounds, perching on the old, hovering cottonwood tree to wait for trout to tarry. The dive bomb was rather dramatic. A big splash, fully submerged. Then, he would flap his wings and elevate, zooming right past us to show off the newest trophy in his talons.

The final showdown was on the afternoon of All Saints Day. I was a stone's throw from downtown Detroit, savoring a runner's high while stretching in front of The Peace and Justice Hive at St. Peter's Episcopal Church. A dozen noisy mourning doves fluttered about, joining the chorus of city sounds. The object of their chaotic coos appeared on the light post above me. Like a drone, the falcon zeroed in on his target and struck a dove mid-flight, carrying her away behind the hulking church. I was stunned.

It is said that Spirit seconds the motions to get our attention. It took her three falcons to get mine. I couldn't call it a coincidence forever. Before this year, I'd never seen a falcon preying. It's probably more likely that I'd just never *noticed*. It is a small sign that I'm slowly becoming awake. Digesting the message of these birds has been a spiritual mini-series. I'm still in season one. Binge-watching is not an option. The Spirit releases episodes on her own time.

The falcon, possessing a vision two-and-a-half times more incisive than humans, is the mascot of the colonial script. These predators lurk everywhere. They see everything. They have immense power and will not stop until they get what they want. The falcon goes rogue. He is individual, manipulative, in control, at the zenith of a vast hierarchy of winners and losers. Perched atop his tower of Babel, the falcon symbolizes what Nigerian author Bayo Akomolafe graphically describes as the "phallic, male-dominated rejection of anything that is 'other.'"[27]

The falcons in my life have awakened me to daily bear witness to all that is predatory—seizing, stalking, selling, scapegoating, commercializing, corporatizing and commoditizing. Developers press for draconian water shutoffs and home foreclosures and then gobble up more real estate. Women and children are sexually objectified and targeted. Tow truck companies collude with local businesses and government and then charge hundreds for owners to recover their vehicles. Credit card companies jack up interest rates in the fine print. The list goes on and on and on and on.

American Christianity easily becomes falconized too. Professional religionists (priests, pastors, professors), mostly white and male, are anointed the experts on God and have the final say on all matters of what is Orthodox and who is officially saved. They preach a falcon God, perched and lurking on the edge of His throne. Omniscient. Omnipotent. Transcendent. Not of this world.

The dove, though, represents the way forward. She is the faithful, trustworthy sign of Noah, week after week, sent forth until she discovers dry land (Genesis 8). She seeks safety for all—from the rising floods that threaten to sweep everything away.

The dove, in Hebrew, is "Jonah," a prophet sent by the God of Steadfast Love to cry out against the wealthy and wicked imperial city of Ninevah, bulging with a population "who do not know their right hand from their left" (Jonah 4:11). It was truly a short-term mission trip—after just one day, the head falcon of Ninevah stepped down from his perch, stripped off his robe and repented in sackcloth and ashes (Jonah 3:6).

The dove was also the metaphor the Gospel writers utilized to describe Spirit, "descending like a dove" upon Jesus as the heavens are torn apart with ominous warnings of catastrophe ahead (Mark 1:9-10). Then, the dove led Jesus into the desert, alerting him to the economic, religious and political falconry that would tempt him along the way.

The mourning dove is one of the few birds that covenants herself to one partner for life. Doves commit to nurturing their young together, but also to doing whatever it takes to protecting and providing for every dove in the flock.

Every life truly matters. No matter what.

In Michigan, the Legislature passed a resolution to make the mourning dove the official bird of peace. It is binding—it is illegal to hunt them anywhere in the state. This borders on the miraculous since so much *is* legal in Michigan, including the right to openly carry a loaded handgun just about anywhere. This, too, is a sign for me.

Descending like a dove is taking on a posture of humility and empathy. Descent is patterned throughout the Gospels. Jesus' preferred title was not Rabbi or Son of God or Master. It was "son of man" (eighty-one times in the Gospels), echoing the prophet Daniel's vision of a coming leader who would champion all those suffering the predatory throne of "a fourth beast, terrifying and dreadful and exceedingly strong" (Daniel 7:7). "Son of man" in the original Hebrew was *kibor enash*, a "vulnerable one" who would secure justice through the paradox of a woundable and defenseless life.[28]

Descending like a dove is a commitment to mourning and then resisting the predatory powers that stalk us. It is a covenant to community, to cooing out the violent and unjust and oppressive policies that are paid for by those filled with an unquenchable thirst for profit and power.

The dove is also a symbol of the short lives of Jesus and King, who were both murdered by the predatory surveillance and strategizing of powerful elites who were threatened by their prophetic messages. Mourning doves are the blessed ones, merciful and meek, pure in heart and thirsting for justice (Matthew 5:1-8). They are abundant and widespread—for those with eyes to see (Matthew 13:16).

My heroes are the mourning doves Jesus called "the least of these" (Matthew 25:31-46). This book contains stories of many doves who have flown into my life, including queer and questioning friends, immigrants (undocumented and otherwise), the unemployed and unhoused, a down syndrome teenager, survivors of rape and abuse, those courageously naming and battling mental illness and addiction, indigenous leaders and, especially, women of color. My intent is not to glamorize, exoticize, fetishize or tokenize. I'm not trying to prove that I've got friends in low places. I'm simply committed to listening and following their lead.

I hope this book charts a practical path forward, toward a spiritual life of connecting the dots and telling the truth. It contains some jottings from my own ongoing journey out of the mainstream and into the margins. It's not a GPS. Every spiritual road trip is different. The divine specializes in diversity.

No matter what, though, our souls long for a promised land, a place to pitch our tents, the final destination of all our wanderings, a space to start shoveling deeper, tapping into what fuels and fulfills. May this book be a prayer that grants you strength, courage and boldness to join up with the masses moving out of the mainstream. Thankfully, these mourning doves are descending just about everywhere.

I.
Genesis

"Even religion and the Bible were used to justify slavery and crystallize the patterns of the status quo."
Martin Luther King Jr.
April 27, 1965, UCLA

4

Putting the Fun Back into Fundamentalism

"It's not a religion. It's a relationship." This was the quick rebuttal that I learned early on to combat anyone questioning my Evangelical faith. A *religion* was equated with ritual, working one's way to heaven, just another competing claim to absolute truth. A real, thriving personal *relationship* with Jesus, on the other hand, required nothing but a heart commitment from those "justified by faith." This could never be questioned.

Especially when I was singing, eyes closed and hands raised, with hundreds (or thousands) of my fellow "believers:"

> *You came from heaven to earth*
> *To show the way.*
> *From the earth to the cross*
> *My debt to pay.*
> *From the cross to the grave,*
> *From the grave to the sky,*
> *Lord I lift Your name on high.*[29]

Since that day, at age ten, when I invited Jesus into my heart to be my personal Lord and Savior, I was assured that I was "not of this world" (John 18:36). It didn't matter how bad things got, in my own life or the lives of others around me, or even those half way across the globe in Africa—someday soon, Jesus *would* return in full force. I would be rescued by the Rapture.

I was taught to love the sinner and hate the sin and to pray for them to get saved too. The world was lost and broken. We white Evangelicals served the poor and marginalized because we were called to love them, but more importantly, it gave us the opportunity to "share the gospel with them." This meant that we would tell them the good news about Jesus dying on the cross for their sins so that they could go to heaven when they died. Or get raptured when he returned. I wanted to make sure none of my friends got left behind.

Early on, I learned "The Romans Road," a series of Bible verses from Paul's letter to the Romans that simplified the path to Jesus and eternal salvation. I still have them memorized:

1. For all have sinned and fallen short of the glory of God (Romans 3:23).
2. But God demonstrates his love for us in that while we were still sinners Christ died for us (Romans 5:8).
3. For the wages of sin is death, but the gift of God is eternal life through Jesus Christ our Lord (Romans 6:23).
4. If you confess with your mouth that "Jesus is Lord" and believe in your heart that God raised him from the dead, you will be saved (Romans 10:9).

I was taught to pray for my unsaved friends and then, when the opportunity arose, I would "share Christ" with them by quoting these passages in formulaic succession. Four easy steps to salvation. If they didn't respond affirmatively, then they had a hard heart and there wasn't much I could do about it. Except pray more.

No doubt about it: *I was a sinner.* And so was everyone else. Only Jesus' death could save us. The blood of Jesus' sacrifice covered the sins of those who sincerely asked God for forgiveness. You had to mean it though, and it became obvious whether you did (or not) by how you lived your life. The passion of this message thrived on a methodical mixture of rock music and personal piety. We poured our hearts out to God:

Through the power of Your blood
Through the wonder of Your love
Through faith in You

I know that I can be
White as snow.[30]

Academic theologians call this "penal-substitutionary atonement." It is the old belief that Jesus' death was and is the only way to erase the stain of sin and to bridge the chasm that "the sinful nature" creates between every human and the righteous God. This was why Jesus had to die.

During my high school and college basketball career, my goal was to play for an "Audience of One." Jesus. Despite setting three-point records and winning championships, I was there to make God famous, not me. I embraced the duty to "be Christ" for everyone in the gym and to guard against doing anything that might hurt my witness. I wrote "Phil 4:13" on my basketball shoes: "I can do all things through Christ who strengthens me." I revered athletes on TV who openly shared their testimonies. In my Evangelical imagination, though, no one was greater than A.C. Green, the thirty-something Los Angeles Lakers power forward who was still a virgin. Abstinence was everything.

In college, I attended a "Man Makers" conference hosted by Campus Crusade for Christ. It was a refresher course on what I had already heard over and over since puberty. Men are the spiritual leaders in dating and marriage relationships and, at all costs, masturbation must be suppressed. After all, Jesus taught his disciples, "If your right hand causes you to sin, cut it off" (Matthew 5:30). The author of Hebrews pounded it even more into our consciences, "In your struggle against sin you have not yet resisted to the point of shedding your blood" (Hebrews 12:4).

Meanwhile, the young women were at their own gathering, learning the hard truth that tight shirts and short shorts were causing their brothers to stumble. This was a few years before the organization True Love Waits was introducing purity rings to teen girls and Promise Keepers was beckoning fathers and sons to fill stadiums.

Ultimately, a masculine God was in control and everything happened for a reason. During my morning quiet times, I would pray, "Lord, just help me submit myself to your will." Inevitably, He would place people on my heart. If they were "believers," I would find time to ask them about their "walk." By this, I meant, their "walk with Jesus." After all, it was easy to get caught up in the affairs of the world. But, no matter how far off the path we were walking, Sunday and midweek services were there to remind us of the power and the undefeated record of the God we invoked. Always victorious. Over and over and over, we rhythmically belted out the classic Rich Mullins worship song:

> *Our God is an awesome God*
> *He reigns from heaven above*
> *With wisdom, power, and love*
> *Our God is an awesome God.*[31]

Despite this, I sensed that the world was a scary, spiritual battlefield. Sin was real and temptations were everywhere. Halloween captured my heart for a reason: it was a non-Christian holiday with roots in devil worship. That said, it was important to keep "Christ" in Christmas. I was horrified when friends or family members referred to it as "Xmas."

Meanwhile, an entire Evangelical book and music industry emerged as the cornerstone of a subculture, equipping us with robust resources to defend the faith:

> Always be ready to make a defense to anyone who demands from you an account of the hope that is in you. (1 Peter 3:15b)

I was riveted by works like Josh McDowell's *Evidence That Demands a Verdict* and Lee Strobel's *The Case For Christ* that claimed to prove the inerrant truth of the Bible. My passion was fueled by John Piper's *Desiring God* and *Don't Waste Your Life*. Robert Coleman's classic *The Master Plan of Evangelism* and Rebecca Pippert's *Out of the Salt Shaker and Into The World* blessed me with a robust strategy for saving my non-Christian friends. C.S. Lewis was required reading, infusing intellectual credibility into Evangelical passion.

In my late twenties, when I started volunteering for the high school ministry at Saddleback Church, the second largest congregation in North America, there were two signs on either side of the stage. One said, "God's Way." The other: "The World's Way." Everything was either sacred or secular. Saddleback's immaculate campus combines the look and feel of a university and an amusement park. It's 72-acre campus has a worship center that seats thousands, magnificent classrooms, a coffee house and food court, water fountains and a youth center with a gymnasium and outdoor sand volleyball courts. Saddleback sparked an epidemic of mega-church plants all over Orange County, one of the wealthiest and whitest regions in the United States (at 2.1 percent, the OC is the only top 25 metropolitan area in the U.S. with an African-American population of less than 5 percent).[32]

Meanwhile, I was one of the few "Christian teachers on campus" at the large public high school where I worked. I was the faculty advisor for The Fellowship of Christian Athletes (FCA) club. I hosted Bible studies in my room at lunch. I met with students for prayer early in the morning at "See You At The Pole" rallies. This was the most important thing in the world for me. Sure, I was a government and economics teacher and basketball coach, but these roles were simply vehicles for "ministry" and "evangelism." It was all about getting opportunities to get young people saved for eternity. At FCA meetings, our strategy was pizza, games, skits and testimonies from popular students. I always made myself available to meet up with students during lunch and after school.

During the summers, I coached a Christian basketball team of high school and college all-stars that traveled through Western Europe. We conducted week-long clinics and played against club and pro teams at night. During halftimes, while our opponents went to the locker room, we sang worship songs to the crowd, and one of the players would share a testimony about how his personal relationship with Jesus changed everything. We passed out programs that explained our mission. Then we signed autographs. These short-term mission trips were highly relational, gifting me with some of my deepest and most meaningful friendships.

This brand of Evangelicalism was putting the "fun" back in fundamentalism. It, most certainly, was *not* my grandparents' Midwestern, early 20th century, Church of the Nazarene fire-and-brimstone faith. We distanced ourselves from Jerry Falwell calling out the purple Teletubby for "modeling the gay lifestyle" and Pat Robertson's daily dose of the 700 Club cringe-worthiness. Just a few weeks after I graduated from high school, Robertson made an announcement on his show that feminism "encourages women to leave their husbands, kill their children, practice witchcraft, destroy capitalism and become lesbians."[33]

This style, I thought, was harsh and unloving. But I agreed wholeheartedly with the *substance* of Robertson's rants. Nevertheless, I preferred Rick Warren who would humorously proclaim, "I'm not right wing or left wing. I'm for the whole bird." He shimmered a quick-witted, warm glow that masked the inner judgments that had everybody who didn't accept Christ going to hell. Pastor Rick would adamantly claim political neutrality, and, in the next breath, speak out against legalized abortion and same-sex marriage. In the Evangelical imagination, "below the belt" issues are not political, but about piety. They are moral and biblical.

While I was caught up in these *below the belt* issues, a gigantic wedge was driven to shelter me from *below the poverty line* convictions, like ending unemployment or denouncing war or combating racism. Somewhere along the line, I came to believe that environmentalists were "lost" too. While they were expending all their energy saving whales, millions of unborn babies were being murdered. The Evangelicals taught me to cherry-pick a "pro-life" worldview, focusing on fetuses and newborn orphans while forsaking tragic deaths from the Middle East to the middle of the American ghetto, barrio and reservation.

Just after 9/11, I planted a church with a few fellow twenty-somethings in Southern California. These guys were sincere, creative, service-oriented and fun. It was a daughter church of Saddleback, thriving on young energy and image-consciousness. The lead pastor and worship leader got the memo on the latest styles (while Pastor Rick stuck with his short-sleeve Tommy Bahamas button downs and khakis). We didn't have altar calls, nor did we pass the offering basket.

These younger Evangelical leaders opened up heart space to take my spiritual journey to another level. The theological lens was simple: everyone is a sacred child of God. It was an even kinder, gentler Evangelicalism, a "soft" fundamentalism[34] committed to fulfilling felt needs while keeping the hardline theology unspoken. The shorter, smaller Sunday services fed off humor, warmth and a yearned-for intimacy for Gen Xers and Millennials who grew up in the megachurch.

My first decade of Presidential voting went George H. Bush, Bob Dole, George W. Bush. In 2000, I stayed up until 2 a.m. watching the ping-pong election returns coming in from Florida. I prayed for a victory. It paid off. I was relieved to finally get a win and was certain that hanging chads were God's Will. There was no doubt in my mind that W's faith-based initiatives would restore religious liberty and shed the country of its sinful, big-government liberalism.

More than anything, the pull of Evangelicalism

intensified in my early adult years as conservative Christian churches grew exponentially in the mostly white middle-class suburbs all over the U.S. There was strength in numbers. Besides, how could all these good people be wrong? It was more than just me and my personal prayer and Bible study. It was a movement of millions.

5
Sagging My Soul

The word "Evangelical" itself comes from the Greek word *euangelion*, translated roughly as "gospel" or "good news." The Evangelical message is focused on a *dualism* that erases complexity and paints everything black and white—God and sin, heaven and hell, saved and damned, believer and non-believer, the Bible and everything else there is. More than a century ago, many Evangelicals left *denominations* to the liberals and *dogmatics* to the hard-core fundamentalists. Instead, they placed their focus on convincing the world to do one simple thing—make a *decision* for Jesus that guarantees eternal salvation.

In 1989, the British historian David Bebbington wrote the book on what an "Evangelical" looks like.[35] He homed in on the four pillars of this uniquely American faith:

Activist Evangelism:
The conversion of "non-believers" is central.

Biblical Authority:
God's perfect Word is "inerrant" or "infallible."

Cross of Jesus:
Sin is erased, ensuring that believers will go to heaven.

Decision:
A prayerful conversion experience is a prerequisite.

Evangelical Christianity thrives in the suburbs and crowds the halls of corporations, college campus crusades, country music concerts, the military and national and state legislatures. I like to describe this movement with five simple concepts starting with P.

It is *powerful* and well resourced.
It is about *passion* for God and Absolute Truth.
It infuses a sense of *purpose* into the lives of adherents.
It is a list of *proper beliefs* about God and the world.
It is about a *personal relationship* with Jesus.

When it comes to politics, though, a vast majority of white Evangelicals support the status quo by claiming neutrality. They became foot soldiers in the massive white backlash to Civil Rights gains of the late 1960s. An entire private Christian school wildfire was sparked that spiritualized "school choice" into a new form of segregation. Evangelical politics swelled into a Moral Majority movement that emphasized "traditional" sexual norms and "law and order" crackdowns against addiction and immigration. These red-flag conditions crested as eighty-one percent of white Evangelicals cast their vote for Donald Trump in 2016.

Evangelical Christians pour time, energy and financial resources into philanthropy. They fight against sex trafficking, world hunger and the invisible children of Uganda. These efforts are sincere and deeply connected to Jesus' emphasis on neighborly love. Yet, only a very small percentage of Evangelical leaders will openly condemn war and economic policies that devastate poor and working people. In the Evangelical imagination, "social justice" is about addressing *symptoms* instead of transforming *systems*.

Arguably, the most popular American Christian in the past one hundred years has been Billy Graham. He is the enduring face of Evangelicalism. He captures the Evangelical perspective in concise fashion:

My one purpose in life is to help people find a personal relationship with God, which, I believe, comes through knowing Christ.[36]

According to American church historian George Marsden, Graham was a "purebred fundamentalist" until he became a national celebrity in the 1950s. He was part of a movement of "new evangelicals" who tempered their militant opposition to liberal theology and secular culture.[37] His popularity grew out of his charismatic personality and he translated this into a connection with the highest form of social and political power in the United States.

Graham was a falcon preaching from his perch high and mighty. His version of the gospel, communicated at well-attended "crusades," focused on a personal decision for Christ that transcended the ugly socio-economic and political realities of the world.

Graham became known as "the Preacher to the Presidents," especially Republicans. Texas oilman Sid Richardson introduced him to Dwight Eisenhower in 1952. Ike was baptized as a Presbyterian after "consulting" with Graham. "I don't think the American people are going to follow anybody," he purportedly said, "who's not a member of a church." Graham held Sunday services in the Nixon White House and advised him on how to campaign in the Evangelical community. Graham even wrote at least one speech for "Tricky Dick."

Nevertheless, throughout his life, Graham maintained the "pietist" position that churches and religious leaders should stay out of politics and strictly focus on "spiritual matters."[38]

For Graham, our only real hope is in Christ's return and admission into heaven when we die. His response to King's 1963 "I Have A Dream Speech" was telling:

> Only when Christ comes again will the little white children of Alabama walk hand in hand with little black children.[39]

The outward pietism and inward militarism of Graham is the nearly universal standard for those trained up in the American Evangelicalism of the past fifty years. It unveils a fundamental incongruity that covers up a distrust of "the other" (whether non-believer, immigrant, queer or liberal) with a smile. It goes a long way to explain its massive attraction for millions of white suburbanites seeking a holy container for middle class values. It is a non-confrontational, glass-is-half-full brand of faith. Evangelicalism brims with passion, warmth, generosity and a deep desire to change the world for the better—one heart at a time. It cherishes introspection, discipline and hard work. It also draws a hard line between right and wrong, sinner and saint, saved and damned, family values and a loose liberal lifestyle.

*   *   *

I am deeply grateful for the Evangelical ethos that energized me throughout my adolescence and early adulthood. It instilled in me spiritual disciplines like Bible-reading and prayer. Thriving on a theology of grace, love and forgiveness, it introduced me to a dynamic, intimate God who created everything, but still knows me more than I'll ever know myself.

Evangelicalism gifted me with older men (teachers, pastors, coaches and members of the church) who provided mentorship and modeled what an intentional, sincere, service-oriented, kind-hearted life resembles in real time. I was inducted into a style of organizing that exuded sincerity and kindness, radiating in the absolute truth of Young Life's missional reminder, "They'll never care how much you know until they know how much you care." I swore an oath of loyalty to this and I'm deeply grateful for it.

On its best days, Evangelicalism transcends the materialism, narcissism and apathy of the American suburban culture I grew up in. It gifted me with compelling alternatives that openly valued humility and sacrifice. Consider Kanakuk. The motto of the summer camp in Missouri that I worked at for two summers in my twenties is "I'm Third" (as in God first, others second, I'm third). This philosophy confronted my selfishness and greed with self-donating love and service.

In a complex and chaotic world, I was offered a simple relationship that would change everything, perfectly articulated by my role model, A.C. Green, proud virgin and power forward of the World Champion Los Angeles Lakers, "Jesus Christ became my best friend, my Lord, my Coach with a capital 'C.'"[40]

Nevertheless, despite the nurturing aspects of this Christian subculture, something began to percolate within me, a sense of uneasiness and incongruity that I simply couldn't shake. More and more, I was second-guessing the pietist position. I was beginning to realize that it was an awfully convenient perspective for middle-class Christians, shielded from the most brutal collateral damage of the colonial script— poverty, violence, decrepit schools, substandard housing, unemployment, the inaccessibility of nutritious food and clean water.

Plain and simple: the mourning doves were getting slaughtered by the colonial script, and the church was painfully silent about it all. First, this jadedness nagged at me during my daily quiet times, holding the Bible in one hand and the newspaper in the other. Then, it started sagging my soul, a spiritual weight that stayed with me throughout my days. It was dragging me down. Something had to change.

II.

Exodus

"We've broken loose from the Egypt of slavery.
We have moved through the wilderness of legal segregation.
We stand on the border of the promised land of integration."
Martin Luther King Jr.
April 27, 1965, UCLA

6

Redemption

While Billy Graham was preaching revivals to sold-out stadiums, Martin Luther King Jr. was hitting the streets in the poorest neighborhoods of America. In early 1965, a few months before he preached to my dad and thousands of other students at UCLA, King joined efforts in Selma, where protests and marches were met with harassment from Nazi thugs and beatings from Sheriff Jim Clark and his officers.

Leaders of the civil rights movement knew that Dr. King would need to go to jail again in order to get media attention. Things started to heat up on February 1 when more than a thousand demonstrators were arrested, including King. As usual, he spent his time in the cell fasting, praying, meditating, singing and exercising.

The next day, more than five hundred teenagers marched and got arrested. A few days later, these same teens posted up outside of the hospital to pray for the speedy recovery of Sheriff Clark who checked himself in for exhaustion.[41] Jesus' clear challenge to embrace nonviolence and enemy love were requirements for those who signed up for a movement committed to "saving the soul of America," the motto of the Southern Christian Leadership Conference that King led in the 1950s and 60s. This soul salvation, though, had everything to do with both a personal and political liberation from the giant triplets of evil: racism, militarism and materialism.

King was in the trenches, spiritually and emotionally pelted by the onslaught of death threats he was receiving. He was exhausted and scared, but it was his hope, somehow and someway, that the likelihood of his oncoming death would have the value of saving his white brothers and sisters in a very real spiritual sense. At the beginning of a massive march in Detroit during the summer of 1963, he proclaimed,

> If physical death is the price I must pay to free my
> white brothers and sisters from the permanent death of
> the spirit, then nothing could be more redemptive.[42]

A few months after prophesying his martyrdom, King preached at the funeral of the four little girls who died in a Birmingham church bombed by KKK terrorists. He agonized and theologized over their deaths too:

> God still has a way of wringing good out of evil. And
> history has proven over and over again that unmerited
> suffering is redemptive. The innocent blood of these
> little girls may well serve as a redemptive force that will
> bring new light to this dark city.[43]

A year later, King was more certain than ever that he would die soon. He confessed to his wife and aide after a plane they boarded received a bomb threat:

> I've told you all that I do not expect to survive this
> revolution; this society's too sick.[44]

More and more, he talked openly of being coffin-ready, of putting on his cemetery clothes every day.[45] As he continued to courageously confront the colonial script, he expected to be slain by the powers. Just like Jesus.

*   *   *

Coming to grips with the massive contrast between the ways Graham and King narrated and lived out their Christian faith was a tipping point for my own spiritual rearrangement. Although both "Christian," their realities on the ground were paved by completely different paths. King's raw and robust

animation of redemption was groundbreaking, calling me back
to the beginning of Paul's letter to the church in Colossae:

> God has rescued us from the dominion of darkness and
> transferred us into the kingdom of his beloved Son, in
> whom we have redemption, the forgiveness of sins
> (Colossians 1:13-14).

During my two-decades tenure in Evangelicalism, I read these
words from Paul as a concise summary of "the gospel message."
It was about how, through the death of Jesus, God saved me
from my sins (redemption, forgiveness), a guarantee that, when
I died, I would be rescued from hell (the dominion of darkness)
and then go to heaven for eternity (the kingdom of the beloved
son).

It wasn't until I was in seminary that I learned that
Paul was echoing Exodus language, the ultimate liberation
event in Jewish history. He was inviting non-Jews into this old
journey out of the dominion of darkness (Egypt) into the
kingdom of the beloved son (the Promised Land). At the same
time, he challenged fellow Jews to reanimate it around the life,
death and teachings of Jesus, who broke ranks with the
powerful religious establishment of his day and, after forty
days of fasting in the wilderness, reframed Moses' teaching in
his Sermon on the Mount.

Three decades later, Paul was calling residents of the
Roman Empire to break free from their imperial shackles and
experience redemption and forgiveness, economic concepts
meaning "buying back" and "releasing"—the opposite of "selling
out" and being "obligated." It represented the ultimate
liberation from all that is dehumanizing.

King utilized this old story of Exodus as a lens through
which to understand the historic Black American experience. It
was not enough to just "break loose from the Egypt of slavery"[46]
and then wander in the wilderness of legalized segregation.

King was constantly casting the dream of a future promised land of equality and freedom from oppression. Getting saved, for King, was never about being rescued from hell when we die, but rescuing those who are catching hell right now.

Over and over again, from jail cells to university campuses to suburban high school gymnasiums, King prophetically prodded white America to join a movement that could save them from the captivity of the colonial script, and start working for a promised land where "the milk of prosperity and the honey of equality" flowed for all.[47] Only then could America really be "great."

This exodus motif is precisely where my own journey through Evangelicalism and out the other side intersects with the gospel of King Jesus and the dream of Dr. King. In my story, Egypt was the colonial script dictating my consciousness and built into the social, political and economic structures that order and oppress our world. I was indoctrinated into an Evangelicalism that kept me in the dark about King's giant triplets of evil, the principalities and powers that continue to impoverish billions of mostly darker skinned people all over the globe. Eventually, I came to the realization that I needed a conversion of the imagination, a redemption from the conventional wisdom that shaped my heart and mind.

7

Evangelexit

When I first started grappling with my own captivity to the colonial script, I was still actively participating in the Evangelicalism of my upbringing and young adulthood. I was attending a church in Southern California with weekend attendance in the tens of thousands. The pastor prayed at Obama's Inauguration. But dread was percolating inside of me as I took inventory of what was happening all around me.

The more I researched and experienced the deeper, more complex realities of life in the world, the more I found myself mired in what psychologists call *cognitive dissonance*, the deep discomfort experienced by an individual holding two or more contradictory beliefs, ideas or values at the same time. It was like I had different shelves in my head and heart to quarantine my personal relationship with Jesus from everything else.

When Jesus met his soon-to-be-disciple Nathaniel, he turned to his friends and proclaimed, "Here is a true child of Israel. There is no duplicity in him!" (John 1:47). Duplicity was splitting my soul in half! I was a desperately seeking child of suburbia. I yearned for what Parker Palmer calls "a hidden wholeness."[48] I sensed a need to get free—to decolonize my spirit—but I didn't have words for it yet.

As I gained more experience teaching in my surprisingly diverse suburban classroom, my ingrained conservative platform began to be humanized. Immigration, addiction and sexual orientation, it turns out, are real people. I traveled to Kenya three weeks before 9/11 and went to Kibera, the largest slum on the continent. I spent one full afternoon walking around like a zombie, baffled by this devastating existence. My Evangelical mind agonized, "Were these precious children of God saved for eternity?"

There were all sorts of factors within Evangelicalism that were leaving me wanting, best summarized by professor of church history Mark Noll, "The scandal of the Evangelical mind is that there is not much of an Evangelical mind."[49] The error-free-and-self-evident Bible, hell as an afterlife destination for "unbelievers," all the repressing and obsessing over sexuality (including the condemnation of queer folk) and the all-powerful, all-male, everything-is-under-control falcon God on his perch: these formed the four walls that eventually became a prison cell for me.

About a decade ago, I finally made my Evangelexit.

Some might say that I evacuated Evangelicalism before I got excommunicated from it. But here's the thing: I had to leave, but I simply could not leave Jesus behind. I was not seeking a choose-your-own-adventure "relativistic" Christianity. My newfound, liberating spirituality is part of a humble-yet-determined attempt to reclaim what it means to follow Jesus in the lively tradition of Christian trailblazers who have lived and spoken in compelling ways about what it means to be human. Part of the good news, it turns out, is that Evangelicalism does not have a monopoly on Christianity.

My exodus and journey through the wilderness was sparked by friends like Dale, a pastor in Colorado who was FedExing me books by authors like Brian McLaren, Rob Bell, Shane Claiborne and N.T. Wright who, in compelling ways, were coloring Evangelicalism outside the lines. I found myself sitting on the beach for hours, pouring over biblical commentaries and Howard Thurman's classic *Jesus and the Disinherited* (1949). Thurman wrote this book while he was pastoring the nation's first interracial church in San Francisco, a few years after he traveled to India to meet with Gandhi.

Meanwhile, the Evangelical-laden Presidential administration that I voted for invaded Iraq under false pretenses. Secret war memos were uncovered. Defense Secretary Donald Rumsfeld applied Bible verses to depict the U.S. military as the faithful fighters of justice: 'Whom shall I send and who will go for us? Here I am Lord, send me "(Isaiah 6:8). On Sundays, I was singing to Jesus, "You are the Prince of Peace and I live my life for you." The rest of the week, politicians were prostituting the Prince of Peace to justify their war games and torture. Then, Charles, the valedictorian at our high school graduation, started emailing me links prodding me to deepen my race, class and gender analysis. The stars were aligning.

Lindsay and I got married in early 2005, and, for our honeymoon, we attended seminary together. While cruising

through my teaching career by day and attending theology and
Bible classes by night, James Cone's *A Black Theology of
Liberation* (1970) dropped a bomb on my white Evangelical
privilege:

> Persons who live in the real world have to encounter the
> concreteness of suffering without suburbs as places of
> retreat. To be oppressed is to encounter the
> overwhelming presence of human evil without any place
> to escape.[50]

Cone and a handful of other scholars were blowing my mind
and expanding my heart at the same time. I had a deep sense
that the same Spirit that raised Jesus from the dead was
giving new life to my mortal body (Romans 8:11).

Fortunately, at this Evangelical seminary, we got a full
buffet of Anabaptists, mystics and liberation theologians. In
the midst of this spiritual and theological makeover, I
happened upon Ched Myers' *Binding the Strong Man: A
Political Reading of Mark's Story of Jesus*. It opened the
floodgates. It was also the nail in my coffin labeled
"respectable." It had major implications. Myers named the
"radical discipleship" movement and its call to repent from and
resist the four horsemen of the apocalypse—empire, militarism,
economic exploitation and environmental revolt. These
galloping ghosts connected the dots for me. To Kibera. To the
Iraq War. To Evangelical Christianity itself.

Meanwhile, this awakening was being nurtured and
supported by a beloved community that valued robust inner
work. After a few short-lived house church experiments,
Lindsay and I were invited to join Kristen, Sam, Courtney and
Kyle in weekly, structured, 12-step style meetings. For the first
time, I was being introduced to the language and lifestyle of
recovery, for myself, our marriage and the whole world. The
purpose of our gathering was not to give advice or try to fix one

another, but rather to create a safe environment where we supported each other through the vulnerable sharing of our experience, strength, hope, pain and joy.

Like everyone else, we were mired in various forms of addiction and codependency and we were learning to admit daily that we were *powerless* over these forces and that our lives had become *unmanageable*. It was a whole new understanding of sin. I had attended many churches and small groups, but had never experienced a community of confession quite like this. It was both transparent and transformational.

*   *   *

While many of my Evangelical friends suspect that I've gone down the slippery-slope of "liberalism," I'm more convinced than ever that the biblical Jesus tradition itself led me out of Evangelical Christianity. His primary message was to repent and trust (Mark 1:13-14). My exodus out of Evangelicalism was an act of repentance (Greek *metanoia*), an active verb meaning "to change your mind" or "turn around."

In the writings of the ancient historian Josephus, *metanoia* was used to describe someone changing sides during a war. [51] A traitor! This gets at what my own journey of repentance has meant for me. I couldn't compartmentalize any longer. I couldn't shelve beliefs that I could no longer buy. I had to find another team. Free agency beckoned.

The more I reflected on the Evangelical convictions that were driving my life, the more I felt incongruent and, quite frankly, disturbed. The more I studied the Bible and the world around me, the more I felt called to something altogether different—to both a way-of-life and a spirituality that resonated with what was true and compelling.

The problem was that I didn't know where to look for faith communities that were compelling. I sensed that there were others struggling through similar tensions, but the maddening thing was that I wasn't finding this different kind of Christian faith really being lived out anywhere—at least, not in my South Orange County suburban bubble. Where were the real live "radical disciples" who were living out a Christian faith in alternative ways than what I had always known?

I read about these stories and ideas in books, but I wanted to see it actually happening. For me, even in my deepest, darkest days of fundamentalism, faith was never fiction or fantasy. It wasn't just a make believe nursery rhyme to read in a book or listen to on a Sunday morning so that I could feel good about my life and the future. Faith was more gritty than that. It had to reflect reality.

8

Getting Rearranged

In the spring of 2011, we met Ched Myers and Elaine Enns who invited us to make frequent weekend drives 150 miles north to Bartimaeus Cooperative Ministries in Southern California's Ventura River Watershed. Their hospitality and pastoral wisdom provided a safe space to ask questions and experience a "tradition" of following Jesus in an alternative way. They accepted us whole-heartedly for who we were: two jaded-yet-eager spiritual pilgrims, still early in the journey. Eventually, they commissioned us on a 75-day road trip across 12,000 miles of fresh terrain. Our friend Mike loaned us his Prius.

We met all kinds of disciples who were descending like doves. We stayed with nuns who have spent years in prison actively resisting the military-industrial-complex. We attended a service at a Catholic Church that ordains women and blesses same-sex marriage. We donned orange jumpsuits with the holy fools just outside the gates of the White House protesting torturous conditions at Guantanamo Bay prison. We hiked with Bible scholars and activists and ate meals with pastors who flew into war zones.

We were exposed to a brand of faith that engaged biblical scholarship and social analysis with a lived reality. These communities were keenly aware of the life of the Spirit in ordinary, everyday life. They prayed and sang, fasted and got arrested. Sure enough, the world still needed saving, individually and institutionally, from austerity, alienation, aggression and addiction.

A few years ago, at the ripe old age of forty, I retired from teaching and Lindsay and I made our exodus out of suburban Southern California. We moved to Detroit, a city where government and corporate elites were proclaiming "a comeback" while the vast majority of residents were attempting to survive water shutoffs, home foreclosures, school shutdowns, joblessness and plenty more.

We threw in with the quirky congregants of St. Peter's Episcopal, a church (boasting an attendance of a whopping two dozen on any given Sunday) that seeks to name and resist this structural injustice. I volunteered at Manna Meal, rubbing shoulders with everyday, ordinary saints like Marianne Arbogast who has been serving in the basement soup kitchen for thirty-eight years.

We got a daily dose of the compelling neighborhood activism of Lydia Wylie-Kellermann and Erinn Fahey who, with a few others, started experimenting with a "visionary organizing" project in an old Polish neighborhood in Southwest Detroit that has since become majority Latino—mostly Mexican and Guatemalan immigrants.[52]

They plant urban gardens in abandoned lots and sell vegetables, honey and eggs at their driveway farmers market.

They organize to protect undocumented families against ICE raids and design protest signs with their children as arts and crafts activities.

They host "clarification of thought" gatherings to share

45

ideas and experiences, implement resource-sharing for the neighborhood (access to cars, power tools, washers and dryers, firewood and more) and set aside time for baking, cooking, canning and pot-lucking their way to beloved community.

We teamed up with Lydia and Erinn to start up a little Wednesday night *lectio divina* group of reading and sharing. Together, we curate RadicalDiscipleship.Net, a blog site dedicated to posting daily samples of alternative Christian experiments all over North America.

I am often dismayed when folks on either the political right or left try to "pull Jesus into their camp," as a friend of mine says. However, I truly believe that something different has been going on with me than most of the conservative-liberal Jesus tug-of-war characteristic of the colonial script. I grew up in white middle-class wealth, comfort and obliviousness. Amazingly, a cadre of conversation partners compelled me to migrate away from the hyper-spiritualized, God-Family-and-Country Jesus that perfectly catered to my own social location, economic agenda and political perspective.

Lindsay and I were gifted with new spiritual blueprints, crafted from the margins, reconstructing the way we understand both the world and the Scriptures. These share a deep sensibility fueled by the pain and suffering inflicted by people and policies, but also the hope and solidarity cultivated in a community of struggle.

Am I "political?" Of course. What I came to realize, though, was that even when I was claiming political neutrality during my years as a pastor at the young Evangelical church, it was simply a vote for the status quo, which was terrible news for those catching hell. And, that too, was extremely political. However, I became compelled by a Christian faith that cut against the grain of my comfort and convenience. I didn't pull Jesus into my camp. He pulled me into his.

*　　*　　*

The impact of marginalized testimonies on my own faith has been both stimulated and intensified by the work of three white baby boomer theologians. It was a beautiful coincidence when I stumbled upon Ched's writings at Fuller Theological Seminary on a non-required reading list in one of my elective courses. A few years later, I received a text from my friend Dan, inviting me to join him and Ched for coffee. Ched changed my life even before I met him. After that coffee, my transformation became caffeinated.

Then we were introduced to Rev. Bill Wylie-Kellermann and Dr. James Perkinson, Detroit-based theologian-activists who we had never heard of before our "radical road trip" in 2013. Like the blind man in the Gospel of Mark, these three came to faith in adolescence, but each, in different ways, were hobbled by a faith blurred by the colonial script: "I can see people, but they look like trees, walking" (Mark 8:24). Later, at various moments in the 1970s, each caught wind of a different angle of Jesus, who clarified their vision of discipleship.

Wylie-Kellermann, a native Detroiter, went to seminary in New York and became compelled by Daniel Berrigan's Spirit-driven civil disobedience. Since then, he's been hauling the sanctuary on to the street, cultivating holy mischief, culminating in hundreds of arrests while organizing what he calls "liturgical direct actions."

After college, an Evangelical organization recruited Perkinson to move from suburban Cincinnati to a Detroit ghetto to "do ministry." Instead of saving the city, he got saved, being ministered to and converted by "the immense creativity and heart-rending ferocity" of Black neighbors. He was, and continues to be, thoroughly "rearranged."[53]

Myers, a fifth-generation Californian, ironically found Jesus at Berkeley. Unfortunately, he didn't recognize him in any church he attended. He hitchhiked across the country to Baltimore to throw in with the militant nonviolent resisters at Jonah House, dumpster-diving for food with Phil Berrigan who challenged him to a deeper commitment to confronting social, political and economic realities.

All three of these men, each in his own unique way, cast a clear vision of the Jesus of the Gospels who was shaped by the margins. Myers calls this "the perspective of the periphery."[54] We can only see clearly when we view the world through the eyes of those left behind and cast aside by the colonial script. The writings and life-commitments of these three, like spiritual Lasik surgery, have sharpened my post-Evangelical sight lines and challenged me to live more congruently with the original message of the gospel. These men have boldly called me to a discipleship of decolonization.

*   *   *

Following Jesus, it turns out, is both relationship and religion. From the Latin *religio* meaning "bond," a religion is simply a commitment of supreme importance. Yet, this adventure in decolonizing Evangelical Christianity is also a partnership that connects the depths of my life to the spirit of Jesus and everything else, whether personal or political. But it is even more. It is radical, an ancient tradition that calls followers to dig deeper. All the way to the roots.

The rest of this book is about a rearranged Christian faith that takes the origins of the way of Jesus seriously and seeks to embody it subversively in the context of the American empire. It is about reimagining and reconstructing a faith after our sight has been restored—for the second or third or fourth time. I hope these chapters resist dogma and simply serve as a collection of glimpses overlooking the Promised Land of a decolonizing discipleship. I hope you enjoy my view. And then descend with the doves in your own challenging context.

III.

The Margins

"I recognize that there are between forty and fifty million of our brothers and sisters in this country who are perishing on a lonely island of poverty in the midst of a vast ocean of material prosperity."
Martin Luther King Jr.
April 27, 1965, UCLA

9

The Other Side

During my teaching years in suburban Southern California, many students commuted to my classroom from across the tracks—literally. They lived in the neighborhood locals dubbed "the barrio," on the other side of the railroad tracks from the old Mission of San Juan Capistrano built by colonizing Christians in 1776. These students, dubbed "Dreamers," crossed the border, less than a hundred miles south, with their parents or other relatives when they were very young. Many of these young immigrants did not know that the United States officially considered them "illegal" until they were deep into their high school years.

One day after class, one of my favorite (and brightest) students, Aida, told me she was undocumented. She asked if she needed a birth certificate to apply for a Pell Grant so she could attend a local community college. She was pursuing her dream of becoming a nurse. Like a migrating mourning dove, Aida didn't ask permission when she crossed the border six years prior with her dad and two younger sisters. They were living with her uncle because her dad was a seasonal construction worker and her mom was still in Mexico, paralyzed after falling off a roof.

During the same season Aida was rearranging my soul with her compelling life story, Lindsay and I attended a Ched Myers lecture on immigration, delivered to a standing-room-only auditorium at a college in L.A. Like a scribe trained by the kingdom of heaven, Myers was pulling out treasures old and new (Matthew 13:51-53). He weaved critical biblical scholarship with current events and the latest political and economic analysis.

Jesús and his parents (Jose y Maria, as Ched calls them) were undocumented refugees. They lived in Nazareth, but could not find any place to stay when the imperial census beckoned them to report to Bethlehem, the ancestral town of Jose's family. Sure enough, not one of his ancestors lived there anymore. Economic policies and wars fought by the Herodian regime had cleared them out. To add insult to injury, every hotel had the "No Vacancy" sign lit up.

After the birth of their firstborn, Jose y Maria crossed the border into Egypt to flee more violent policies of Herod. Like the holy family, the current influx of immigrants into the United States has been pushed by social, economic and political policies crafted by the colonial script. In other words, immigrants don't come to "our country" because we have Disneyland and Obamacare. They come to survive.[55]

Residents of Mexico and Guatemala and Nicaragua (and many other countries) head north when they are tired of working long hours for very low pay or cannot find a job or when they fear for their lives because of war, violence or terrorism. American tax dollars subsidize American farmers, encouraging overproduction of corn and other food staples. These cheap products flood the market south of the border, destroying and displacing countless communities of small landowners and subsistence farmers.[56]

As billions of dollars of corporate produce flows south, millions of campesinos are priced out of the market. They find jobs in the U.S. where the demand for seasonal migrant work remains steady. Meanwhile, the U.S. government has poured billions of tax dollars into militarizing the southern border.

These policies are flavored by Donald Trump's crude characterizations of immigrants as "criminals" and "rapists" from "shithole" countries. These stoke the fear-based spiritual fire lighting up demands for a heavily fortified border wall. Meanwhile, more than three-quarters of white Evangelicals support banning all refugees from certain Muslim countries.[57]

Unjust American economic policies led Aida to head north across the border and into my classroom. Despite being demonized as "aliens" by my white neighbors and those in my church congregation, students such as these consistently blessed me with their courage, work ethic, sincerity and appreciation. Karen, Ana-Karen, Marco, Kathleen, Jorge, Maria, Carlos, Yesenia and Alejandra—these valiant young people, undocumented and unafraid, have been a crucial part of my own conversion story.

* * *

The last time Rev. Martin Luther King Jr. visited Detroit, just three weeks before his murder, he courageously crossed the eastern border of the city into suburban Gross Pointe. He introduced his mostly white audience to "the other America," which he described had "a daily ugliness about it that transforms the buoyancy of hope into the fatigue of despair."[58] Just across the border, Detroit remained on high alert, still emotionally processing the July 1967 uprising sparked by police brutalities, joblessness, decrepit housing, defunded education and rampant racial discrimination.

On his car ride to the high school to deliver the speech, the chief of police sat on King's lap to protect him. He was met by hundreds of protesters on the street spewing hateful venom. During his keynote address, he was repeatedly interrupted by members of the audience shouting him down. It was the most disruption he had ever experienced at an indoor gathering.[59] King listened patiently. Then, he lamented that "large segments of white society are more concerned about tranquility and the status quo than about justice and humanity." King was obviously there to tell the truth.

King warned that the most dangerous development in the nation was the building up of Black inner-cities ringed by white suburbs. My friend Jyarland Daniels of the racial equity organization Harriet Speaks laments that the suburbs have historically been white America's answer to Mr. Rogers' question of, "Won't you be my neighbor?" The answer has always been, "No." White folks have always had their overt and covert arsenal to keep others out. Eventually, as Black and Brown residents moved into neighborhoods, white folks rapidly made their exodus.[60] It is a cycle that continues to repeat itself.

King's chronicling of "the other America" was a vital aspect of his Christian discipleship. In fact, the Jesus he knew journeyed with his disciples to "the other side" of the sea to cultivate a deeper sensitivity to justice and humanity:

> On that day, when evening had come, he said to them, "Let us go across to the other side." And leaving the crowd behind, they took him with them in the boat...A great gale arose, and the waves beat into the boat, so that the boat was already being swamped. But he was in the stern, asleep on the cushion; and they woke him up and said to him, "Teacher, do you not care that we are perishing?" He woke up and rebuked the wind, and said to the sea, "Peace! Be still!" Then the wind ceased, and there was a dead calm. He said to them, "Why are you afraid? Have you still no faith?" (Mark 4:35-40).

This was a short-term mission trip to Gentile territory. Today, it is known as "the other side of the tracks." In Detroit: the other side of 8 Mile Road. It was on par with a white suburban Evangelical youth group visiting a barrio, ghetto or reservation. The disciples barely survived a stormy sea on their trek to the country of the Gerasenes. When they arrived, they were met by a man possessed by "Legion:" the violent demons of the colonial script (Mark 5:1-20).

In their two journeys to "the other side" (see also Mark 6:35ff), the disciples encounter vicious wind-swept storms. In both journeys, they totally freak out. In both journeys, Jesus saves them. First he's asleep and speaks the word "peace;" in the second, he walks on water. In both journeys, they arrive safely "on the other side," and then Jesus heals people of another race and ethnicity. They're weird: they eat, worship, dress and speak differently than Jews from Galilee or Judea.

The first trip to "the other side" was so traumatic that Jesus had to force his disciples into the boat the second time around: "Immediately *he made his disciples* get into the boat and go on ahead to the other side" (Mark 6:45). The author of the Gospel invites the reader to identify with the disciples. They are saturated with fear. So am I. Journeying to the other side is scary. The storms mirror what brews inside of me when I respond to Jesus daring every disciple to ditch the safety of comfort and convenience.

In every age, fear has proven a decisive factor. It easily paralyzes me from answering Jesus' call. The message of these "get in the boat" episodes is clear: following Jesus' Way requires a commitment to justice and humanity for those on "the other side"—not just tranquility and the status quo for ourselves.[61]

10

Those People

I grew up in what Rev. Dr. Martin Luther King Jr. called "the sunlight of opportunity," a middle-class housing development in Southern California. It was a tranquil neighborhood that was virtually all white. In my home, at school, on the playground, on vacation, I had what King described that day in the Detroit suburbs as "the milk of prosperity and the honey of equality" overflowing into our laps. I *did* have one Black friend. Same suburban story.

I was taught to fear "the other America," sometimes subtly, sometimes aggressively. The fires of the 1992 Los Angeles "riots" (fifty miles north) burned into my consciousness, "Don't ever go up there. Those people are dangerous." The colonial script was constantly and subconsciously invoked, plenty of insinuations from adults in my life about "those people." It didn't need to be any more specific than that.

"Those people" went beyond race and class. My formative years basking in the sunlight of opportunity were also fueled by a hyper-toxic masculinity. My Jesus was athletic and he was kicking ass. All of us neighborhood boys wasted the summer away playing "smear the queer" in backyards. In high school, my friends in the stands interrogated the sexuality of my opponents on the charity stripe: "H-O-M-O: Homo on the free throw!"

Meanwhile, pastors and teachers justified our banter with a boys-will-be-boys shrug, while condemning "the gay lifestyle" with Bible-quoting quips about "abominations" and universalized rhyming assurances that "it was Adam and Eve, not Adam and Steve." The enduring, ongoing process of repenting from my built-in homophobia is decades in the making.

I still remember when the scales started falling from my eyes. A glorious tension grew within me as Lindsay and I listened to testimony from our good friends Dale and Stacy Fredrickson, who were the first to let us in on the secret that there wasn't just one clear-cut Christian conviction on gender and sexuality. They introduced us to pastors, Bible scholars and theologians who affirmed and welcomed queer folk into the fold.[62]

Then along came Ty, a former children's pastor at Saddleback Church, who was outed, and then promptly fired. When sexuality swims upstream, the falcons start hovering. Ty's friendship was authentic, refreshing and vital for our process. Here was a gay Christian whose courage, compassion and self-deprecating humor and grace were a stark contrast to most of the straight followers of Jesus we knew. Ty was the first to challenge us to become straight *allies*. He prodded us to go beyond welcoming and affirming—to stand up in solidarity and speak out for the queer community. After all, the doves remain vulnerable when the rest of us sit silently on the sidelines.

As I researched, I learned that there are seven Bible verses that condemn "homosexuality," which I wedge in quotation marks here because Scripture was written in Hebrew and Greek and neither language has one clear-cut word that translates "homosexuality" in English. The kind of same-gender-loving coupleship that 21st century church and society is currently debating did not exist in the ancient world.

Back then, "homosexuality" meant (1) a wealthy man who hired a pre-pubescent boy to be his sex slave and protégé, or (2) the humiliating act of anal rape performed by victorious soldiers after a village was conquered in war, or (3) an act of "worship" with same-sex prostitutes during services at a pagan temple. These were non-consensual, non-covenantal, commodifying acts. They are clearly harmful and destructive. However, these do not resemble the contemporary concept of "sexual orientation," something we are born with or develop very early in life. This issue, more than any other, has taught me how important it is to be careful, critical and contextual when quoting the Bible.

What Evangelicals have often referred to as a "lifestyle" or "agenda" is really about two people who want to join in a covenant of love, service and fidelity recognized by the state they live in and the faith community they belong to. This kind of relationship-bound-by-promise is a powerful practice of discipleship. It also makes society a stronger, more secure and stable place to live. Furthermore, when it came to same-gender love, Jesus was silent.

In my experience, the intramural Christian debate over inclusion of queer and questioning neighbors does not boil down to what one knows about the issue, but rather, whom one knows. Most Evangelicals I have dialogued with reject the notion that it is both natural and nurturing for someone to have sexual and romantic feelings toward members of their same gender. Most Evangelicals, in my experience, are not in authentic relationships with folks who are out. In addition, too many leaders of churches and non-profits refuse to speak out in full support of queer and questioning folks for fear of alienating donors and members. This has left the Evangelical masses with a mentality of "I love you, but I do not approve of your lifestyle or your partner." This has driven queer and questioning folks away, to the margins, all the way to "the other side."

Lindsay and I cherish our relationships with the gay, lesbian and trans friends with whom we share meals, study the Bible, attend church and protests, and for whom we facilitate marriage retreats. Their willingness to share painful stories of coming out, and the courage and joy that comes with being themselves and experiencing deep love and tenderness with their partners, have been gigantic gifts of nurture and support for our own coupleship. As it turns out, instead of threatening our "traditional" marriage, these sojourners from "the other side" continue to encourage, challenge and help us thrive.

11
Root Causes

When Jesus called me and Lindsay to "get in the boat" and journey to Detroit, a city with more than forty percent of the population living below the poverty line, we were given daily opportunities to bear witness to the American social divide that Dr. King spoke about in the suburbs. Sure enough, "the other America" still exists fifty years after his speech.

We arrived just a few months after the governor of Michigan appointed an emergency manager to usher the struggling city into bankruptcy proceedings. The water department contracted a wrecking company from the suburbs to start shutting off water to all households two months behind on their bills. More than ninety-nine percent of these victims of shutoff were poor Black residents.

Every Thursday we delivered eight gallons of drinking water to Deborah on the east side of town. Her water was shut-off by the city because of an outstanding $4,000 water bill that included charges for the repair of old leaky pipes. Deborah is the youngest of ten children, a college graduate who had lived in the same house for sixty years. Unable to find a job anywhere, she was spending much of her time volunteering at the soup kitchen down the street.

While canvassing in the northwest section of the city with the grassroots organization We The People of Detroit, we met an elderly woman hooked up to an oxygen tank. She had lived downtown in low-income housing for years until a billionaire bought the building and dramatically increased the rent. She and her special-needs daughter moved across town into another home, only to learn that they did not have access to water because the prior owner hadn't paid the bill.

On Detroit's east side, we met Connie, a single mother with four children under ten years old. She had heart issues and her oldest daughter was diagnosed with asthma. She was renting the home from a guy who owed $4,260 to the water department and turned the water back on illegally before he conned Connie into renting the place. When we delivered forty gallons to her, she shared the details of her covert hydration operation. Connie was toting jugs and buckets down the street to a neighbor who was charging her for it.

Before our friend Tangela died on her 40th birthday, she owed $787 on her water bill while trying to cobble together odd jobs to support her family. She described the contrast of two Americas as the difference between those who have the privilege to *owe* money and those who have *no* money. She told us true stories about properties owned by corporations and old white billionaires, from golf courses and professional sports stadiums, owing tens of thousands in unpaid water bills. Their water kept flowing.

During our first bitterly cold winter in the city, my friend Dan asked if I would help him move—three times in four months! First, he was evicted from the place he was renting a half mile from our church because the owner wasn't paying taxes. He and his wife moved into the basement of their son's house. Then, the city turned off their taps because they couldn't afford to pay the water bill. They moved into a two-story pad on the west side until his wife was robbed at gunpoint just before Christmas.

The last place they moved to was in a neighborhood that appeared to have been hit by a hurricane. Across the street, where three homes used to stand, there was nothing but old mattresses and a couch. Half of the houses that remained standing were boarded up, ready for demolition. The street pavement looked like it was the site of a grenade-tossing contest.

These are just a few of tens of thousands of Detroit residents who, echoing straight from King's final Detroit speech, are "perishing on a lonely island of poverty in the midst of a vast ocean of material prosperity." Within a half-mile radius of where we lived on Cecil Avenue in Detroit, there were four dollar stores, four gentlemen's clubs, four cash advance outlets, four liquor stores, a McDonald's, a Church's Chicken and the famous Telway, where you can get four burgers in a bag for three bucks. Our neighborhood was not only toxic, it was terrorized by violence—domestic abuse, rape at gunpoint and robberies. The house across the street was a hub for drug-dealing and prostitution. These, however, are all *symptoms* of the predatory root causes.

In the mid-twentieth century, "the other side" was further downgraded by the creation of the Federal Housing Authority (FHA), which bolstered neighborhood borders built on race and class. In a process called "redlining," the FHA refused to insure mortgages in Black neighborhoods while subsidizing builders who were mass-producing subdivisions for white folks (with requirements that none of the homes be sold to Black families). White neighborhood organizations and real estate brokers ensured ongoing segregation through "restrictive covenants," neighborly agreements to only sell homes to white families. To add insult to injury, in a practice some call "bluelining," police either neglected to offer protection to certain neighborhoods or intensified their presence with arrests and stop-and-frisk procedures.[63]

The Black population of Detroit, like every community surviving on the margins, has been systematically oppressed by long-standing policies and practices that have created misery:

- massive job loss
- pay cuts
- slashed pensions
- skyrocketing medical bills
- bloated heating bills
- the highest water rates in the state (twice the national average)
- water shut-offs
- predatory mortgage lending
- over-inflated property taxes
- auto insurance more than double that of the suburbs
- abysmal schools
- pitiful public transportation
- meager access to nutritious food
- a continuation of "de facto" systemic racism—especially with job interviews, bank loans and the criminal justice system.

Meanwhile, in suburban spaces blessed by a coalition of government and business and church:

- property values steadily rise
- insurance rates remain low
- bank loans with low interest rates and inheritance money provide needed capital
- a multitude of grocery stores make nutritious, organic food plentiful and cheap
- high performing schools are funded by property tax monies
- access to higher education equals access to secure, high-paying jobs

The issues plaguing American ghettos, barrios and reservations are not due to culture, family values or work ethic, as I was told time and time again growing up in the suburbs. King's words still haunt us because predatory root causes are neglected, creating a deeper divide between the margins and the mainstream. Then, the Bible is quoted to justify the whole arrangement.

12

The Poor Among You

Toward the end of the earliest Gospel ever written, a woman anoints Jesus with really expensive perfume. The disciples explode with judgment. She should have sold it and given the proceeds to poor folks! Jesus exhorts everyone to settle down, reminding them, "You'll always have the poor among you" (Mark 14:3-9).

Over the decades, I've consistently heard Evangelicals quote these very words of Jesus to dismiss policies and provisions that attempt to systematically help low-income residents. "See," they say, referencing the Scripture, "Jesus, is telling us it's a waste of time to try to alleviate poverty. He promises that the poor will always be with us no matter what we try to do." In other words, we can't stop the inevitable.

Far too often, American followers of Jesus justify inaction, particularly in regards to policy change, by misrepresenting his teachings. This is why context is crucial. In this episode, Jesus is actually quoting Deuteronomy 15, one of the most crucial junctures in the history of Israel. God is preparing the former slaves of Egypt to live in a new kind of way in the Promised Land. As the old African-American proverb illuminates, it is easier to get the enslaved out of Egypt than it is to get Egypt out of the enslaved. The exodus wilderness was a school, a 12-step-program for recovery from the colonial script.

The God of Steadfast Love threw down the gauntlet, "Every seventh year you shall grant a remission of debts." A clean slate. A Sabbath year release! Those searching for the biblical prescription to end poverty find it right here.

After giving the command, Steadfast Love says, "There will, however, be *no one in need among you*...if only you will obey the Lord your God by diligently observing this entire commandment that I command you today." If only.

Two verses later, God reiterates: "*If there is among you anyone in need*...do not be hard-hearted or tight-fisted toward your needy neighbor."

First, God says (A) there will never be poor people in the land...as long as y'all practice Sabbath economics.[64] Then, God says, (B) "If there *are* any poor among you, then see A." There's a slippery learning slope at play here. A few verses later, God summarizes:

> Since there will never cease to be some in need on the earth, I therefore command you, "Open your hand to the poor and needy neighbor in your land."

Translation: The poor will always be among us because people of faith will consistently fail to follow this challenging divine economic policy. Jesus' words in the Gospel episode cue readers to the chronic failure to practice what God called "Sabbath" and "Jubilee." These concepts call us to live with less and redistribute surplus to those who need it (Leviticus 25:8-13). It pinpoints the structural, predatory root of poverty.

As it turns out, "You will always have the poor among you" means exactly the opposite of how I heard it used over and over again during my decades in Evangelicalism. It's not an unfortunate inevitability to relieve the guilt of the privileged and powerful. It is a prophetic call to ensure that communities do not structure economic growth around the plundering of poor people.

When Paul was given the green light to invite non-Jewish people to join the Jesus movement, leaders offered one caveat:

> They asked only one thing, that we remember the poor, which was actually what I was eager to do (Galatians 2:10).

Over and over, the Bible calls people of faith and conscience to do something serious about poverty. In fact, there are more than one thousand passages urging believers to care for those plagued by economic oppression.

The year I started attending the fundamentalist Christian elementary school, the most popular song was from Prince: "This is what it sounds like when the doves cry." It is an apt soundtrack for the ancient script that refused to leave the most vulnerable standing alone in a world so cold. In fact, it is the cry of poor and marginalized doves that consistently finds the ear of the God of Steadfast Love throughout the Bible.

This ancient cry starts with the recently murdered Abel, a nomad who lived off the land, his blood prayerfully weeping to the Creator (Genesis 4:10). So, too, God hears the groans and moans of the enslaved Israelites in Egypt (Exodus 2:23-25).

After God liberates them, the immigrant, the orphan and the widow are prioritized in policy (Exodus 22:21-25). Steadfast Love promises to hear their cry whenever they are abused or neglected.

In the wilderness, God teaches the community of the formerly enslaved that the key economic principle, for the health of everyone, is to abstain from taking too much. God's gift economy centered on a daily practice of gathering *just enough* food to sustain a simple diet (Exodus 16:1-36). Manna was a reminder to them that, back in Egypt, they were tasked with brick-making to build gigantic warehouses to store the grain produced by industrial agriculture (not coincidentally, the career choice of Cain, the world's first murderer). Pharoah's economic policy hinged on hoarding all the food so the masses would stay perpetually imprisoned in debt and dependence (Exodus 1:8-14; Genesis 47:13-22). Unfortunately, the wilderness people eventually settled for the way of Pharoah (1 Samuel 8).

For four hundred years of Israelite monarchy, the marginalized movement of prophetic faith committed to crying out on behalf of those oppressed by the colonial script (Isaiah 40:6-8; Jeremiah 8:18—9:11). This is the tear-stained tradition that John the Baptist and Jesus took up. They covenanted to grieve with those groaning under the weight of a dehumanizing socio-political and economic system (Matthew 2:17-18). Early Christian communities connected the dots and told the truth—unjust economic practices never go unnoticed by God:

> Listen! The wages of the laborers who mowed your fields, which you kept back by fraud, cry out, and the cries of the harvesters have reached the ears of the Lord of hosts (James 5:4).

The deep groan of the Spirit keeps on crying out from the depths of creation (Romans 8:18-27) and it is the blood of the prophets (from Abel to Jesus to Dr. King) that is finally unveiled at the end of the story, underneath what Jim Perkinson describes as "the Babylon concentration of goods and gore, pirated from everywhere" (Revelation 18:1-24).[65]

Just as poverty was the prism through which the earliest followers of Jesus viewed the world, so it was for Dr. King and the Civil Rights movement in their mission "to save the soul of America." The last months of King's life were consumed with organizing a Poor People's Campaign to expose hidden suffering all over the country. He was murdered in Memphis, where he traveled to support 1,300 sanitation workers on strike. The night before his assassination, he got to the core of what the gospel meant:

> It's all right to talk about "streets flowing with milk and honey," but God has commanded us to be concerned about the slums down here, and his children who can't eat three square meals a day.[66]

Jesus wasn't dismissing his disciples' meager attempts to eliminate poverty, but challenging them to live in close proximity to poor and marginalized people. "For you always have the poor with you," Jesus proclaimed and then added, "and you can show kindness to them whenever you wish" (Mark 14:7a). The authenticity of our kindness is fully dependent on our consciousness. When we can see for ourselves the concrete conditions that produce poverty in the first place.

Jesus wasn't dissing the critical work required to get at the roots of poverty, but questioning the creative tricks utilized to flee from it. As Ched writes, folks are either living *insulated from* the poor or in *solidarity with* the poor. Where one lives determines what one learns. Jesus knew what the colonial script refuses to acknowledge—that the poor have plenty to teach *us*.[67]

13
Reverse Mission

The poor among us are living reminders of Martin Luther King's conviction that "we are all caught in an inescapable network of mutuality, tied in a single garment of destiny." These words flow from his legendary letter from a Birmingham jail in 1963. King explained that he traveled from Atlanta to Birmingham to protest because "injustice anywhere is a threat to justice everywhere."[68] Everything is connected to everything else.

Psychotherapist Francis Weller calls this "an interpenetrating reality:"

> We are not isolated cells partitioned off from other cells; we have semipermeable membranes that make possible an ongoing exchange with the great body of life. We register in our psyches, consciously or not, the fact of our shared sorrows.[69]

While the wretched web spun by white supremacy led King to travel, protest and get arrested on behalf of his oppressed brothers and sisters in Birmingham, Weller laments that most of us learn to cope with shared sorrows through either *amnesia* or *anesthesia*. Reality is too painful. The strong tendency is either to deny it with distractions or to numb it with addictions. The goal is to both name it and address it with a few, rare soul friends who possess the courage to stay connected to pain and discomfort.

For followers of Jesus, the sorrow of the marginalized is sacred. Refusing to deny it or numb it gets to the core of what we call "spirituality." There is something deep in every living thing that is made up of what is invisible and indestructible. Spirit. Being. Essence. This is who we really are. We are "inextricably connected" to everyone else. We belong to each other.[70]

The same Spirit that raised Jesus from the dead dwells in everyone and infuses life into our decaying days (Romans 8:11). A Power greater than ourselves aligns us so that we spontaneously rejoice with those who rejoice and weep with those who weep (Romans 12:15). We experience true solidarity and intimacy.

This Spirit gives us the courage to speak on behalf of those on the margins in our social circles. In this vocation, we will often feel like we are standing alone. But we are not. We are inextricably connected with those on the other side. We are not isolated cells. By design, our sorrows are intended to be shared.

Lindsay and I believe that it was this Power percolating in us that eventually prodded our move to Detroit. We had the middle class privilege to raise financial support to live and serve in a marginalized context where we could learn from leaders who had been working intimately with poor and marginalized neighbors for decades. We are deeply grateful for this opportunity, knowing full well that most folks do not have the financial or family situations to even dream of something like this.

However, we remain convinced, that everyone can journey to the other side wherever they find themselves. Jim Perkinson, in fact, challenges his suburban students, thirty miles north of the city, to live there and regularly raise issue with who is being excluded from there.[71] A commitment to decolonization does not require us to move two thousand miles to descend like a dove. It simply beckons us to start paying attention to what is going on right in front of us—to experience the deep spirituality of shared sorrow and then do something about it.

Over the years, I've discovered that when I journey to the margins, I tend to be the one getting saved. Somewhere along the line, the missionary enterprise got flipped in my soul.

The margins represent a reverse mission.[72] My own salvation has relied heavily upon it. The more I'm around people who experience and observe life from a completely different vantage point— immigrants, Black and Brown folks, those who identify as queer or questioning, the elderly, survivors of abuse and trauma—the more I become whole and complete.

My barber in Orange County left his native Vietnam in the early '90s and has never returned. He explained to me in broken English with sorrow in his eyes that his three children have become Americanized because he "didn't want to confuse them." Native Detroiter Cecily McClellan stayed and paid while so many left her city for the suburbs. When she isn't fighting pension cuts or getting treatment for multiple diagnoses while navigating the wretched health-care system or caring for her own children, she's at the St. Peter's Peace and Justice Hive organizing emergency deliveries to victims of water shut-offs.

When I look into the eyes of these two mourning doves and listen to their stories, I experience a depth of soul that only comes from the well of grief. The pure in heart and the poor in spirit, the meek and the merciful—these are the "blessed" ones whom Jesus lifted up as the gospel people (Matthew 5:1-8). Their way-of-being evangelizes me constantly. I become rearranged in the process.

Howard Thurman called this work "the gospel of creative love for the abandoned."[73] The original Jesus movement was rooted in a deep concern for those who are tragically abandoned to the margins. The book of Hebrews exhorts readers to share hospitality because "through it some have unknowingly entertained angels" (Hebrews 13:2). The world is mysterious and enchanted. But my own soul bears witness that these recipients of our service—these angels incognito—entertain us far more than anything we are directing or producing for them.

This is the miracle of Jesus' missionary enterprise—only

those on the margins can save the rest of us from the colonial script. When we get in the boat we are confronted by our mutual humanity. Fear floats away. On the other side, there's no longer any need to take sides. We are in this together.

IV.

The Mainstream

"History has proven that social systems have a great last
minute breathing power, and the guardians of the status quo
are always on hand with their oxygen tents to keep a hold on
our lives."
Martin Luther King Jr.
April 27, 1965, UCLA

14
Lost in Translation

On a perfect summer afternoon in 2013, Weldon Nisly, the pastor at Seattle Mennonite Church, treated me and Lindsay to lunch at a hole-in-the-wall Persian joint a few blocks from his office. Just weeks away from retirement, Weldon recapped his life growing up in Iowa where he clearly heard the call to ministry on September 1, 1973 (two days before my birth). It was a unique summons to a life dedicated to prophetic preaching and peace witness.

He told us about traveling to Iraq after the U.S. military invasion in March 2003, an extremely dangerous mission on which his church and family prayerfully sent him. He was there with a Christian Peacemaker Teams delegation "getting in the way of war."[74] They wanted the world to see the war through Iraqi eyes—different than what was portrayed in the American media.

While in Iraq, the car he was riding in blew out a tire and careened off the side of the road during an air raid by U.S. forces. The crash dislocated Weldon's shoulder, breaking bones and gashing the back of his head. While U.S. bombers flew overhead, the people of the local village of Rutba carried him to safety.

The doctor who came to his aid lamented that U.S. bombs destroyed their hospital just three days earlier. He asked Weldon:

> Why would your country bomb our hospital? But don't worry, we help anyone here—Christians, Muslims, Jews, Iraqis or Americans. You are our brothers, and we will take care of you.

The doctor apologized for the lack of medical supplies and

stitched up Weldon's head without anesthesia. The Americans tried to pay the doctor when they were leaving, but he refused to take it. He asked, instead, that the team tell the world about Rutba.[75] Weldon did just that. Years later, he traveled back to Iraq to thank the group of Good Samaritan-Iraqis who saved his life.

As Weldon shared about his commitment to being a pastor, activist and monastic, Lindsay and I were struck by how he embodied both tender compassion and fierce conviction in his pursuit of a deeper connection with the God of Steadfast Love. This fueled a robust commitment to serving others. His life remains a witness to a brand of refugee discipleship that prioritizes an exodus out of empire—like the Israelites out of Egypt and like the first Christians resisting Rome.

* * *

In his book *Democracy Matters*, Dr. Cornel West contrasted a Weldon Nisly prophetic faith with the mainstream version that I grew up with—what West calls "Constantinian Christianity." Since the fourth century, when the emperor Constantine strategically infused Christian faith with Roman world dominance, this brand of faith has sought respectability and legitimation by combining a passionate praise of Jesus with a patriotic pledge to the colonial script.[76]

Today, Constantinian Evangelicals sponsor Presidential prayer breakfasts, sing "God Bless America," rebuke NFL players for kneeling during the national anthem and endorse "One Nation Under God" on coinage. The myth is aggressively promoted: there is strength, safety and security in numbers. Anything associated with the military is held in highest esteem.

Back in the 1980s, during my early Evangelical years, I vividly recall the men at my church raving about Colonel Oliver "Ollie" North, a prized member of President Reagan's

National Security Council. To them, he was both an American hero and a man after God's own heart. A falcon of the highest order. He courageously stood up to the enemies—both the liberals at home and the communists abroad.

After Congress refused to allocate funding to the Contra rebel group fighting the "socialist" Sandinista government in Nicaragua, Ollie supported the cause by illegally transferring profits from (A) weapons sold to Iran and (B) crack cocaine covertly peddled in Black neighborhoods.[77] He was convicted of three felonies.

Ollie was granted immunity and then lost his bid for the U.S. Senate in the mid-'90s after raising more than $15 million through direct mail donations. For the past couple of decades, his own show on Fox News and his many published books have been prized by millions of Evangelicals, thoroughly committed to a foreign policy that paints Muslims as "terrorists" and defends the unregulated "free enterprise" of corporate America. In the spring of 2018, he became the President of the National Rifle Association. His goal: to increase NRA membership to "14 million activists on the streets."[78]

I also remember, in 5th grade at my private Christian school, going on a field trip to the headquarters of Wycliffe Bible Translators in Costa Mesa. I loved it. These people were committed to learning rare languages so they could travel to "the deepest, darkest jungles" of Asia, Africa and the Amazon to save souls for eternity. Some years later, I finally connected the dots. Wycliffe was translating the Bible by eliminating the Spanish and indigenous words for certain concepts that threatened their Constantinian worldview: class, community, conquer, exploitation, oppression, repression, revolution, revolutionary, rebellion.[79] Jesus' politics were lost in translation—intentionally.

As it turns out, at the same time my class was taking a field trip to its headquarters, Wycliffe missionaries were in Guatemala partnering with former President Efrain Rios

Montt, himself a devout "born again" Evangelical. According to
one Wycliffe representative, they served as "a bridge between
the military and the people." The "model villages" they helped
establish and facilitate were nothing less than concentration
camps. Montt's notorious "frijoles y fusiles" campaign
murdered more than 80,000 Guatemalan civilians, mostly
Mayans.[80] A member of Montt's own church claimed it wasn't
genocide, based on his logic right out of the colonial script:

> The Army doesn't massacre the Indians. It massacres
> demons, and the Indians are demon-possessed; they are
> communists.[81]

Constantinian Christians confronted the Cold War with a
colonization funded by suburban collection-plates. Montt
received millions of dollars from Pat Robertson's Operation
International Love Lift program.[82] In fact, many U.S.
Evangelical missionaries and organizations supported Montt's
regime through public outreach, fund-raising and congressional
lobbying, greatly influencing U.S. relations with Central
America during this period.[83]

Unfortunately, these stories are the rule, not the
exception. For decades, Evangelicals have either supported or
stayed silent about policies that consistently inflict pain and
death on inner-city ghettos and barrios, native American
reservations and communities all over the global South. These
stories are seldom (if ever) told by an American imperial
mainstream devoted to "making America great again."

15
An Epic Gravestone

In the early 1980s, while I was praying against the evils of
Communism in my private school classroom and Colonel North
was winning the hearts of deacons and elders at my church,

historian William Appleman Williams published his aptly titled book *Empire As a Way of Life*.[84] Williams chronicled how the colonial script, for centuries, had imposed American political, social and economic policies on people all over the world. Lowlights include the near-genocide of native Americans in "the new world," importing kidnapped and enslaved peoples from Africa, launching imperialist wars with countries from Mexico to Iraq and then stealing their land, resources and cultures.

The United States was, and continues to be, built on what Dr. Lily Mendoza, one of our beloved mentors, calls "the undeniable debris of dead bodies, stolen wealth, and the enslavement of other beings, both human and non-human."[85] This tale hits close to home for me. The way of the falcon is the backdrop of my own family's "success" story too.

A little more than a century ago, my great-grandfather Tom immigrated to the United States from England with his Scottish wife, Mary, and their four sons. They settled on a plot of "old sage brush land" in the little town of Omak, Washington. They arrived just after the completion of the Conconully Dam, a grand irrigation project to industrialize agriculture production. Tom planted a large apple orchard in a region with very little rainfall. The government tamed the river so that white folks like Tom could funnel that water into profits.

Tom's son, Valentine (born on Valentine's Day, 1901), my grandfather, was nine at the time. He graduated from high school, attended pharmacy school and then moved seventy-five miles away to operate a drugstore in the town of Mason City, after President Roosevelt signed into law the construction of a high dam that would provide jobs for about 5,000 white men who were unemployed during the Great Depression.

My dad was born just months before the completion of the Grand Coulee Dam, the largest concrete structure in the world, providing irrigation to a million acres of farmland and electricity to the entire Pacific Northwest. It powered the nuclear facility that created plutonium for the atomic bomb and enabled Boeing to design and build planes to fight the Nazis in WWII.

Before any of these projects were initiated, a dozen tribes were forced to sign treaties and were then corralled into the Colville Indian Reservation, which shrank and morphed over time, as white settlers demanded the choicest of lands, flush with natural resources. The mourning doves were caged up and the key was thrown away. The building of these dams destroyed what sustenance remained, killing off 645 miles of seasonal salmon runs and flooding plains of rich land and sacred burial grounds.

The Indian population had depended on the free flowing Columbia River for centuries. Their work, recreation, diet and most sacred ceremonies revolved around the summer migration of salmon.[86] Author Sherman Alexie calls the Grand Coulee Dam "an epic gravestone:"

> Spiritually speaking, the Spokane Indians and all other Salish tribes worshipped the salmon as passionately as any other people in the world worship their deities...What is it like to be a Spokane Indian without wild salmon? It is like being a Christian if Jesus had never rolled back the stone and risen from the tomb.[87]

During the fall of 2016, Lindsay and I made the pilgrimage to Grand Coulee to sprinkle some of Dad's ashes off a bridge over the Columbia River, in full frontal view of the epic gravestone. Two blocks away, I discovered the Colville Indian Museum where I met the curator, Jennifer, who's about a decade younger than my dad. She grew up an hour from the dam, but moved there after extensive research and study in archaeology and anthropology.

Jennifer told me about participating in a conference at

Gonzaga University in 1999 where she testified about the Catholic Church's role in the abuse that her mom suffered as child at an Indian boarding school in Eastern Washington. Immediately after her presentation, a priest got in her face and shouted her down. Then an amazing thing happened. A 4-foot, 10-inch female Colville elder charged through the crowd to shove the falcon back in his place.

Memories like this, she said, keep her going. Jennifer, though, confirmed my deep suspicion. Access to the Grand Coulee Dam's electricity and irrigation was promised to the Colville people, but wasn't delivered for decades. To this day, the tribes endure high electric and water bills and shoddy irrigation.

The colonial script privileged the men in our white family for a hundred years, opening the doors wide as they were welcomed into the country. It funded grand water projects, interstate highways and low-interest loans and cleared the way for education and jobs and homes for white folks by pushing people of color into reservations, barrios and ghettos.

Eventually, the Rexall Corporation recruited Grandpa Val to follow the growth generated by even more government subsidies. He moved his business to suburban Seattle, the new home of Boeing, contracted to build the B-29 bomber. They were the first family on the street with a TV and their home had a beautiful view of Lake Washington. Long before my dad left for college, Val was making six figures.

In his final sermon, just a few days before his assassination, Rev. Dr. Martin Luther King Jr. contrasted the intergenerational story of his family with mine:

> [The federal government] simply said "You're free," and it left him there penniless, illiterate, not knowing what to do. And the irony of it all is that at the same time the nation failed to do anything for the Black man—through

an act of Congress it was giving away millions of acres of land in the West and the Midwest—which meant that it was willing to undergird its white peasants from Europe with an economic floor.[88]

The genealogies and genograms of my family system powerfully subvert the success stories I've been told and assumed. They help me connect the dots so I can tell the truth. The intergenerational arc of the moral universe is long and it begins with a holy groaning, unsettling me out of my privilege and entitlement. The creation waits with eager longing for the revealing of the children of the God of Steadfast Love. And for the return of the salmon to the Upper Columbia River.

*　　*　　*

Equality and justice for all is far from a reality in the American mainstream. In fact, this gap has only intensified since King subversively called the United States the "greatest purveyor of violence in the world" in his speech at Riverside Church in New York City exactly a year before his assassination. There are more than 800 military bases in 70 countries all over the world. The War on Terror has cost U.S. taxpayers more than $5 trillion. The Pentagon's annual budget is more than $600 billion. The Defense Department even paid a PR firm $500 million to make fake al Qaida videos.[89]

At the height of the Roman Empire, it is estimated that the top 1 percent of society controlled 16 percent of the wealth. This is less than half of what the top 1 percent of Americans control today![90] It is the expected result of a profit-driven U.S. capitalism infused with predatory "neoliberal" policies that prioritize and protect corporations and wealthy investors over those on the margins.

In the late 1990s, neoliberal evangelist Thomas

Friedman warned that economic growth necessitated a military on steroids:

> The hidden hand of the market will never work without a hidden fist. McDonald's cannot flourish without McDonnell Douglas, the designer of the F-15. And the hidden fist that keeps the world safe for Silicon Valley's technologies to flourish is called the US Army, Air Force, Navy and Marine Corps.[91]

Many neoliberal advocates refer to these policies as "austerity measures." It conjures the need for Americans to be serious about the budget and to make severe cuts so that the national economy will be sustainable.

In reality, and ironically, austerity proclaims the glories of low government regulations and minimal taxation. Then, it pours billions of government dollars into militaries that invade foreign lands to secure precious resources. It subsidizes stadiums and skyscrapers owned by billionaires. The benefits never trickle down.

Austerity cheats poor countries out of trillions of dollars by lending them more money than they can possibly repay and then taking over their economies.[92] Then it ships jobs overseas, closes schools and libraries, cuts or eliminates pension and retirement plans, slashes Social Security, collapses minimum wages, weakens workers' rights to organize unions, bails out Wall Street, militarizes police forces and builds high-tech prisons. Investors shout with glee. [93]

Austerity boldly blames Black and Brown folks for outcomes designed by austerity itself. Three weeks before his assassination, Dr. King gave this assessment to more than a thousand striking sanitation workers in Memphis:

> When there is vast unemployment and underemployment in the black community, they call it a

"social problem." When there is vast unemployment and underemployment in the white community, they call it a "depression."[94]

Many Americans are quick to blame globalization, technology and China for the ongoing stagnation and struggle of those in the middle and lower classes. Not so according to a recent report by leading economists who released "The Inequality Report 2018." They conclude that the unique American austerity experiment has been disastrous. But it can be changed: "Bad policy can have a real impact on millions of lives, for decades. But what governments have done, they can still undo."[95]

As long as federal and state governments commit to austerity policies, we will always have the poor among us. Sister Marianne Arbogast has worked at the Manna Meal soup kitchen in Detroit for the past four decades. I asked her when the kitchen was most stretched to the limit of its resources. She said it was in the early 1980s, after Reagan started to make cuts to the social safety net. This was the beginning of a new era of "welfare reform"—back when Manna Meal was the only soup kitchen in town. Since then, austerity has multiplied charities to keep up with demand.

And since then, Bill Clinton's rebranded Democrats joined the austerity party. The Dems pledged allegiance to big donors and military-industrial corporations. This left the poor and working class, especially Black and Brown Americans, with nothing more than the crumbs that fall from the master's table.

The wealthy are not those who work harder and persevere more than anyone else. Those at the top simply have access to capital (through inheritance and social connections) and have strategized how to utilize that capital to make even more money for themselves and their families.[96] Both major political parties advance austerity measures that cater to these elite families. Both major political parties spin distracting and distorting messages that divide the rest of us.

As King lamented time and again, the American economic system puts "profits before people." As early as 1952, King wrote to his soon-to-be wife Coretta lamenting that "capitalism had outgrown its usefulness." King was a democratic socialist who spoke out against the predatory violence of the American economic system. He believed in a political system ruled by the people and that protected the rights of everyone.

But King also believed in tax and regulation policies that would ensure that the economic system gives opportunities to everyone. Dr. King called for a universal minimum income paid for by the federal government. This conviction flowed naturally from his faith:

> God intends for all of his children to have the basic necessities of life, and he has left in this universe "enough and to spare" for that purpose.[97]

As it turns out, King was more socialist than Bernie Sanders. Over the past fifty years, the anti-poverty policies that he endorsed have been blasted by a Constantinian Christian establishment who have consistently utilized fear-based tactics to scare the American public. The hypocrisy runs deep. They preach the evils of "big government" while supporting subsidies to corporations and bloated military and police budgets.

Unfortunately, the results have been disastrous for the doves. There is a direct connection between economic policies supported by white Evangelicals and recent reports that racism, poverty and militarism are worse today than they were five decades ago.[98] This can change—and the change can begin by changing the way we read the Bible.

16
The Original Gospel Message

Tragically, mainstream Christian narratives have failed to follow King's critique of devastating policies and practices of the U.S. government. Within American Evangelicalism, King's prophetic sensibilities have been shelved in favor of personal and patriotic impulses—propped up by three key theological pillars, heavily influenced by over-spiritualized interpretations of Paul's letters:

1. Good works don't get me into heaven—I'm "justified" by faith.

2. Jesus died for me so that my sins can be wiped away.

3. Jesus is my personal Lord and Savior.

From early on, these Evangelical fundamentals instilled a confidence in me that God was on the side of the American masses who made a decision for Christ. This was all that mattered. "Politics" was a waste of time because these issues were obsessed with "earthly matters." However, the more I studied the Bible, the more I discovered a tension between what Paul wrote from prison a few decades after the death of King Jesus and what I was quoting from suburbia a few decades after the death of Dr. King.

     The Evangelical emphasis on "justification by faith" has been erected entirely on a reading of Paul interpreted through the lens of Augustine in the fourth century and Martin Luther in the 15th. Paul, according to these men, was focused on individual sinners becoming "justified"—as in "just-if-I'd never sinned." In my Evangelical imagination, this sin stain removal was vital so that I could go to heaven when I died. At least, this was how my leaders at Campus Crusade for Christ broke it all down to me in college using their "Four Spiritual Laws" tracts.

Over the course of the past fifty years, however, many Christian scholars have questioned the accuracy of this interpretation. Krister Stendahl, a Lutheran pastor and Harvard professor, wrote a legendary article in the 1960s entitled "Paul and the Introspective Conscience of the West." He proposed that every time Paul uses "justification" (or "righteousness": it's the same Greek word *dikaiosyne*) in Romans and Galatians, he is referring to how it is that Gentiles can join Jews in a divine movement to redeem the world (as opposed to how an individual can be made righteous before an angry and/or perfect God).[99]

Justification is actually a social and political concept. It is about identity and vocation, not eternal destination. It is about Jews and Gentiles eating at the same table and worshipping together, equal in the eyes of the God of Steadfast Love. Justification emphasizes racial and ethnic equity, an end to all prejudice and discrimination. Stendahl, who had the original Greek text of the entire book of Romans memorized, courageously offered a reading of Paul that means far more than relieving *my* guilt, a clean slate to save *my* soul.[100]

Justification is not about getting into heaven after death. It is about participating in the healing of the world now. Justification unveils an inclusivity that vetoes the old definitions of what is clean and unclean, pure and impure. All are welcome to join in the work.

Paul opposed Peter "to his face" because he stopped sharing meals with Gentiles when certain exclusivist Jews disapproved of it (Galatians 2:11). This is the specific context of Paul's famous words: "We ourselves are Jews by birth and not Gentile sinners; yet we know that a person is justified not by the works of the law but through faith in Jesus Christ" (Galatians 2:15-16). In short, anyone and everyone is a child of God.

Justification is not a call to invite Jesus into my heart to "get saved" once-and-for-all. It beckons everyone to participate in a way-of-life that is salvific, alternative to a mainstream fueled by the colonial script. By the grace of God, justification fuels good works that lead to real justice.[101]

According to Bible scholar Neil Elliott, Paul narrates in his letters that Jesus was following in the centuries-old tradition of the Hebrew prophets who proclaimed "the justice of God" as an alternative to "imperial injustice."[102] Jesus was shunned, shamed and scapegoated by religious and political elites accommodating to the mainstream. The scandal of the cross (1 Corinthians 1:18-25) is how power, in every era, exploits, abuses, tortures and crucifies the vulnerable and marginalized among us. When we gaze at the cross, it exposes our own unjust and oppressive purity codes and litmus tests, used to disqualify or exclude others.

*   *   *

Paul's "gospel" message proclaimed the good news of a God of Steadfast Love who was determined to save the population of Caesar's empire by calling them to pledge allegiance to a different kind of citizenship altogether. Caesar's Rome represented what theologian Walter Wink called "the Domination System," an order built on the myth of redemptive violence, fear and intimidation. It was a deeply unequal economic system run by a few wealthy patrons. It was a hierarchy. Everyone knew their place.

Historically, the mainstream grows stronger and swifter by siphoning from those trying to survive by swimming upstream on the margins. This is how it has worked for the last ten thousand years of colonialism. Nations are made "great" through the thievery of indigenous lands and the exploitation of immigrant hands.

Paul's "good news" was that God was determined to redeem the world through people of faith and conscience committed to *decolonization*. These anti-imperial gatherings, known as "churches" (from the Greek *ekklesia* meaning "town hall meetings"), were energized and inspired and guided by the spirit of Jesus, who modeled and taught what a "Domination-free order" was all about. These thrived and multiplied, going against the flow of the mainstream.

When Paul wrote his letter to the church in Philippi, he was confined to a prison cell because of his defiance of Emperor Caesar, the one patriotic Roman citizens called "the Lord and Savior of the world." In some areas of the empire, loyalty to Caesar was tested with a required ritual of emperor worship. All people, slaves and citizens alike, were required to take a pinch of incense and place it on burning coals before a statue of the ruler of the world, the bringer of peace and justice. As the smoke ascended, each worshiper was to say, "Caesar is Lord." The Christians refused to participate in this patriotic pledge. They confessed with their mouth that "Jesus is Lord" (Romans 10:9). Instead of removing their caps and placing a hand on their heart, they took a knee. As a result, they were subjected to severe persecution.

Counter to a mainstream that considered sickness to be the result of fate, bad luck, or punishment, those pledging allegiance to Lord Jesus continued his ministry of healing the sick, cleansing the lepers, and casting out demons.

Counter to a mainstream that believed in revenge and the power of the sword, those pledging allegiance to Lord Jesus risked their lives by putting their bodies in the way of oppression and injustice.

Counter to a mainstream that focused only on their own families, those pledging allegiance to Lord Jesus gathered food for the hungry both inside and outside their fellowship.

Counter to a mainstream that believed in the strict separation of spirit and flesh, those pledging allegiance to Lord Jesus celebrated the God of Steadfast Love in flesh—in water, bread and wine, in all creation.

The "Jesus is Lord" movement spreading all over the

Roman Empire threatened the well-organized world of rewards, status, hierarchy, points, distinctions, enemies, oppression and the large gulf between the haves and the have-nots.

Before his conversion to Caesar's rival, Paul was well-situated in Roman society. He was a well-educated, well-heeled, well-fed Jewish elite male. He had nothing to gain (socially, politically, economically) by converting to the way of Jesus. For Paul, salvation was intimately tied to Jesus' own life and teachings. For Paul, like Jesus, it meant downward mobility. He descended like a dove, committing to a process of decolonization. He was undoing all the things that propped up his identity and status. Compared to the "surpassing value of knowing Christ Jesus my Lord," his résumé was "rubbish." Or, more precisely and dramatically, in Greek *skubala*: shit (Philippians 3:4-8).

Earlier in this same letter to the Philippians, St. Paul exhorted followers of Jesus living on the fringe of empire to "work out their salvation with fear and trembling" (Philippians 2:12b). Fear is real when the faithful commit to resisting and rising above the colonial script. It takes courage and grace in the context of a beloved community.[103]

The Lord Jesus was thoroughly political, calling his followers to subvert the colonial script that became common sense to that culture. When he taught his disciples to "give to God what is God's and to Caesar what is Caesar's," he was riffing off the foundational Jewish belief that everything belonged to God (Mark 12:17). If everything belongs to God, then Caesar is left empty-handed!

When he forgave people, he was releasing them from certain obligations that only credentialed religious leaders were supposed to perform (Mark 2:1-12).

When he broke Sabbath law (John 5:5-18) and when he shared meals with those considered "unclean" (Luke 11:37-41) and when he was healing (Luke 8:43-48) and talking with women (John 4:7-26), he was breaking social mores engraved in public policy.

When he stormed the Jerusalem Temple and overturned the tables, it was a direct action. He was leading a protest that sought to expose the ways that religious leaders blessed violent revolution, economic exploitation and substitution of worship for justice. Mainstream religion, tragically, had become a sacrificial system that bypassed solidarity and advocacy for the oppressed and marginalized (Mark 11:15-18). It was tragic because it embraced a politics that anointed the status quo.[104]

17
Why Did He Have To Die?

Jesus' lifestyle and teaching were so dangerous that he was constantly under surveillance. The establishment in Jerusalem sent their loyalists to check his allegiances and then conspired to destroy him (Mark 3:1-6). According to Wink, Jesus represented "the most intolerable threat ever placed against the spirituality, values, and arrangements of the Domination System."[105] Those with the most power and comfort—those with the most to lose in a world envisioned by Jesus—conspired to kill him.

In the first volume of their series *Ambassadors of Reconciliation*, Elaine Enns and Ched Myers challenge readers to keep the main thing the main thing—that Jesus was killed as a dissident of the mainstream:

> The primary meaning of "Jesus died for our sins" is that he was killed because of sinful humanity...the inevitable consequence of prophetic practice in a world of violence and injustice.[106]

In other words, the way he lived out his life led directly to his death.

Theologian James Cone lamented that an overwhelming majority of contemporary American Christians miss the main point of Jesus' death because of their inability to connect its historical context to what mirrors present imperial realities. Cone emphasized that Jesus' death on the cross was not necessary. It was *inevitable*. As was the assassination of Rev. Dr. Martin Luther King Jr. Crucifixions and assassinations are the responses of empires to prophetic preaching. When you are a "troublemaker" like King and Jesus, then it's bound to happen.[107]

Cone's work is vital because he calls white Americans to ponder a long-silenced perspective largely hidden from the Evangelical Christian masses. When they gaze at Jesus on the cross, Black Christians cannot help but see a God of Steadfast Love who intimately knows their deep sorrow. They are also reminded that the cross was a "public service announcement" from Roman imperial authorities: know your place...or else.[108]

According to Cone, Jesus' death was nothing less than a first century lynching, a brutal reminder to those on the margins that they'd better obey:

> As I see it, the lynching tree frees the cross from the false pieties of well-meaning Christians...the lynching tree reveals the true religious meaning of the cross for American Christians today.[109]

In the eighty years between the end of the Civil War and World War II, more than four thousand Black Americans were lynched. These were violent and public events, tolerated by state and federal officials and well-attended by picnicking spectators. Black victims were tortured and murdered for violating social mores like bumping into a white person or not addressing white folks with appropriate titles. Lynchings were acts of terrorism. Just like crucifixions.[110]

Allowing the cross and the lynching tree to interpret each other unveils the reality about God and our context. This is a God of solidarity. This is an anti-imperial God that calls us to see the world through the eyes of those crucified by the colonial script. The cross and the lynching tree together prod us to repent from and resist the illusions of the colonial script and to work for the rebirth of a world built on what King called "the beloved community."[111]

*   *   *

This historically accurate vision of the death of Jesus illuminates a more compelling meaning of baptism. Jim Perkinson describes this old Christian ritual as the decisive moment of conversion, that "at once 'drowns' everything connected with empire."[112] Today, I remind myself of my baptism by wearing a black band around my wrist with a silver pendant—a cross with a pair of running shoes draped over it. I received it as a gift in my late twenties while working summers at Kanakuk, an Evangelical sports camp in the Ozarks of Missouri.

The cross reminds me that the death of the Lord Jesus is vital to my own spirituality, although it means something very different than it did when it was given to me a few weeks after 9/11. I've come a long way on this spiritual journey. I'm still running, but I've entered a different kind of race.

The cross around my wrist calls me to the hard work of *decolonization*. It daily reminds me that I pledge allegiance to something that opposes the colonial script, with all its comforts, conveniences and benefits for straight white middle class males like me.

The cross interrogates the American trinity of God, Country and Family.

The cross rejects the kind of patriotism that assumes that the United States is the greatest country in the world and that our "freedoms" have all been earned through the benevolent sacrifice of wars.

The cross calls me to "support men and women in uniform" by advocating for what is in their best interest—for the U.S. government to stop invading and occupying other countries and for the public policies to prioritize protecting and serving the most vulnerable and marginalized.

The cross openly questions and calls out the American mainstream commitment to an economic policy that produces cheap goods and services through labor exploitation and resource extraction.

The cross around my wrist is a commitment to alternative virtues and practices—simplicity, humility, sharing, caring and bearing the burdens of the majority of the human community who have been killed, displaced and dehumanized by U.S. policies.

The cross lavishes humanity and dignity on all peoples of the world, regardless of nationality, tribe, ethnicity, gender or race.

The cross prods me to pray against and resist idolatrous political, economic and social systems, to make this kind of witness central to my "ministry."

The cross inspires me to keep running, carrying with me divine love, grace and forgiveness as I confess my own complicity with the colonial script.

The cross reminds me that only when I descend like a dove and die to the mainstream can I experience the newness of life rising up on the margins of reality.

The cross around my wrist beckons me to descend with the doves and openly oppose every personality and policy that is predatory.

The bottom line: the cross of Jesus confronts the flag of America. I must choose which symbol garners my ultimate allegiance. I choose the cross. This is a daily spiritual practice of disobeying the colonial script.

V.

Disobedience

"If he puts you in jail, then you go into that jail and transform
it from a dungeon of shame into a haven of
freedom and human dignity."
Martin Luther King Jr.
April 27, 1965, UCLA

18
At the Water Department on Randolph Street

Just a week shy of his 66th birthday, despite aching knees from decades pounding the basketball court, Bill powered up three flights of stairs to my office in the old Episcopal Church overlooking downtown Detroit. I knew he was up to some holy mischief. On a normal morning, he would whip out his flip phone and shoot me a text. On this morning, though, Bill greeted me breathless with an eye-of-the-tiger stare down. Obviously, it was game day.

Rev. Bill Wylie-Kellermann is a pastor who takes his prophetic call seriously. The first time Lindsay and I met him, we just had to ask: How many times have you been arrested for civil disobedience? His response was automatic: "After fifty, I stopped counting." So it came as no surprise that he lumbered up the stairs that morning to break the news that the city's water department would be voting on renewing its contract with a suburban wrecking company to shut off water to homes of low-income residents who were $150 or two months behind on their water bills. The department had already forked over $6 million to do the dirty work. This was for another million.

The residents of the city of less than 700,000, 40 percent of whom are surviving below the federal poverty level, continue to get pummeled by water bills with rates twice the national average. As of that spring, 14,000 homes did not have running water and 30,000 more were estimated to be shut off by the end of summer. Most of these were occupied. It's the new normal in the municipality formerly known as "The Motor City."

Bill scraped together a rag tag group of us, a thrift store version of Oceans 11. He was determined to do whatever he could to block the inevitable—even if it meant getting arrested. First, he wrangled his thirty-something sidekick Luke, an urban farmer who has squatted on abandoned land for a half dozen years, selling his kale, garlic, tomatoes, beets and raspberries at Eastern Market.

Luke was sporting wire-framed glasses and a dirty blonde dreadlocked mohawk. He learned how to resist evil in high places when he lived at Jonah House in Baltimore with the septuagenarian nuns known for their civil disobedience at military bases and the Pentagon. He's the nicest guy you'll ever meet. Just ask any of the guests he serves each morning at the soup kitchen.

Bill recruited more friends to testify during public comment. He also coaxed a socially conscious filmmaker to get video coverage. I was drafted to bail him out of jail. When we arrived for the pre-game scouting report at Checker Bar in downtown, he handed me his keys, the card to the parking structure, a list of phone numbers to call after he's arrested and $500 in cash to bail him out. He'd obviously done this before—decades of resistance work in dozens of locales, from military bases to board meetings to the middle of the street. His mentors Daniel Berrigan and William Stringfellow compelled him long ago: If the Lord Jesus and Dr. King did it, why shouldn't Pastor Bill?

We walked to the water department on Randolph Street and rode the elevator to the 5th floor. The water commissioners met in a large room, only a quarter of the space devoted to public seating. A three-foot wooden barrier with a single gate separated us from the appointed officials and their staff. It reminded me of the design of an airplane. We weren't the ones sitting in first class. Five of the commissioners were white men and four were people of color—odd in a city with a population that is 83 percent Black.

There were about twenty of us in coach that afternoon. Bill's friends spoke with eloquence and clarity: a seminary professor, a marriage and family therapist, another pastor and even the presidents of the Sierra Club and the Rosa & Raymond Parks Institute. A resident none of us knew came to the microphone. Her name was Donna. She testified that, in

March, her monthly water bill jumped from $294 to $928. The department sent someone out to check for leaks. None. Either she takes hourly showers and is fracking for oil in her backyard, or the department is making a major mistake. DWSD demanded she pay it and, of course, she couldn't afford it.

At 2:55p.m., the meeting finally got to our agenda item: the one million dollar contract renewal with Homrich Wrecking Co. Immediately, Bill stood up and approached first class to hijack the proceedings: "Stop the water shut-offs! Stop the water shut-offs! Stop the water shut-offs!" Three security guards immediately took their position at the gate. One of them looked just like Shaq's bodyguard who used to sit behind the bench of every Laker game: a large Black man with a neck as thick as my waist.

After they carried Bill down the aisle and through the doors, it was Luke's turn: "Stop the water shut-offs! Stop the water shut-offs!" A sixty-something white guy immediately body-slammed him to the ground. When he got up after being hauled out, Luke was mostly concerned that the older man might have been hurt. As Luke apologized, the man cursed him out. Later, right after apprehending Rev. Denise, another normally well-behaved pastor who went rogue with shouting and singing, he apologized to Luke for his temper.

Another white sixty-something security guard with a shaved head stared me down when I came out to the lobby, which was serving as a holding tank. The Black chief of security, though, struggled to hide his appreciation for this holy spectacle. My wife, the licensed therapist, came out of the commissioners' boardroom and shook his hand. She thanked him for doing his job, graciously allowing her to stay in the room when she led activists chanting "Shame!" after they voted unanimously to approve the million-dollar contract. "I'm smiling," he said, "because back in the '60s and '70s, we were doing the same thing." That was before forty years of police work in the suburbs.

Thirty minutes later, five Detroit cops calmly strolled out of the elevator, and after a short period of deliberation, decided to let the holy rebels go with a warning. Outside in a cool spring drizzle, Bill retrieved his keys and cash from me. He half-jokingly suggested that he might be getting too old for this. I shook my head and told him he'd better wear his knee braces next time.

19
Consider

Before the Apostle Paul joined the movement called "the Way" (Acts 9:2) he was Saul, a murderer of members of the Way. In his own words, he was "violently persecuting the church of God" (Galatians 1:13), hell-bent on stopping the Jesus cult from spreading its heretical tentacles all over Palestine and beyond. He threatened, intimidated, projected and scapegoated—what happens when a religion becomes unsafe and destructive.

The Way proclaimed an inclusivity that defied tradition. It threw open the doors, inviting just about anybody into its fold: women, slaves, sell-outs, the physically unclean, the sexually impure and uncircumcised. To their opponents, the Way posed a dire threat to any dream of Making Israel Great Again.

On his way to Damascus, chasing refugees of the Way into Syria, Saul had an epiphany—his zeal was fueling the wrong side of history! As it turned out, his murderous threats and tactics were not of God. He was blinded and started hearing voices. Was he crazy? Or was this his conscience getting his attention—what addicts know all too well as hitting rock bottom? This was the moment he knew it was time to drop his power and privilege and descend like a dove into this Spirit-driven movement.

Eventually, Saul was embraced by leaders of the way and threw in with the holy revolution. Actually, it wasn't really a conversion. More like a transition. The voice of Jesus on the road to Damascus was seconding the motions of what had always been calling him. It was a voice crying out from deep within him, a divine spark lighting a fire in his soul that never fully extinguished, even on his most angry, hateful and violent days.

He changed his name to Paul and his passion led him into the streets and synagogues of imperial Rome. He taught that the Lord Jesus was the reality for which Lord Caesar was the counterfeit: that humble service, unconditional love and tenderly forgiving ourselves and others was the Way to authentic life. Every living thing imaged God. No exceptions. No hierarchies. No scapegoats. The way into eternal life was the way out of empire. It was a beautiful conspiracy that interrogated the colonial script. It was a new kind of exodus.

Eventually, imperial forces arrested Paul and locked him up. His teachings were widely considered subversive, unpatriotic and blasphemous by Roman citizens committed to the colonial script. He wrote about Christ Jesus (not the Roman Emperor) sitting on a "judgment seat" and a "throne" (2 Corinthians 5:10). He borrowed political jargon like "church" and "gospel" and "fellowship" to describe key elements of the Way. Paul was a political prisoner, like John the Baptist and Jesus, following the alternative script of the Hebrew prophets who spoke truth to power.

Paul was carrying the prophetic torch of the Hebrew midwives who refused to obey the commands of the Egyptian Pharoah to kill every newborn male (Exodus 1). He was following in the line of the subversive, anti-imperial antics of Shadrach, Meshach and Abednego who rejected the king's firm mandate to bow down to the dehumanizing idols of empire (Daniel 3). He was echoing the ways of "the wise men" who refused to report back to Herod after they found the baby Jesus in Bethlehem (Matthew 2). There was plenty of precedent for Paul's holy disobedience.

* * *

The Apostle Paul was a model for Rev. Dr. Martin Luther King Jr., who was arrested for civil disobedience nineteen times. In October 1960, King joined several dozen student-activists from the newly formed Student Nonviolent Coordinating Committee (SNCC) in a sit-in at the lunch counter at Rich's Department Store in Atlanta. They were arrested, jailed and refused bail. King was singled out and sentenced to four months of hard labor at a prison 200 miles from home.[113]

In 1963, his "Letter From a Birmingham Jail" was written on the margins of a newspaper and toilet paper and smuggled out of his cell. King the "outside agitator" wrote the letter in response to eight white pastors from Birmingham who published an editorial questioning the bold nonviolent direct action of the civil rights movement which led to numerous arrests. King lamented:

> You deplore the demonstrations taking place in Birmingham. But your statement, I am sorry to say, fails to express a similar concern for the conditions that brought about the demonstrations.[114]

Rosa Parks, too, was a model for the young Martin Luther King Jr. "From my upbringing and the Bible," Parks once wrote, "I learned people should stand up for rights just as the children of Israel stood up to the Pharaoh."[115] When she was forty-two years old, she refused to give up her seat on an Alabama bus after working all day as a seamstress at a department store. After she was arrested, her co-workers refused to speak to her. She and her husband Raymond both lost their jobs as a result of her action.

Contrary to popular myth perpetrated by the colonial script, Rosa Parks did not refuse to give up her seat because she was tired. Trainings and organizing meetings prepared her for her intentional act of holy rebellion, designed to challenge structural racism in the city. It sparked a bus boycott that lasted 381 days, leading to the U.S. Supreme Court ruling that bus segregation was illegal. Eight months later, unable to find work and facing death threats, the Parks family moved north to Detroit.

Consider also Bayard Rustin, one of the godfathers of the Civil Rights Movement, who wrote, "We need in every bay and community a group of angelic troublemakers."[116] Rustin was arrested for defying segregated seating in restaurants, buses and trains. He also refused to serve in the military. He believed that the true power of resisting the colonial script was in the ability to make it unworkable, to utilize human bodies as nonviolent weapons to lodge in the spokes of the system so that the wheels can no longer turn.

Consider the rebellious Catholic nuns at Baltimore's Jonah House who confront the atrocity of nuclear weapons by sneaking onto military bases and pouring their own blood (in the shape of a cross) on nuclear warheads. This nonviolent movement calls itself "Plowshares," drawing attention to violence with their hammers, as they "beat swords into plowshares" (Isaiah 2:2-4) until they are arrested.

Consider the poet and priest Daniel Berrigan who, when asked how many times he'd been arrested, responded, "Not enough." After a non-violent direct action in the late '60s, he was sentenced to three years in federal prison. He wrote from his cell explaining that he "would neither remain silent nor passive before the pathology of naked power, which rules our country and dominates half the world."[117] The real question was not "Why?" but instead "Why not?"

Consider Bree Newsome, a thirty-something Black woman who was arrested in 2015 after she shimmied up the flagpole at the state capitol in South Carolina, took the Confederate flag in her hand and, before she recited Psalm 27 and the Lord's Prayer, she proclaimed:

> You come against me with hatred and oppression and violence. I come against you in the name of God. This flag comes down today![118]

Consider Rose Berger, the senior associate editor of *Sojourners Magazine*, who joined fifty-three mostly-senior-citizen activists in a flash mob at the headquarters of Environmental Resources Management (ERM), the firm hired by the U.S. State Department that gave approval to the Keystone XL pipeline. These rebellious retirees were arrested and charged for "unlawful entry" after blocking the elevators by chaining their arms together inside a PVC pipe and chanting a "public liturgy" about Big Oil, Mother Earth and the need for a transparent democracy.[119]

Consider my friend Cait De Mott Grady who grew up in an extended family of resisters committed to a life she describes as "walking in a closer relationship with structures of power." From a very young age, Cait learned about the colonial script in community, in courtrooms and in the streets. Her parents met at a Plowshares action in the early '80's and, after an arrest for civil disobedience and sentencing, passed love notes to each other while serving in prison together.

Cait's dad, Peter, was a Marine who went to Vietnam where he came to understand war as "organized mass murder," a conviction directly tied to his discipleship to Jesus who commanded his followers to love one another and their enemies and to do good to those who persecuted them. Peter committed the rest of his life to working with his hands and participating in organized direct actions at military bases and recruiting centers.[120]

*   *   *

A cursory examination of U.S. prisons testifies to the system that Parks, King, De Mott, Newsome and Pastor Bill have been resisting for decades. Over the past forty years, American prisons have become bloated with poor people of color, mostly Black and Brown men who have been racially profiled and slapped with heavy sentences for "crimes" like possessing small amounts of marijuana. These are some of the real victims of the colonial script.

In 2015, *The New York Times* published an article entitled "1.5 Million Missing Black Men."[121] Anyone daring to take the complete tour of American prisons would eventually find most of them. Michelle Alexander wrote *The New Jim Crow* (2010) to expose this hidden reality, connecting mass incarceration to previous eras of slavery and Jim Crow. Alexander unveiled a criminal justice system no longer concerned with prevention and punishment of crime, but instead primarily about "the management and control of the dispossessed."[122] In reality, it is a criminal (in)justice system that captures and cages the doves of American society.

In the mid-1980s, President Reagan officially declared his "War on Drugs," punishing "crackheads" with a minimum five-year sentence for anyone possessing 5 grams. When it came to powdered cocaine, the wealthy white drug of choice, it would take 500 grams to receive the same five-year minimum sentence.

These Republican policies percolated at the end of my elementary school years in suburbia. I vividly remember a friend's dad consistently driving me home in his Jaguar while sipping on his post-work cocktail. However, Reagan never ordered a War on Drunk Driving. When politicians eventually strengthened new penalties for DUIs, they paled in comparison to the automatic five-year sentence for first time crack users.[123]

Decades later, the United States leads the world in

prison population. There are more than 2.3 million Americans locked up. Many of these prisoners provide cheap labor for governments and corporations (making from eight cents to about forty-four cents an hour and, in some states like Alabama, earning nothing). Journalist Chris Hedges asks, "Why pay workers outside the walls the minimum wage when you can pay workers behind walls only a couple of dollars a day?"[124] Only a system that prioritizes profit over people demands more prisons.

Alexander proposes that the current condition of this system leaves people of faith and conscience with a choice—either extend care, compassion and concern for those locked up (what anyone would seek for their own children), or continue to shame and blame the most vulnerable among us. Unfortunately, this latter option is the path that American society has chosen.[125]

Prisons are the first clue that American society is in serious trouble. Jim Perkinson proposes that the colonial script might just be the most mentally disturbed in history, an ironic form of American "exceptionalism:"

> We are Number One on the planet in murder. Drug use. Incarceration. Child abuse. Clinical depression. Divorce. Debt. Weapons ownership. Total crime. Defense spending. Carbon-footprint. Obesity. And we often take our own lives.[126]

King called upon the United States to, instead, lead the world in a "revolution of values."[127] For John the Baptist, Jesus, the Apostle Paul, Martin Luther, Dietrich Bonhoeffer, Dr. King, Father Berrigan and so many others, a vital aspect of Christian faith is actively disobeying laws that value profit motives and property rights over people.[128]

20
Living in a Mess

Christian disobedience has a long and holy history. Many have been inspired by the life and teachings of Jesus to use their own bodies as obstacles to and witnesses of the injustice embedded in our society. This nonviolent tactic can effectively expose the poverty and oppression created by what Alexander has called "a tightly networked system of laws, policies, customs and institutions."[129]

The Evangelical Christianity of my youth, however, trained me to embrace a mentality of "law and order." To pledge unquestioned allegiance to God and country. Following Jesus was, ironically, about obeying authority—the Bible, our teachers and coaches, our parents, our pastors, our bosses, the Republican President—no matter what. I've often observed Evangelical leaders reacting to civil disobedience or just "activism" in general, by "proof-texting" from Paul's letter to the Romans: "Let every person be subject to the governing authorities" (Romans 13:1). In these circumstances, they use this passage as a timeless, universal command. Obey your elders—no matter what.

However, in historical context, Paul's plea for obedience was a check on first century Christians who believed that their faith in the Lord Jesus gave them license to do anything and everything they wanted. Paul was warning that this kind of anything goes "freedom in Christ" was foolish. He was also being strategic. Paul knew that the little house church in the capital of the empire had no chance whatsoever against the power of the Roman state.

However, twenty-first century American society is a slightly different context. Sure, the power and excess of the state is massive. But, today, at the very least, North Americans have a semblance of constitutional democracy. There is an entire tradition of nonviolent direct action—from the Boston

Tea Party to the Montgomery Bus Boycott—that has changed society by creatively disobeying its unjust rules. Civil disobedience has never been an argument about "just being rebellious." It is about refusing to cooperate with evil. It is about exposing injustice and oppression with our bodies.

The trouble with white Evangelical quoting of Romans 13:1 is that it is an argument for passivity. It over-spiritualizes Christian faith. It is a defense for the unjust and oppressive status quo. Preserving law and order at all costs props up a system governed by the colonial script. What is preserved is a whole unjust state of affairs dictated by race, class and gender.

Demanding full obedience to every governing authority also silences what Paul writes immediately prior. Romans 12 charges members of the subversive house church "to present your bodies as a living sacrifice" (12:1) and "not be conformed to this world" (12:2). Paul called for humility and "sober judgment" (12:3) and an organized movement of people with different gifts and roles (12:4-8). He challenged them to "hate what is evil" (12:9), to "not lag in zeal" (12:11), to be "patient in suffering" (12:12), to "associate with the lowly" (12:16) and to refuse revenge (12:19).

Another major problem with white Evangelical dismissal of civil disobedience is that it scans over the angelic troublemaking of Jesus himself. He broke the law to bring life to his people. By doing this, he confronted the unjust distribution of social, economic and political power. In at least one instance, the sacred text unveils the subversive fact that Jesus was a fugitive of the law: "Then they tried again to arrest him; but he escaped from their power" (John 10:39). This is what happens when one pledges allegiance to a movement diametrically opposed to the colonial script.

Historian Howard Zinn believed that real change would only come if those the system benefits—those Zinn called "the somewhat privileged"—would possess the conviction and courage to revolt. The real problem, Zinn lamented, was that "people are obedient all over the world in the face of poverty and starvation and stupidity, and war, and cruelty."[130] Unquestioned obedience to a system built on the colonial script is the opposite of authentic faith.

* * *

The same summer that Lindsay and I road-tripped in search of alternative brands of Christian faith, Dr. Willie Jennings (at the time, a Duke Divinity School professor) joined a large group of religious leaders getting arrested at the state Capitol building in Raleigh, North Carolina. After his short stint in jail, Jennings reflected that "there comes a point when the words you write crowd into the life you live and demand that you reorganize your space or you will live in a mess."[131] In other words, it is what he had to do in order to maintain his own integrity—for his actions to remain congruent with his convictions.

The constant prospect of "living in a mess" haunts my own life. The more I learn about the "tightly networked system of laws, policies, customs and institutions" that scripts American culture, the more I realize how much I've both benefited from and been complicit in it. I am a walking, talking paradox. An ongoing ethical dilemma. A mess. I know, deep down, that the only way to live congruently is to confront the dysfunction and dehumanization. To connect the dots and tell the truth. In the face of evil and tragedy, "free people," as Berrigan wrote from prison, "cannot remain free *and* silent."[132]

Like Jennings, my conscience has long been screaming out for my attention. My clean arrest record was interrogating the world around me. It unveiled an unjust system that has granted me virtually infinite opportunity while members of my college basketball team, who grew up in poor, Black neighborhoods, were constantly reminded of old felonies every time they applied for a job or housing or anything else—

because they got caught coping with small amounts of marijuana (while I got drunk on beer) or because they were arrested for stealing to survive (while I asked my parents for money).

My clean arrest record was also interrogating myself. It raised an eyebrow to a lifestyle of talking the "radical" talk and walking a rather comfortable and convenient walk. It prodded me to imagine what kind of beautiful society might be realized if everyone in my shoes organized and strategized with the kind of robust nonviolent direct action that Dr. King and the civil rights movement utilized to "turn the world upside down" (Acts 17:6) in the 1960s.

Lindsay and I both got arrested in nonviolent direct actions with the new Poor People's Campaign (PPC) in the spring of 2018. This movement initially grabbed our attention because it was directly connected to the substance and spirit of the original Poor People's Campaign that Dr. King helped start in the 1960s. PPC 2.0 organized to raise awareness by shifting the narrative away from Trump destruction and distraction to the real heroes and heroines resisting and rising above poverty and oppression all over the continent.[133]

Ched has wisely encouraged us to take civil disobedience seriously, but slowly. The focus, according to Myers, should be on "making the resistance more holistic." Reconstructing our lifestyle is more important and more challenging than one act of political spectacle. It starts with taking inventory of the dehumanizing ways that we obey this tightly networked system of laws, policies, customs and institutions. Where and when are we called to simple acts of civil disobedience today?

The goal is a whole lifestyle of civil disobedience. Sometimes, this may lead to arrest. But most of the time, it will involve connecting the dots and telling the truth *wherever we are standing*—at work, online, at church, around the dinner table. Sometimes, this will involve whistleblowing on our bosses or people in power in our social network. Most often, unjust policies will never change unless major social pressure is applied. This part of making the resistance more holistic is serious, courageous, inconvenient and awkward business.

*   *   *

Today, Americans find themselves prisoners to what Dorothy Day, the co-founder of the Catholic Worker movement, called "this rotten, decadent, putrid industrial capitalist system."[134] The way of Jesus, Paul and King and Wylie-Kellermann is fundamentally about disobeying everything that dehumanizes, the first step toward freeing ourselves from the prison of the system.

Paul greets readers of his letters in a scandalous way, identifying himself, not as a citizen, but as a "prisoner" of the empire (Philemon 1). The ancient text compels readers to take personal inventory: why not me too? This is a sacred tension. I continue to be prodded by the words of Dr. King who warned white audiences that, far too often, we live as "protectors of the status quo." This tension I live in calls for humility, confession and, sometimes, more questions than answers. I'm slowly learning that this is a big part of what it means to descend like a dove—what it really looks like "to have faith."

VI.
Faith

"There is still a need for more people to become actively involved in the movement, to become involved participants instead of detached spectators."
Martin Luther King Jr.
April 27, 1965, UCLA

21
Conspiracy Theories

I'll never forget the day I met Monica Lewis-Patrick. She showed up to the church late that Tuesday afternoon, after ubering her teenage daughters all over the city—from school to practice to organizing meetings. She was invited to join a panel of white Bible experts jargoning over "hermeneutical circles" and "the scandal of particularity." Five minutes after she took her seat, she harkened St. Peter's proclamation that "love covers a multitude of sins" (1 Peter 4:8) all over impoverished neighborhoods of Detroit. Monica broke into sermon, her passionate story-telling splashing wave upon wave of new life all over the mostly-white audience. Spirit was descending like a dove.

This postmodern Pentecost was playing out just a few months after the Republican governor of Michigan appointed an emergency manager (EM) to take the reins from the mayor and city council of Detroit. Monica explained that the EM served as the city's dictator, ushering in the historic bankruptcy proceedings while slashing pension and health-care obligations to longtime city workers.

Yet, despite an all-out assault on longtime, low-income Black residents of the city, corporate and government leaders, as well as media outlets, had consistently reported that this was the start of a "comeback." Monica, the point-guard of Detroit's grassroots struggle for clean and affordable water, reframed this "comeback" for the congregation. It was nothing less than "a collaborative, well-orchestrated system of evil." Detroit was not really bankrupt. It was being bankrupted.

The sins of power and corruption, according to Monica, cling to her city like late summer humidity—backroom deals, shady business contracts and inhumane water shut-offs. But the power of love rushes in as neighbors come to the rescue via buckets and hoses. Young Black men like "Rome," "Kitchen" and "Razor" deliver gallons of water to those in dire straits all over the 139 square-mile post-industrial apocalypse. Just as she was kicking it into another gear, Monica proclaimed, "Faith is not something I pick up like a book. It's something I walk out with my life." Authentic faith always resists the ever-present temptation of being reduced to a noun.

Monica is a living, breathing, passionate action verb. A native of Tennessee who has been baptized into the struggle against policies hijacking public education, water and housing in Detroit, Monica lost her bid for city council by a few dozen votes. That was a year after she lost her only son to gun violence. Faith breaks the chains of passivity when one battles forces like this. For Monica, being a Christian means wildly trusting in a Power that will sustain her in love—somehow, some way—while she works tirelessly for victims of hate, injustice, violence and oppression.

Monica's theological clarification was a distinct contrast to the Evangelical "belief system" that I grew up with—a formulaic series of postulates claiming to crack the code of eternal salvation. I was taught that "having faith," was about signing on to certain biblical convictions about God and a whole lot more. The inerrant Bible. The perfectly divine Jesus. Original sin that created an everlasting divide between humanity and God. A prayer uttered with a sincere heart that saved us for eternity. A transcendent God in control—everything happening for a reason. In this mode, if you mentally assent to the correct ideas about God, Jesus and the Bible, only then you are on the right path. If not, well…

* * *

In both word and deed, Monica's undomesticated definition mirrors the biblical "faith" (Greek *pistis*) of New Testament authors. It is a commitment to something much deeper than a head game. The Gospel of John, for instance, portrays the disciples of Jesus, after his death, filled with "unbelief" (*apistis*), huddled together inside on a Sunday because they were afraid of the elite coalition of religious and political leaders who had just tortured and executed their unarmed leader in a mockery of justice. They feared that they would be next.

And then, the crucified Jesus rose up and appeared to his posse. One of the disciples, however, was missing-in-action:

> But Thomas (who was called the Twin), one of the twelve, was not with them when Jesus came. So the other disciples told him, "We have seen the Lord." But he said to them, "Unless I see the mark of the nails in his hands, and put my finger in the mark of the nails and my hand in his side, I will not believe." A week later his disciples were again in the house, and Thomas was with them. Although the doors were shut, Jesus came and stood among them and said, "Peace be with you." Then he said to Thomas, "Put your finger here and see my hands. Reach out your hand and put it in my side. Do not doubt but believe." Thomas answered him, "My Lord and my God!" Jesus said to him, "Have you believed because you have seen me? Blessed are those who have not seen and yet have come to believe" (John 20:24-29).

At the time this Gospel was written, fifty to sixty years after the death of Jesus, the Roman Emperor Domitian was referred to as "the Son of God," "the Lord," and the ultimate: "my Lord and my God." After all, imperial propagandists claimed, it was Domitian who brought peace to the entire world.

In every era, the colonial script spins narratives to get her citizens to believe. In fact, variations of English translations of *pistis* that arise over and over in this episode—translated as belief, believe, believing—are rooted in the imperial lexicon. Citizens were required to pledge *pistis* to the Emperor in ritualized incense burning. Those who refused were persecuted and many were tortured and killed. For these first readers of the Gospel of John, this was *not* an irrational fear. They worshipped behind locked doors.

Pistis was not just mental assent to a certain set of religious doctrines. It was about loyalty, an everyday socio-political choice with profound consequences. It wasn't something they picked up like a book. It was something that they walked out with their lives. It was the answer to the question, "Who are you ultimately pledging allegiance to?"

Earlier in John's Gospel, as the chief priests pressed Pilate to crucify Jesus, they wanted to make their "belief" plain, "If you release this man, you are no friend of the Emperor," they testified. "We have no king but Emperor!" (John 19:15). Faith was just as political then as it ought to be now.

*   *   *

The peace of the Lord Jesus (*Pax Christi*) created a tense rivalry with the comfort and power of religious elites who pledged allegiance to the Emperor's *Pax Romana*. In the Gospel story, the risen Jesus eventually bestows the power to forgive on to his followers, hijacking that role from the priests (John 20:22-23). The power to forgive was a fundamental practice stemming from Jesus' critique of how people were valued in his society. He rearranged the imperial rankings of whose lives really mattered.

The powerful establishment, then as now, utilized a mainstream media to script the masses into a conventional wisdom. When the disciples tell the absent Thomas that they had seen "the Lord," he naturally sides with imperial conventional wisdom. Crucified rebels were guilty and cursed by God (Deuteronomy 21:23). And obviously, rising from the dead was pure fantasy. If Jesus was the real Lord, he would have conquered and dethroned the ruling elites, not gotten himself crucified by them.

These mourning doves are spinning conspiracy theories and Thomas isn't buying it. The only way he's going to pledge allegiance to Jesus as the true Lord is if he can see it and feel it for himself. For anyone scripted by the rationale of conventional wisdom, Thomas' skepticism was utterly reasonable.

Conspiracy theories, on the other hand, incessantly question the colonial script. They arise from oppressed and marginalized communities, like the original disciples of Jesus who were attempting to make sense of their plight in the world. Conspiracy theories are not 100 percent factual. They contain hyperbole and a poetic license that serve to flip conventional myths into more faithful renderings of life on the ground. Conspiracy theories testify to the truth in ways that conventional wisdom rarely does.

As Monica explained during a workshop at a national Evangelical conference at the Renaissance Center in Detroit, when assessing the haves and the have-nots, it is vital to question imperial conventional wisdom. Water shutoffs and home foreclosures, she clarified, don't stem from sinners making bad decisions. These arise from powerful people scripting sinful polices that devastate poor communities. When falcons write the rules, doves are decimated.

Conspiracy theorists know that the prosperity gospel—that "God provides" wealth and health based on simple trust—is foolish. They know deep down that decisions are being made behind the curtain that directly affect who wins and who loses in society. Conspiracy theories push back against justifications of the unjust status quo based on personal responsibility narratives—that poverty, imprisonment, dilapidated schools and water shut-offs are a result of bad life choices. If we are actually attempting to solve society's ills, blaming the victim is never an effective strategy.

22
Conventional Wisdom

For decades now, Black Americans have testified to police brutalities and the killing of unarmed friends and family members by the authorities. White folks, by and large, have played the role of the doubting Thomas of conventional wisdom. "No, these aren't victims: they are 'thugs' and 'criminals.'" White folks have schlepped these lamentations aside as silly conspiracy theories, illogical and unproven. And then along came the Smart Phone. YouTube is now chalk-full of horrific videos of these killings. Just Google "unarmed Black man shot 16 times" as exhibit A. The conspiracy theory is, in fact, a reality.

Black communities in the United States have consistently re-narrated the War on Drugs in America as a war on Black people. White folks have played the role of doubting Thomas. "This isn't about race. It's about the real drug problem in our ghettos. Crack kills. Just say no." However, scholarship from Loic Wacquant, Michelle Alexander and others have provided irrefutably data. Alexander carefully documented that the drug war has been waged almost exclusively in poor communities of color, even though the research reveals that people of all races and ethnicities use and sell drugs at the same rates.[135] The ghetto and the suburb have this fact in common.

The detailed analysis from universities is backed by the later confession of John Erlichman, Richard Nixon's chief domestic advisor during the roll out of the initial installation of "The War on Drugs" in 1971. He eventually confessed to an interviewer that they created a false conventional wisdom about their political enemies through an elaborate orchestration of deceit and lies:

> We knew we couldn't make it illegal to be either against the war or blacks, but by getting the public to associate

the hippies with marijuana and blacks with heroin, and then criminalizing both heavily, we could disrupt those communities.[136]

The conspiracy theory is, in fact, a reality.

Yet, in much of white America, the conventional wisdom of "law and order" and "the politics of responsibility" continues to trump the truthfulness of these conspiracy theories arising from the margins. Psychotherapist Edwin Friedman writes that people think *emotionally*, not rationally. Reason, clarity, transparency and analysis is too often vetoed by powerful vested interests, deep fears and unresolved hurts. Hearing about it, researching it, and even watching it online are, often times, just not enough. But Thomas calls us further on, to travel to places of trauma to touch open wounds in order to have a more robust faith:

> Unless I see the mark of the nails in his hands, and put my finger in the mark of the nails and my hand in his side, I will not believe (John 20:25).

Thomas is the mascot for all of us claiming to be objectively weighing reality from the sidelines. The bottom line: If these alternative renderings of reality arising from the margins are just crazy "conspiracy theories," we can go on living as we please. Nothing is demanded from the rest of us. There's no need for repentance. There's no need to decolonize.

The key is confession. Our perspectives are limited by our isolation from those living on "the other side." Everything sounds like a conspiracy that doesn't match our experience. Abject poverty, injustice and violence are all easily explained away. But once we actually go there—when we see it for ourselves and then digest and debrief it—our perspective on reality begins to change.

*   *   *

The conventional wisdom about the downfall of Detroit is that middle-class white folks had to flee for their lives to the suburbs. It was no longer safe. Black folks have been scripted as violent "thugs," addicted to drugs, careless, lazy and dependent on the government. "Those people are what ruined Detroit," the white middle-aged female cashier at Target in the suburbs proclaimed to me one day. She made it crystal clear who "those people" were.

The conventional wisdom about the comeback of Detroit is that the city desperately needs a combination of corporate redevelopment and personal responsibility, in order to grow the economy and balance the budget. Conventional wisdom proclaims that the city needs to "change the culture" when it comes to residents paying their water bills and property taxes.

Conventional wisdom is confronted by longtime residents who have a conspiracy theory—that these policies unfairly target poor Black people who stayed and paid while everyone else walked away from the city in the '60s, '70s and '80s. In actuality, the "comeback" is a clearing out campaign built on both austerity and white supremacy. Detroit can be declared a "comeback" city, in fact, only if it is defined by "what is best for white people."

A few months after we moved to Detroit in 2014, Monica told us about leaders from Flint showing up at a protest in Detroit with bottles of brownish-yellow water from taps in their homes. She testified to an epidemic of lead poisoning in Flint. I listened, but like my namesake, Thomas, I balked. *This can't possibly be true. This just doesn't happen in America.* My own imagination, after all, had been scripted by conventional wisdom for decades. My perspective had been severely malformed by the comfort and convenience granted by my class, gender and race.

It was a humbling wake-up call when, more than a year

later, the Flint water crisis finally went viral. I'm ashamed to say, it took the headlines of mainstream media to finally validate the brutality of reality. Residents of Flint had been drinking water from their taps tainted with lead and other deadly bacteria. Complaints and cries for help were legion. An epidemic of Legionnaires disease erupted. Local, state and federal officials poured on denials, distraction, distortions, rebukes and justifications. Eventually, this conventional wisdom was exposed for what it really was: lies.

Even though I had traveled 2,000 miles, from the mainstream to the margins, my consciousness was still weighed down and blocked by the colonial script. White supremacy and patriarchy, as always, were hard at work, colluding against me, "These women are overreacting." My white male suburban mind demanded hard data. Of course, these women delivered the data, too!

While grassroots organizers in Flint were recruiting an Oceans 11 team of journalists, lawyers, doctors and water engineers to conduct water tests to support their soon-to-be-proven conspiracy theories, the women of We The People of Detroit were partnering with Ph.D. students and faculty at Wayne State University on a mapping project in Detroit that graphically revealed their findings—city leadership targeted certain neighborhoods for water shut-offs, school shutdowns and home foreclosures. It followed a clear pattern of systematic racism, a clearing out campaign to reimage the city with a young, white upwardly mobile face. As Monica bluntly proclaims, "Detroit's not broke. It's been broken into."

One of the more illuminating historic epiphanies from the published project shined the light on the suburbs surrounding Detroit, already heavily subsidized by federal highways, FHA loans and more. This coalition of scholars and community organizers clearly documented the unconventional truth that each and every suburban municipality marks up water rates that the Detroit Water and Sewerage Department sells to them at wholesale. Some suburban city governments tack on almost 1,000 percent to the price of the water they sell their residents.[137]

For decades, white suburban folks grumbled to their city leaders about Black Detroit jacking up their water rates. Suburban leaders rolled with the myth, creating their own conveniently deceptive conventional wisdom. As it turns out, Black Detroit was gifting water to the white suburbs at wholesale prices as white suburban leaders then hiked rates to increase city revenues. In fact, according to state law, Detroit's water department can only legally charge what it costs to treat and deliver water to its suburban customers.[138]

Demanding "data" to block progress is nothing new, an historic trend embedded in the history of white America. White folks in the 1960s had access to plenty of "convincing data" to prod them to make robust commitments to change local and federal policies that were decimating Black people. They saw for themselves, live on their television sets in the suburbs, fire hoses and attack dogs in Birmingham and skull-crushing beatings in Selma.

In the wake of violent uprisings in Watts, Detroit, Newark and elsewhere, Congress created the National Commission on Civil Disorders. After three months of hearings that called in 130 witnesses, it produced a five-inch thick, 1,400-page report that proclaimed it loud and clear (verbatim from the report):

White society is deeply implicated in the ghetto.[139]

The eleven "Kerner Commission" members were moderate-to-conservative white men (and one white woman) who shockingly proposed this solution:

From every American it will require new attitudes, new understanding, and above all, new will. Hard choices

117

must be made, and if necessary, new taxes enacted.[140]

Kerner was a confessional document, calling out the conventional wisdom that reigned supreme in white communities for decades.

Unfortunately, the Democratic President (and his white supporters) ignored the recommendations. Funds were funneled to arm local police forces with high-tech arsenals of tanks, machine guns, nerve gas and more.[141] The data is available and the solutions are clear, but leaders both historic and contemporary choose to travel a different path. The results are devastating. Today, 21 percent of children live in poverty (in contrast to 15.6 percent in 1968) as cities and schools have become re-segregated beyond belief—an abysmal failure of faith.[142]

23
Tending to the Wounds of Empire

To have faith is to pledge allegiance to the way of Jesus as an alternative to the colonial script that governs American culture. It is, as Dr. King challenged my dad and thousands of other mostly white students at UCLA in 1965, "to become involved participants instead of detached spectators." Faith is the substance that fuels us in our mission to actually make King's dream a living reality.

In 1963, King delivered his famous "Dream" speech in front of the Lincoln Memorial in Washington D.C. to an audience of hundreds of thousands of "veterans of creative suffering." These were involved participants in the struggle who, King lamented, "still languished in the corners of American society."[143] A year earlier, in a speech celebrating the 100-year anniversary of Lincoln's Emancipation Proclamation, King defined faith as "taking the first step when you don't see the whole staircase."[144] He portrayed a way-of-life modeled by those first followers of Jesus who "walked by faith, not by sight" (2 Corinthians 5:7).

Debra Taylor, one of the co-founders of We The People of Detroit, says that, if you want to see the whole staircase— the big picture of what this world is coming to—all you need to do is visit Detroit. She warns that her hometown is "the beta test for what the rest of the country is about to experience." Detroit has been used as a laboratory for corporate takeovers, crafty experiments devised by corporate and political leaders who warn of the dangers of big government in order to cut taxes and slash spending on programs that low-income residents depend on. In the next breath, these elites call for subsidizing big businesses with new stadiums, militarized police and rail lines connecting high-end bars and restaurants.

In Detroit and beyond, authentic faith beckons disciples to throw in with mourning doves on the margins—with under-resourced neighborhoods, instead of with the falcon forces of urban redevelopment.[145] Those with access to capital come in from outside the city drooling over a "blank canvas." Detroit author adrienne marie brown describes the whole scene tragically as "...the opportunity available among the ruins of other people's lives."[146]

The blank canvas doesn't just happen. In Michigan, a coalition of high-flying falcons, including the governor, the mayor of Detroit and Quicken Loans multi-billionaire Dan Gilbert have hijacked federal dollars earmarked to help low-income residents pay back predatory bank loans and transferred hundreds of millions toward "blight removal." This wealth, intended to help victims of subprime mortgages, has been redistributed to suburban contractors creating more open land (with their bulldozers) for suburban developers to cash in on their entrepreneurial schemes.[147]

Some people, well-acquainted with the perspective from the margins, will believe the conspiracy theories and pledge allegiance to resisting redevelopment. Indeed, as the Gospel text proclaims, "Blessed are those who have not seen and yet have come to believe" (John 20:29). However, many of us, like Thomas, will only believe the alternative narrative when it affects us directly. Thomas reminds the rest of us that something ground-breaking happens to and through us when we risk social alienation and question conventional wisdom. When we go beyond Googling it and see it for ourselves.

"If you've ever seen a mother going door to door just to get a cup of water for a bottle for her baby," Monica lamented, "then you know it's not a condition that people choose to live in. It's a condition that has been imposed on them." Thomas did not shift his allegiance until he put his fingers in the destructive and dehumanizing wounds pierced by the weapons of conventional wisdom.

The reader of the subversive Gospel story is called to follow Thomas and then circle back to the beginning of the story. There, Jesus invites the disciples to "come and see" the real life behind the conspiracy theories of our world (John 1:39-41). This is how convictions change. It is how allegiance gets rearranged from conventional wisdom to the divine conspiracy of Jesus.

However, the authentic faith defined by Jesus, King and Monica assures me that my unbelief, my caving to conventional wisdom, is not a deal breaker. The risen Jesus shows up anyways, always offering me the "peace" of the dove (John 20:26). This is a Lord who defies falcon aggression, gently pursuing us with Steadfast Love. This is a Lord determined to remind us that theories about this divine conspiracy are, in fact, true. They set us free. I am slowly learning to stop underestimating the forces that propagandize me and dehumanize me with their conventional wisdom. These have taken their toll on me over the decades. It's long past time to stop the bleeding.

Disciples who dig deeper to the root discover that

"conspiracy" comes from a Latin word meaning "to breathe with." Breathing with the God of Steadfast Love. Breathing with those on the margins. Breathing with the meaning of life and the nature of reality. Breathing with those, like Monica and Debra, who have given their lives over to tending the wounds of empire.

These model an entirely different mode of faith altogether—one they walk out with their lives. In order to descend with these doves and then follow them up the staircase, I had to take the first awkward step: to listen carefully to the conspiracy so that its powerful truth could set me free. More and more, I am slowly realizing that faith starts with listening to the conspiracy and trusting that this is where truth is breathing life into the world.

VII.
Listen

"I am not a ceremonial symbol. I am an activist. I didn't just emerge after Martin died—I was always there and involved."
Coretta Scott King (1976)[148]

"We know that no section of our country can boast of clean hands in the area of ~~brotherhood~~ sisterhood."
Martin Luther King Jr.
April 27, 1965, UCLA

24
Icons

Maureen Taylor has spent decades tending to wounds inflicted by the colonial script. She also holds to a strict no-tolerance-policy when conventional wisdom rears its ugly head. In an interview on MSNBC in late 2014, Maureen checked the young white male reporter who deceptively claimed that Detroiters were choosing to pay their cable bill instead of their water bill:

> What's at stake here is that there are tens of thousands of low-income families who cannot pay rising water bill costs. The costs of living are going up, the chances for living are going down and we've got these reporters out here like this guy just standing on the side of the people who have money.[149]

Maureen has been the state chair of Michigan Welfare Rights since 1999, a native Detroiter committed to her self-defined vocation to "intervene and intercede on whatever your survival issue is." She exhorts the unhoused and the unemployed to stay in vacant homes and, back in the late '90's, she set up a circus tent in Detroit so that those who lacked housing would have protection from the elements. Then she moved the subversive carnival to the Capitol lawn in Lansing. This mourning dove moves with some serious moxie.

On a chilly Saturday afternoon in February 2016, a few dozen of us were crammed into a room on the third floor of Michigan Welfare Rights, operating out of the old United Methodist Church with a view of the city's baseball stadium, subsidized by more than $100 million in tax dollars. Maureen kicked off the gathering by lambasting "crony" capitalism, "They make mistakes, apologize, correct it, but *we* suffer the consequences." The "they" she was referring to were elected officials in the state of Michigan, particularly Governor Rick

Snyder who appointed "emergency managers" (EM) to run both Flint and Detroit. According to Maureen, these leaders make decisions in solidarity with "the banks and their hoochie mama girlfriends." She was referring to corporations.

Maureen lamented the EM's decision to switch Flint's water from the Detroit River to the Flint River, quickly poisoning the water supply of the entire city. Every public official involved denied there was any problem for almost two years. The lead-tainted water just kept flowing through household taps. The EM in Detroit, meanwhile, raised water rates and mandated shut-offs to tens of thousands of longtime residents. However, Maureen was not there to give a history lesson. She had a confession to make. She mailed a package of Spanish onions to the Governor-in-denial. She attached a note urging him to slice one of them if he needed help crying for the victims of poisoned and shutoff water.

On another occasion, at a monthly standing-room-only People's Water Board meeting, Maureen squirmed and agitated while the director of a local nonprofit shared the news of his organization's partnership with the city government on an extensive survey of Detroit's neighborhoods. She raised her hand and testified,

> We've been around the block a few times and when it comes to our needs, your partner has given the answer of no, no, no *and then definitely no.* When the wolf starts asking the questions about what the chickens need, we start running for the exits because we've learned that the next thing they do is break out the A1 sauce.

Maureen doesn't just connect the dots and tell the truth. She decolonizes just like Jesus. She speaks in parable.

Maureen and other Black women leading the struggle for water affordability in Detroit have resurrected for me the old Gospel story of the persistent widow (Luke 18:1-8). She comes to the "judge who neither feared God nor had respect for people" and begs him for justice over and over again. In response, the unjust judge refuses her plea over and over again. Eventually he relents "so that she may not wear me out by continually coming." These women refuse to accept an oppressive status quo as they boldly confront those in power. They are committed to wearing them out until justice prevails. A package of onions is just one weapon in their large arsenal.

*   *   *

Women of color, particularly Black women, are the empathic glue holding the suffering world together. They operate on a completely different wavelength than anything I ever experienced from the white Evangelical male-dominated leadership of my youth. I am grateful for the role that many of these white men played in my life, but their voices were amplified, and the visions they cast were overly rigid, logical, formulaic, dutiful and disciplined. They were fixated on a blend of charisma, choreography and control. They spent plenty of time "taking the reins" and "keeping matters under control." Like most white men in America, they were trained to hide their feelings and avoid conflict. Most of them stayed silent on controversial issues of justice and oppression.

Authentic Christian faith yearns for a robust coloring-outside-the-lines emotionality, the compassion that fuels revolution. This is what Harlem native Audre Lorde alludes to in her essay "Poetry is not a Luxury:"

> The white fathers told us, I think therefore I am; and the black mothers in each of us—the poet—whispers in our dreams, I feel therefore I can be free.[150]

As a young girl, Lorde struggled to communicate so she

memorized several poems and recited them when she was
asked how she was feeling. She rejected what she called "the
european mode," an obsession with logic, formula and
rationality. Through her brilliant poetry and prose, Lorde
dedicated much of her life challenging fellow Black women to
get free from the ways they had internalized the european
mode. I know I desperately need this word, too. The colonial
script has dehumanized all of us in different ways.

Life, Lorde prods, is not a problem to be solved, but a
situation to be experienced and interacted with. Our feelings,
in fact, are "the sanctuaries and spawning grounds for the most
radical and daring of ideas."[151] This is what she calls "the
ancient, non-european consciousness." Experiences of great
love and suffering, I am slowly learning, are the main sources
of authentic transformation. It is these, deep within me, that I
seek to tap into.

The theologian Kelly Brown-Douglas proposes that the
best portrayals of Christ in our world are in the faces of Black
heroines, especially those living below the poverty line. She
calls these women *icons* of Christ, from the Greek word for
"image," used for centuries by the church to make the God of
Steadfast Love real and tangible in our worship. Icons spark
our spiritual and theological imaginations. The divine comes to
life! They are sources of encouragement and challenge,
creativity and accountability for the faithful. Brown-Douglas
writes:

> It is only in a commitment to insure the life and
> wholeness for "the least of these" that we can grasp the
> radicality of who Christ is...[152]

The icons of the colonial script—celebrities, politicians,
professional religionists, wealthy white men—are the default
for all of us living in North America. They easily become
mirrors, shaping us in destructive and dehumanizing ways. I

have come to the realization that I desperately need new icons, images that more faithfully illuminate the risen Christ in my own context. This challenges me to flip the script—just like Jesus did.

Jesus challenged the Roman "patronage" system, a hierarchy that determined who mattered most. Life in the first century followed the colonial script, ordering value from almighty Caesar at the top, all the way down to children and household slaves. Jesus flipped it. He exalted the humble (Luke 14:11). He grabbed the last and put them in the front of the line (Matthew 20:16). He made the enslaved and children the models of the movement (Mark 10:44; Matthew 18:3).

Authentic faith keeps calling us to descend from the falcon perch so that we can see more clearly that the American Dream is a nightmare for most. In Detroit, for example, it places the needs of guests at the Manna Meal soup kitchen in the basement of St. Peter's Episcopal Church above the power and prestige of those staying in the penthouse suite at the Renaissance Center, the tallest hotel in the Western Hemisphere, less than a mile away from Manna Meal. Real brilliance doesn't trickle down. It bubbles up.

The cellar dwellers of the American imperial patronage system are Black women who still make just 64 cents on the dollar compared to white men, and 82 cents for every dollar that their white female counterparts make.[153] Black women over 65 have the lowest household income of any group and Black female retirees live in poverty at a rate five times that of white men.[154] Even though they make up less than 10 percent of the overall population, 25 percent of those living in poverty are Black women.

A decade after Dr. King was assassinated, Ronald Reagan took advantage of centuries of racist stereotyping by grotesquely conjuring Black women as loose-living, baby-making, Cadillac-driving "welfare queens" and "crack whores" living large off the government. These false and dehumanizing images are demonically ingrained in the white American mind.

Reagan's chief domestic policy adviser, Gary Bauer, proclaimed, "Even the most casual observer of public assistance programs understands there is indeed some relationship between the availability of welfare and the inclination of many young women to bear fatherless children."[155] I once attended a Bauer keynote hosted by an Orange County megachurch. His political logic was seductive, flavored through with well-timed quotations from Scripture. With our Bibles open and guilt appeased, we guzzled the Kool-Aid.

25
Transphysics

Black women, well attuned to deep suffering, possess the kind of mentality and way of life that have modeled for me, over and over again, the decolonizing spirit of the grace-filled, anti-imperial Jesus. These women endure, from the womb to the tomb, what Lorde has described as a "societal deathwish." Lorde writes, "From that moment on we have been steeped in hatred—for our color, for our sex, for our effrontery in daring to presume we had any right to live."[156] This effrontery, a courageous determination to survive and thrive in the face of racist policies and assumptions, is the embodiment of what King called "transphysics," a spiritual dynamism originating deep in the gut, sparking a "fire that no one can put out."[157]

Despite the death wish, Black women sustain a rare brand of joy. It is a happiness that doesn't depend on what happens. So many of these icons have modeled for me a mystical faith that is both prophetic and poetic, working off the creativity and passion of the right-side of the brain. They refuse to take life for granted. They are rooted in experience and fueled by tender compassion and a creative playfulness.

Black women are the underrated and overlooked Miriams (Exodus 15:21), who get one follow-up verse of song for the eighteen that Moses received after crossing the Red Sea (Exodus 15:1-18). Yet, only the Miriams possess the emotional and spiritual resources to lead us to the Promised Land.

This bias toward the bottom has beckoned me to the work of literary genius Alice Walker, the eighth child of sharecroppers from rural Georgia. Lamenting all the focus that male preachers consistently put on heaven, her spiritual hope is in resisting and rising above the colonial script right now:

> What is happening in the world more and more is that people are attempting to decolonize their spirits. A crucial act of empowerment, one that might return reverence to the Earth, thereby saving it, in this fearful-of-Nature, spiritually colonized age.[158]

Walker, who decades ago brilliantly proposed that the White House should be run by twelve grandmothers, places the emphasis on women's intuitive ability to be rooted in the deeper ways of the Earth. This, she writes, "always leads to revolution."[159]

Walker pushed back on church leaders obsessed with heaven. They quoted the Apostle Paul, who exhorted the little community in Colossae, "Set your minds on things above, not on things that are on earth" (Colossians 3:2). In historical context, Paul was challenging the ancient community with a subversive theology, calling them to pledge allegiance to heaven, "where Christ is, seated at the right hand of God" (Colossians 3:1b). This is a clear-cut challenge to Caesar, who every good Roman citizen believed was enthroned at the right hand of the divine. Paul was confronting "the human way of thinking" (Colossians 2:18b), what I call "the colonial script."

Paul, I believe, would whole-heartedly agree with Walker's assessment. Whenever heaven is manipulated into a future protective paradise, it is counterfeited. It permits oppression to reign. The real heaven is the subversive Way of

Jesus. He taught his disciples to keep praying for the God of Steadfast Love to reign *on earth as it is in heaven.* The point of faith is to pledge allegiance to heaven while we are still on earth. Allegiance challenges followers of Jesus to embrace the tension of reaping joy and amazement from the beauty of the land while we attempt to dismantle the wretched policies that deface it for the profit and prestige of powerful men.

Decolonizing our spirits is the work of liberating ourselves from all the ways that the colonial script has ripped us away from the deepest Source of our being. Mainstream Christianity is deeply implicated in this mess. It stamped its approval on the entire colonial project.

In the 15th century, the pope implemented the "doctrine of discovery" to give power and control to Christian explorers speculating in "the new world." Any land that was not inhabited by Christians was anointed as a blank slate to be "discovered," claimed, and exploited. If the "pagan" inhabitants could be converted, they might be spared. If not, permission was granted by church leaders to enslave or kill them.[160]

This mentality has been a monstrous aspect of the colonial script from Columbus all the way forward. The spiritual practice of decolonization, for me, begins with a confession that I have become well-adjusted to the colonial script, with all of its edges and entitlements granted to whiteness and maleness and the middle-class mentality. I have been greatly malformed in the process. I have an unhealthy need to be in control and know all the answers. I possess a fragile ego and take things too personally (as if everything is about me). These symptoms are at the heart of the epidemic of white male mediocrity.

Decolonization beckons me to repent and exchange my idols of whiteness and maleness for icons that more faithfully express the crucified God of Steadfast Love. I am challenged to listen and learn from women of color who know, through hard experience and deep intuition, what it takes to heal and "get saved."

These women show me time and again that I cannot think my way into newness of life. Ideas and insight, no matter how brilliant, can only take me so far on the journey. They keep me locked in my head. Black women have been my best models for how to feel and move my way into liberation. To embody the Way of Jesus by exiting the european mode.

*   *   *

I see Jesus in the life of Marian Kramer, co-chair of the National Welfare Rights Union, a freedom fighter who advocates for the most marginalized in Detroit. Marian integrated lunch counters and registered Black people to vote in her native South in the '60s and learned to drive when members of the KKK chased her and a fellow civil rights worker down a back road when she was a teenager. After she participated in a nonviolent direct action, the police threw her in a garbage truck and then made her spend eight days in solitary confinement.

I am compelled by the life of Fanny Lou Hamer, a poor sharecropper until her early forties, forcefully evicted from her plantation home for speaking out against Southern racist realities. She refused to be intimidated, remaining ruthlessly committed to the Civil Rights struggle despite severe physical abuse by law enforcement officers. She connected the dots, told the truth and paid dearly.

Valerie Burris, too, is an icon. I met Val one afternoon while we were canvassing door-to-door in a beat down, burned out Detroit neighborhood. On that day, she soaked in the tears of a ninety-year-old woman who had a gaping hole in her roof from a recent storm. Her fierce kindness fueled action as she dialed up a young unemployed contractor who came right over and fixed the roof for free.

Val, who some African friends call "Abrihet," an

Ethiopian word meaning "Light," has endured unexplained tumors for more than twenty years. She does not hold back when she is connecting the dots and telling the truth about her native city ravaged by unjust water shut-offs and illegal home foreclosures:

> Polite language like "this is unfair" ain't gonna' get the job done. Language carries energy, and when we're living in times like this city is seeing, you better expect "this is some bullshit" to come out of my mouth from time to time.

Then there's Oakland Congresswoman Barbara Lee, who just three days after 9/11, was the only leader in Congress to vote against giving the President "all necessary and appropriate force" to invade or bomb anytime, anywhere. She was bombarded with insults and death threats.

I'm moved by the honesty, directness and courage of novelist Chimamanda Ngozi Adichie. She was berated by a young man during a question-and-answer session, "I used to love you. I've read all your books. But since you started this whole feminism thing, and since you started to talk about this gay thing, I'm just not sure about you anymore. How do you intend to keep the love of people like me?"

Adichie confidently responded:

> Keep your love. Because, sadly, while I love to be loved, I will not accept your love if it comes with these conditions.[161]

Michelle Alexander's writing and life challenge me politically and spiritually. Her white mother was disowned by her family when she married a Black man. Then the Lutheran church excommunicated her. Alexander didn't grow up in the church, but she has spoken candidly of the desperate need for a spiritual awakening to bolster our work for peace and justice. Her mid-life crisis led her to resign her post at The Ohio State Law School to become a professor and student at Union Theological Seminary.[162]

Ruby Sales traveled to the South in 1965 to help register poor Black residents. I met her briefly fifty years later when she hosted a moving public memorial service just blocks from the White House, a reverent reading of the names of the 1,000 Black Americans killed by police since 2007. Almost every day, she posts news of police brutalities and murders of people of color on her Facebook page "Breaking the Silence Against Modern-Day Lynching."

Rosa Parks leads this great cloud of witnesses. More than two decades before she famously refused to give up her seat on that Alabama bus, she courageously stood up to a white man attempting to rape her while she was working as a nanny. "If he wanted to kill me and rape a dead body," she wrote years later, "he was welcome, but he would have to kill me first." Rape was a tool of terrorism in the Jim Crow South and it was virtually unheard of for a Black woman to speak out, let alone defy a white man.

A decade later, despite blatant efforts to threaten and intimidate her, Parks launched "The Alabama Committee for Equal Justice for Mrs. Recy Taylor" to defend a 24-year-old Black mother and sharecropper who was gang-raped by six white boys.[163] The true story of Rosa Parks is that a large majority of white folks disagreed with her activism and even many Black folks viewed her as a "radical" and "troublemaker."

In 1965, a decade after her act of civil disobedience on that Alabama bus, White Citizens' Councils plastered huge billboards along the route of the Selma-to-Montgomery march that depicted King and Parks as "Communists." That same year, Congressman John Conyers hired Parks to work in his Detroit office and white folks poured in threatening calls and hate mail, including watermelons, voodoo dolls and other racist symbols. She was hated in the North, too![164]

These icons are not "exceptional" Black women. They are the rule, the stand-ins for hundreds of millions of Black women who, from 1501 to the present, have endured "the double jeopardy" of being both Black and female in America.[165] These women embody the revolutionary spirit of the original Jesus movement described by Paul in his letter to the little house church in Corinth:

> God chose what is foolish in the world to shame the wise; God chose what is weak in the world to shame the strong; God chose what is low and despised in the world, things that are not, to reduce to nothing things that are (1 Corinthians 1:27-28).

Christian faith represents an "upside-down kingdom." The last are first. The humble are exalted. Black women flip the script, pouring out inspiration, strength and love, creatively and compassionately thriving in spite of all that empire dishes out.

26
A Feminist Masculinity

Evangelicalism, by and large, stifles the voices of all women. It is a movement that hero-worships charismatic white men. I am ashamed to say that I was completely oblivious that the megachurch I attended two to three times per week in early adulthood was governed by a small cadre of white men while women were not permitted to preach. As far as I know, this is still the case.

The entire Evangelical movement remains caught in the net of patriarchy, defined by bell hooks as "a political-social system that insists that males are inherently dominating, superior to everything...and endowed with the right to dominate and rule over the weak."[166] This demonic power confines women to second-class citizenship—to submitting and serving and nurturing and supporting and feeling and being constantly overlooked—while the men go about the business of deciding and voicing and earning and competing and being praised.

The Civil Rights Movement itself often fell victim to the patriarchy of its context. King's voice, then as now, dominated a landscape that mostly cherished its male leaders. Women were "helpmates" to the men in charge. They were expected to be the secretaries, to do the "shit work," and to service the sexual needs of the men. Brilliant women like Ella Baker, Diane Nash and Marian Wright (and many more) were supporting actresses. It takes intensive labor to mine the few words and deeds recorded by them and about them.

King's wife, Coretta, stayed at home with their four children while Martin traveled the country. Coretta, though, often led Martin in the struggle against racism, militarism and poverty. When they met in Boston where they were both attending university, she was more politically active than he was. When they got married in 1953, she insisted that "obey" be removed from their vows. Coretta openly and publicly spoke out against the Vietnam War as the only female keynote speaker at Madison Square Garden in 1965. This was two years before Martin's "A Time to Break Silence" speech at Riverside Church.

After she spoke at a peace rally in 1965, a reporter asked Martin if he educated his wife on the issues. He responded: "She educated me."[167] After his assassination, Coretta carried forward the Poor People's Campaign even though many of the male leaders asked her to step aside. At the end of her life, she spoke out against the American invasion of Iraq and became a vocal advocate of gay rights and same-sex marriage.[168]

Ella Baker, described by a biographer as "a middle-aged

hell-raiser who defied categorization" was so brilliant and subversive that the FBI secretly followed her for decades.[169] Her leadership, through both word and deed, critiqued the male-dominated, hierarchical, "charismatic" mentality of King and others. She famously proclaimed that "Martin didn't make the movement. The movement made Martin." The leading male figures, though, consistently took it for granted that Baker and other women, at organizing meetings, would prepare and set-up the food and coffee for everyone, and then join the meeting itself and contribute out of their intellectual and intuitional genius.

Contrasting Baker with King, Cornel West has assessed her overlooked leadership as "a joy in serving others that is qualitatively different than a pleasure in leading others."[170] That perfectly pinpoints the vital contrast between women and men that I observe over and over again: *a joy in serving* rather than a pleasure in leading.

*　　*　　*

Women have been robbed and oppressed and silenced and abused and neglected over the past several millennia. Men, playing the role of oppressor, have also been damaged by this system: both through entitlement and victimization. They have been stripped of permission to be open-hearted and emotionally expressive, a toxic masculinity foisted upon us from every angle. With patriarchy, everyone loses.

Americans are shocked when men in public are vulnerable, ask for help, admit they don't know something or cry. The careful reader of the Gospels discovers Jesus doing all of this and more. He weeps at the funeral of his friend Lazarus and pours out mother hen tears on a hill overlooking Jerusalem, lamenting the city's leadership all caught up in violence and greed as they schemed to make Israel great again.

Jesus, time and again, displays what bell hooks calls a

"feminist masculinity": an ethical sensibility that enables men to love justice more than manhood.[171] Jesus, in fact, models a completely different brand of masculinity than King David, that mighty man of valor (1 Samuel 16:14).[172]

Jesus displays tenderness and empathy and tells stories about men who do the same.

Jesus takes a clear stand on issues that matter, rejecting the safety of being objective and "staying above the fray." He is direct and honest, yet respectful and humanizing.

Jesus asks clarifying questions, pursues intimacy, listens to others, refuses to avoid conflict, shows a deep appreciation for the gifts of others and empowers them through the delegation of leadership. Ironically, Jesus doesn't have a messiah complex.

Admitting he was wrong, Jesus praises the faith of the foreign woman who calls him out on his own prejudice (Mark 7:25-30). In word and deed, he highlights the faith and love of Gentile leaders and scapegoated Samaritans, subversively placing people with "funny accents" on pedestals.

In his greatest sermon (Matthew 5-7), Jesus animated what it means to recover our humanity and live with dignity and compassion. The God of Steadfast Love, it turns out, takes sides, favoring the underdogs, calling us to live in solidarity with and to advocate for the poor in spirit, the persecuted, the pure in heart, the peacemakers, those mourning, the meek, the merciful and all those who hunger and thirst for justice.

Brown-Douglas proposes that Jesus' biological characteristics were not significant factors in the cultivation of his healing and prophetic brilliance. It was not who Jesus was (particularly as a male) that made him Christ. It was what he did.[173]

According to author Riane Eisler, in her book *The Chalice and The Blade*, all societies have been patterned by either (A) *dominator* models based on the use of force (the Blade), or (B) vintage *partnership* societies, based on sharing, caring and bearing one another's burdens (the Chalice), where women shared power with men. Jesus, Eisler proclaims, preached the gospel of a partnership society, rejecting the "traditional" notion that high-ranking men were favored by God. He mingled freely with women and refused to go along with the myth that they are spiritually inferior to men.[174]

In mainstream American culture, the media, the military, the machismo of athletics and the muscular Evangelical version of Christianity are well-oiled machines of the colonial script that, over time, hoodwink young men into living out the ultimate dominator message. While men are charged with the task of being the breadwinner and the "spiritual leader of the household," women are domesticated and silenced in a variety of serious and subtle ways.

These factors have worked tirelessly to counterfeit my own masculinity. I was trained to suppress my tears and tenderness, to have all the answers, to be in control, to be self-sufficient. I was taught that the worst thing I could be was a woman or queer. My coaches and pastors and others were simply passing along the colonial script that they were raised on. Most likely, no one ever encouraged them to question it— especially since it tirelessly privileged their voices around every corner.

A few years back, Chimamanda Ngozi Adichie's Ted Talk on feminism went viral. Then she parlayed it into a book, which the Swedish government now annually distributes to every 16-year-old in the country. She wrote:

> The problem with gender is that it prescribes how we should be rather than recognizing how we are. Imagine how much happier we would be, how much freer to be our true individual selves, if we didn't have the weight of gender expectations.[175]

An authentic spirituality rooted in the Way of Jesus is

liberating. It frees followers from the confinement of the colonial script, with its counterfeit notions about gender, including the "binary" assumption that we must be either/or. People are far more unique and dynamic and mysterious than what any two categories might (superficially) offer. That is to say: the God known in Jesus has created every single human being, through a delicious blend of nature and nurture, in the image of divine self-donating Steadfast Love.

27
Apprenticeship

Listening to and following Black women ought never be mistaken for idealizing or fetishizing them. Furthermore, I hope this focus on Black women does not, in any way, minimize or neglect the suffering and abuse that other women, particularly women of color, continue to face on the daily. Indigenous and immigrant women continue to be particularly vulnerable.

Jyarland Daniels, the executive director of Harriet Speaks, has convinced me, though, that racism in North America functions as a hierarchy with whiteness at the top and blackness at bottom. In this caste system, power and perks are given or denied based on one's proximity to blackness.[176] It is vital to place a priority on Black women because their liberation would necessitate the full deletion of the colonial script, making everyone else free in the process.[177]

The simple point I'm trying to make is that both the brilliance and oppression of Black women has been schlepped aside, or altogether overlooked, by white Americans for the past 500 years. Every Christian has her role models, her icons, her standards for what faith looks like. Where I come from, these are, almost universally, white men. Radical discipleship, though, descends to discover what is divine at the very depths of our dehumanizing and destructive society.

I'm absolutely *not* proposing that we seek out more Black women to fill slots in the already-existing system set up by the colonial script. As my friend Sarah Thompson recently reminded me, "Decolonization is not the same thing as diversification." The goal is liberation, not tokenization. It starts with imagining a society that transcends the white supremacy, patriarchy and corporate capitalism that have dehumanized it for centuries.

Decolonization demands that those of us in the mainstream let go of our grip on power and control and allow those on the margins to take the lead with how the system is set up in the first place. It is a matter of taking cues from the Black church, a tradition that goes beyond the walls of the sanctuary to all the "historic efforts toward complete liberation," as Black theologian Dolores Williams describes it.[178] Now is the time for the rest of us to listen, to take on lesser, more appropriate roles.

This form of apprenticeship, I have experienced, is not fueled by some sort of sacrifice. It is in everyone's best interest for leadership to be decentered from the heroic white male. Following Black women has refreshed my soul with a kind of fierce tenderness. I am convinced that if the voices of Black women were given the airtime they deserve the result would be a far more humanizing and just world for everyone. After all, they are experts at delivering healing and wholeness and nurture and support to the entire community. This is what they have had to do in order for their families and neighborhoods to survive perpetual demonization for the past five centuries.

The built-in segregation and polarization of contemporary culture are massive obstacles to the kind of "iconography" I'm proposing. Brown-Douglas, in a panel discussion at the Proctor Institute in 2016, shared a sobering statistic: 75 percent of white Americans do not have a non-white friend in their social group.

How, then, does one listen to and follow Black women if one does not know any Black women? Denver-based author Toi Marie Smith offers a solution with a simple, soul-searching question for white folks: "Where are all the Black women?" This, she challenges, is *the* question that follows us everywhere—to the grocery store, the conference, the board meeting, out to dinner, on Facebook, at the airport, at a retreat, on our bookshelves, on our podcasts and news sources. She summarizes:

> Your eyes should always be open to where black women are not present in your world and your mouth should always be questioning, to yourself and others, why we aren't there.
>
> Because lack of representation in the places you frequent means you need to seek new places to frequent, or it means you need to work to make sure more black women are present and their voices are heard.
>
> If you start asking yourself this question on a regular basis it will force you to confront yourself in a real honest way.[179]

It comes down to connecting the dots and telling the truth.

The colonial script teaches that white men are the first and final authority. The falcons. This must be actively, intentionally unlearned. For white men like me, it demands a real process of repentance, taking on a posture of humility and generosity. To learn the value of finding joy in serving, rather than seeking pleasure in leading. Listening has always been an underrated spiritual discipline. The focus here is on intentionally shifting *who* we are listening to. Only then will wisdom and strength be able to speak from a different script.

VIII.

Speak

"It may well be that we will have to repent in this generation, not only for the vitriolic words and the violent actions of the bad people…but also for the appalling silence and indifference of the good people…"
Martin Luther King Jr.
April 27, 1965, UCLA

28
What the (Bleep) Happened?

My faith journey eventually led me to the basement of the old Unitarian Universalist Church in Detroit's Cass Corridor. I was invited to come listen in on "What The (Bleep) Happened to Hip-Hop,"[180] a gathering of local artists to address the ways corporate power is co-opting music, dance and other arts. They created this unique space to cast a vision of what it might look like to build a movement to end corporate dominance.

Until that morning, I was under the impression that hip-hop was just a genre of music. In this circle, though, I was schooled in what has been a long spiritual tradition. Martin and Malcolm gave birth to a whole generation of storytellers, philosophers and teachers. These Detroit-based artists taught me that hip-hop is a consciousness, an underground resistance, a way of viewing the world where everything is rhythm.

Hip-hop is committed to a life of peace, love, unity and fun experienced through the four practices of break dancing, graffiti, dejaying and emceeing. "The courage to be yourself is the essence of hip-hop," KRS One proclaimed back in the late '80s. This is a tradition known for its vulnerability, boldness and raw honesty.

A Detroit-based artist named Supa MC highlighted the passionate dialogue with an improvisational sermon about the watering down of their tradition. "We've become the mutant bastard of what we made!" he lamented. The tradition has been hijacked by the corporations, which are only "about selling and selling and selling and selling and selling." Too many artists have sold out and "become a clone of a clone of a clone of a clone of a clone." This version of hip-hop was wasting his ear time:

> We need to be able to say: "That shit is whack. Go home and read a couple books and pen that shit up again." We are all too afraid of being haters.

One after another, each artist weighed in on what was trending—too many of their peers have been trying to make a name for themselves instead of staying centered on the essence of hip-hop—connecting the dots and telling the truth. One young upstart spoke up, horrified that Quicken Loans billionaire Dan Gilbert was recruiting graffiti artists from the east coast to paint murals on his recently-purchased buildings in downtown Detroit.

One of the organizers, a young woman who was clearly the inspirational glue of this intimate group, praised the creativity that is paramount in the 'hood—young people installing home speakers in car trunks to get it bumpin'. She lamented, though, that "stripper culture" had become normalized. It was an assault on their community.

A veteran artist in the room let his frustrations flow, reminding the vibrant congregation that, more than a decade ago, the Dixie Chicks got kicked out of *their* genre. They broke the rules of country music by speaking out against the imperial policies of the U.S. government. Every genre needs their standards. He pleaded that, if hip-hop artists took theirs more seriously, they, too, would realize that many in their own ranks don't even come close to passing the test. Truly, this was a community focused on reclaiming the roots of their spiritual tradition.

*   *   *

Those of us in the Jesus tradition desperately need a gathering too. What the (bleep) happened to Christianity? Like hip-hop, it has been hijacked. Like hip-hop, most people know only the watered-down, corporatized version. Those of us committed to reclaiming the tradition need to take its litmus test a lot more seriously. Not every brand of following Jesus is legitimate. But what qualifies for authentic faith? The very essence of Christianity is, of course, a contested concept.[181]

In the last century, Evangelicalism has overwhelmingly won the intramural contest over what Christianity is in the American psyche. In attempts to make Christianity palatable to the American mainstream, the Evangelical movement created a name for itself by distancing itself from hard-core fundamentalism.[182] It has become wildly popular.

In the last fifty years, white Evangelical Christianity has been massively shaped by its response to the Civil Rights Movement of the '50s and '60s. Evangelical leaders and their congregations were courted with a combination of Republican Party race-based branding known as "the Southern Strategy" and "law and order," as well as "the Moral Majority," a pitch of personal piety to whites in the Bible Belt, trickling into suburban contexts all over the nation.

White folks, by and large, swallowed the narrative whole. They eagerly and overwhelmingly endorsed the War on Drugs, the War on Terror, Three-Strikes sentencing laws, a cutting of "welfare" funding for low-income residents and the disavowal of affirmative action employment and admissions policies. Meanwhile, they hyper-focused on sexuality issues, condemning abortion and same-sex marriage. In addition, Evangelicals have increasingly taken on a defensive posture, claiming that liberals are erasing their religious liberty. They pay heed to Fox News warnings of a "War on Christmas."

In the decades since his death, white Evangelicals have stripped Rev. Dr. Martin Luther King Jr. of his Christian faith, replacing him with a kind, meek and mild black man petitioning for a color-blind society with a kumbaya dream. Cornel West laments that the real legacy of King's prophetic struggle has been "sanitized," "sterilized," "deodorized" and "Santaclausified."[183] What the (bleep) happened to Rev. Dr. Martin Luther King Jr.?

Author Arundhati Roy has chronicled King's sanitation succinctly. She digs to the roots, explaining that the King Junior Center for Non-Violent Social Change was organized and funded by corporations: the Ford Motor Company, General Motors, Mobil, Western Electric, Procter & Gamble, US Steel and Monsanto. The Center works closely with the United States Department of Defense, the Armed Forces Chaplains Board and others. It co-sponsored a lecture series called "The Free Enterprise System: An Agent for Non-violent Social Change."

Foundations and corporations have reinvented King "to fit a market-friendly format."[184] This is mostly the image of Martin Luther King Jr. that is celebrated every January during the federal holiday that honors his life and work. In 1983, the King holiday was signed into law by Ronald Reagan emphasizing King's courage and love and a "true patriotism that cherishes America's ideals."[185] Reagan joined the business of remanufacturing King into an icon of depoliticized color blindness.

This is painfully ironic. Back in the 1960s, Reagan campaigned against the national Civil Rights and Voting Rights Acts and defended California's Proposition 14, the overturning of the state's fair housing law. Reagan reasoned, "If an individual wants to discriminate against Negroes or others in selling or renting his house, it is his right to do so." One of his commercials in 1966 referred to Black neighborhoods as "jungles."[186]

The real Rev. Dr. Martin Luther King Jr. was feared and demonized by most white folks, especially business and government leaders. In the lead-up to his famous Dream speech at the March on Washington in August 1963, several congressmen condemned the gathering, calling it "un-American." The Kennedy administration rigged the microphone so that it could be turned off if necessary. Every D.C. cop was on duty and more than 150 FBI agents monitored the crowd.[187] The day after the 250,000+ person march, one FBI agent who was assigned to monitor King's activities referred to him as "the most dangerous Negro of the future in this nation."[188]

In his "Beyond Vietnam: A Time to Break Silence" speech, given in New York City exactly one year before his assassination, King connected the dots and told the truth about capitalism, imperialism, racism and war. The next day, 168 newspapers denounced him. *The Washington Post* lamented that King had done a disservice to himself, his people and his country. President Johnson disinvited him to the White House.[189]

In the white imagination, King's dream threatened their centuries-old grip on power. In 1966, only 28 percent of Americans had a favorable opinion of him. By 1987, however, his approval rating skyrocketed to 76 percent.[190] In two decades, the American public appeared to change their mind about Rev. Dr. Martin Luther King Jr. In reality, though, the American public simply changed who Rev. Dr. Martin Luther King Jr. was in their minds.

29
Koinonia

Now more than ever, Jesus is threatened by counterfeits too. A litmus test is desperately needed to clarify what is authentic. I believe it starts by re-claiming a small passage from Paul's letter to Philemon:

> I pray that *the sharing of your faith* may become effective when you perceive all the good that we may do for Christ (Philemon 6).

From middle school through my early adult years, I was taught by Evangelical leaders, passionately quoting this verse, that we needed to "share our faith" with others so that they, too, could be saved (i.e., go to heaven when they died). Only when we boldly "shared the gospel," my youth pastor explained, could we "perceive all the good that we may do for Christ." This imperative came with a tutorial of manipulative strategies that

I could utilize to transform normal conversations into conversion opportunities.

It was awkward and dutiful. It was also a bad interpretation of the Bible. "The sharing of your faith" is a translation of one Greek word: *koinonia*. In the New Testament, *koinonia* is often rendered as "fellowship," a concept that places a strong value on spending time with other like-minded believers. I've often heard it transformed into a verb, as in: "We had an incredible time fellowshipping with each other over appetizers at TGI Fridays." For Evangelicals, these times are vital to sustain the hard work of "being *in* the world, but not *of* the world" (John 17:16).

However, *koinonia* actually has very little to do with either telling non-Christians about Jesus or hanging out with fellow converts. A more faithful rendering is "solidarity" or "partnership." It is about joining the God of Steadfast Love in the adventure of healing the world. *Koinonia* is a vocation.

This important reframing of *koinonia* takes seriously the relationship between the mainstream and the margins. Ched Myers challenges readers who are "politically free, socially mobile, and information-and-resource rich" to "take the side of the Hebrews even though citizens of Egypt."[191] *Koinonia*, from this perspective, means being in solidarity with all those exploited and abused by the colonial script.

Before he was assassinated by the American Evangelical-sponsored Salvadoran army in the late '80's, the theologian Ignacio Ellacuría proposed that *koinonia* requires a "copro-analysis" of American culture. A study of its feces![192] A copro-analysis reveals that so much of what is consumed and digested by mainstream Americans comes at the expense of "the Global South" (Latin America, Asia and Africa)—invading land, stealing resources, exploiting labor, decimating culture.

Jon Sobrino, another Salvadoran theologian, proposed that to be "Christian"—to experience a truly biblical understanding of *koinonia*—is to be in intimate relationship with those he calls "the crucified people" of the world—to listen to them and follow their lead. It is only through them that those on the perch can descend to learn service, simplicity and the readiness to receive God's gifts.[193]

This more authentic understanding of *koinonia*, I believe, is the litmus test for authentic Christianity. It demands courage to boldly speak out against every form of oppression and then to work for its eradication. It commits to naming hard, unpopular truths that, in many of our social settings, tend to ferment an awkward and tense atmosphere.

*   *   *

While many are turned off by Christianity's focus on sin, theologian Kelly Brown-Douglas proposes that sin is precisely what those participating in a more compelling Christian faith ought to home in on. However, she proposes that most of us have been emphasizing the wrong sins.

Brown-Douglas reanimates "original sin," in the American context, as the inhumane treatment of Native Americans and the enslavement of African-Americans. Sin is rooted in a 500-year narrative about American exceptionalism—that the United States of America is the greatest country in the history of the planet, a beacon of freedom that can do no wrong. A key aspect of this old story, according to Brown-Douglas, is that making America "great" has always been defined by white people, for white people.

The seed of this good 'ole American white supremacy, according to Douglas' compelling research, was planted by Roman historian Tacitus in his thirty-page propaganda piece *Germania*, written in the forests of Germany at the end of the first century. About the same time as the New Testament Gospels. Tacitus proposed the greatness of "an unmixed race" of blue-eyed warriors successfully fighting off the Romans.

The Nazis famously utilized Tacitus' work to bolster

their claims of a master race. However, Tacitus also had a massive influence on the "Founding Fathers" of the U.S. who were propped up by a white mainstream Christianity seeking to convert the foreign masses to their version of "Christian civilization." To "Make America Great Again" has always meant to "Make America White Again." Our original sin, planted 500 years before 81 percent of white Evangelicals voted for Donald Trump.[194]

Back in the late 1700's, Peru's Tupac Amaru II and his African-descent wife, Micaela Bastidas, organized a rebellion against the Spanish colonial script by recruiting a coalition of Peruvian doves —the indigenous, mestizos and slaves. Although the insurrection was put down and Tupac was executed, the indigenous uprising became an inspiration for holy rebellion in South America for centuries afterwards.

At the same time, and in dramatically different fashion, a cadre of falcons organized a revolution to protect their slavery, property and political power in Great Britain's North American colonies. Thomas Jefferson and his white posse looked to European philosophers for inspiration and rational justification for slavery, the seizure of indigenous lands and controlling the unruly masses.[195]

Viewing American events and policies, both historic and contemporary, through the lens of white exceptionalism reveals that this sin sets the terms of just about everything. White people lament, "Why do you always have to make it about race?" The clear answer is because it always has been about race. In fact, white folks have been "playing the race card" (in their favor) for over 500 years.

Four days before his death, King laid it out loud and clear for the mostly white congregation at the National Cathedral in Washington D.C.:

It is an unhappy truth that racism is a way of life for

the vast majority of white Americans, spoken and unspoken, acknowledged and denied, subtle and sometimes not so subtle—the disease of racism permeates and poisons a whole body politic. And I can see nothing more urgent than for America to work passionately and unrelentingly—to get rid of the disease of racism.[196]

Yet fifty years after King, in the wake of a two-term Black President, American society still suffers greatly from the disease of structural racism. On average, white households possess seven times as much wealth as Black households and, according to a recent study, Black families making six figures live in more disadvantaged neighborhoods than white families making $30,000. These statistics provide a small sample of what journalist Ta-Nehisi Coates calls a "pigmentocracy"—rule by color.[197] Similar statistics abound, ranging from inequity in school funding, in voter suppression laws, in emergency managers and in Congressional district boundaries.

Contrary to popular belief, this massive wealth gap is not the result of white folks working harder and saving better than Black folks. The opposite is actually true, according to another study. When comparing white and Black folks who both have college degrees, full-time jobs, two-parent families and similar spending patterns, it revealed that whites were far better off.[198]

Why? Inheritance is a huge factor. Whites are five times more likely to receive gifts and inheritance money passed down from previous generations, and when they do, they receive far more than Black folks. All the policy discrimination that benefited white baby boomers and their parents ("the greatest generation"), from the GI Bill to redlining to much more, is still playing a huge factor in who gets what in the United States.

This is just the icing on the racism baked into the mainstream American cake. Consider, for instance, "racial steering" in the mortgage industry. Just a few years ago, Wells Fargo was forced to pay more than $175 million to settle allegations that it steered thousands of Black and Brown borrowers into subprime mortgages with high interest rates while white borrowers with similar credit profiles received loans with the lowest rates possible.[199] Examples like this abound.

Saying "that was then, this is now" only perpetuates white supremacy. Claiming that one is color-blind or that one lives in a color-blind society is even worse. Even Barack Obama, during his 2008 Presidential campaign, subscribed to the well-worn idea that American society is almost to the post-racial promised land. He claimed that the civil rights generation "took us 90 percent of the way there, but we still got that 10 percent in order to cross over to the other side."[200] Many argue that this is what he had to say in order to get the white votes needed to win. Probably true. And yet another piece of evidence to make the case that racism is alive and well.

Rev. Dr. Martin Luther King Jr. never signed off on the kind of color-blindness that many white Americans claim he was all about. King hoped for a color-blind society, but only once oppression and racism were destroyed. This, he realized, was a distant dream. He predicted that supremacy was so imbedded in the white society that it would take many decades for color to cease to be a judgmental factor.[201]

King articulated a strong conviction that the prospects of real change relied upon precisely those claiming color-blindness. The real problem, he said time and time again, was the well-worn practice of good and sincere people staying silent about issues of grave importance.

Michelle Alexander proposes that, when it comes to race, our goal should not be color-blindness, but what she calls "color-consciousness." She writes, "Seeing race is not the problem. Refusing to care for the people we see is the problem."[202] When white folks proudly say that they "don't see color" they show their hand, admitting that they don't see the oppressive forces weighing down people of color in American society. The real problem is a lack of *koinonia*.

Fueling this problem is the historic fact that white people have been raised up like falcons—by the media, the government and, yes, the church—as the standard for everyone else. Oakland-based pastor Lynice Pinkard calls this "white ubiquity," a deeply ingrained belief that what matters to white people is all that matters.[203] The colonial script infuses a "white normativity" that keeps us oblivious to what is happening on "the other side." This is why it is vital for white Christians to name, out loud and often, the ongoing racist reality still plaguing every aspect of American culture.

30
De-Godding Whiteness

Over the past few years, I've learned three simple things about race: (1) *everyone is infected* with the disease of white supremacy, (2) healing will take *a long time* and, (3) everyone can actively work to dismantle it *right now*. In short, a lot of humility and hard work is required.

To remind himself of its omnipresence and omnipotence, Jim Perkinson capitalizes Whiteness and defines it as "a hidden Power that inhabits institutions, influences policies, whispers in psyches, and colors perceptions without itself appearing."[204] Whiteness is demonic. It impacts us personally and politically. In order to identify it and uproot it both from our own lives and the structures that order our world, it will take some real intentionality.

Perkinson talks openly and honestly about his own need to confess that he is a "settler" on someone else's land and that he consistently has access to resources and goods because of someone else's labor. He calls his recovery from Whiteness a process of "becoming unsettled."[205] This is the key to what I've learned from Perkinson's deep analysis: it's not about pointing out individual "racists," but about coming to terms with the racism lodged both within us and in the social, economic and political structures that organize our world. Racism has gone viral, personally and politically.

White supremacy is not just my grandfather yelling the n-word at the TV and proudly campaigning for George Wallace in the '60s or the KKK and neo-Nazis lighting torches in the streets of present-day Charlottesville. These overt forms of racism are real and must be named and dealt with appropriately. White supremacy, however, is much more. It is not just "out there." It is "in here" too.

My friend, mentor and Detroit high school teacher and activist Kim Redigan, reflecting on her own white working class roots, commits herself to the ongoing process of unlearning Whiteness. She writes:

> I have come to believe that to be white in this country is to be either a racist in denial, a racist by choice, or a racist in recovery.[206]

Kim names the vital first step of doing the work for all of us possessed by the demon of Whiteness: confession. It is a long road to recovery, requiring vast amounts of grace. Fortunately, as the Apostle Paul wrote, the power of God is made perfect in our imperfection (2 Corinthians 12:9). The social analysis is important for us white folks, but, too often, we pile on the fear, guilt, shame and fragility. These are obstacles to becoming accomplices in the cause of dismantling white supremacy.

Kim's confessional commitment has been an important model for my own journey of unlearning racism. In addition to being schooled by a society that holds Whiteness to be supreme and works tirelessly to keep me oblivious about it, I was steeped in the coded language of 20th century suburban white supremacy. Every beach-going Orange County white boy knows what "Here come the 909ers!" means. 909 is the area code of the mostly Black and Brown residents of Riverside County who, during summer weekends, would head west for relief in the Pacific Ocean. It's plain and simple: "The 909ers," then and now, is a racist term.

Area code dog whistling was the tip of the iceberg. Suburban living rooms and locker rooms are littered with jokes flippantly demonizing Black and Brown folks. I am ashamed to admit that I was in on these jokes, readily joining the chorus of laughter and passing them along to new audiences whenever possible. In addition, language like "thugs" and "ghetto" and "welfare" weave through discourse easily. These, either consciously or subconsciously, are racialized jargon.

The bottom line is that I have been trained to treat my Whiteness as supreme. My psyche has been shaped in such a way as to think and feel, consciously or subconsciously, that Black and Brown neighbors are lesser. I am an addict in recovery. All I can do is start at step one, admitting my powerlessness over the addiction. Only a rigorous process of recovery can reclaim my right mind.

Perkinson's wife-partner is Dr. Lily Mendoza who was born in the Philippines and came to the United States a few decades ago for her Ph.D. work. Lily commutes to the suburbs forty miles north of Detroit to teach "multiculturalism" classes to mostly white undergraduates at Oakland University. But she isn't just teaching. She's pastoring students out of their Whiteness and offering paths of liberation from it.

Lily utilizes ethno-autobiography curriculum to gently challenge her students to "decenter" the superiority of their Whiteness by committing to a process of digging into past generations to uncover "an indigenous self."[207] Ethno-autobiography guides white folks back to their family origins in pre-colonial Europe. All the way back to the days before the nation-state.

Decentering Whiteness is a vital aspect of a Christian spirituality that takes racism seriously. It heals by going straight to the root—the prior generations, caught up in the civilizing and colonizing, so much of it justified by racist Bible quoting. This is a confessional process that refuses name-calling and projecting.

Lily embraces the Iroquois tradition of "the long body." Life decisions are made with the next seven generations in mind, and from the wisdom of seven generations past. She starts by asking her mostly white students: "Who are your ancestors?" Specifically, Lily presses her students to dig deeper to "submerged ethnicities"—who their ancestors were before they became "homogenized into a white 'European' identity"?[208]

For me, this has become a spiritual practice of generational digging. I am attempting to reconnect with my line, long before my Scottish great-grandmother Mary Moore immigrated to the States in 1906 and settled in central Washington just a few decades after Native Americans were rounded up and forced on to the Colville Indian Reservation. With the aid of a little imagination, I'm going all the way back to my Celtic heritage, even before Roman Christians forcibly colonized them. This is the starting line in my long marathon to reclaim the roots of my own indigenous self.

I come from the people known by ancient Greeks and Romans as *keltoi*, the "strangers" or "hidden ones" living on the northwestern fringes of empire (eventually Ireland, England, Scotland, Wales). These rural, tribal Celtics emphasized relationship and action over rational knowledge and doctrine. They practiced an earth spirituality of hospitality and blessing. The divine was mysterious and on the move and could be accessed through "thin places" anywhere and everywhere. The world was filled with wonder and enchantment. The mundane was sacred. When they converted to Christianity, they synthesized their indigenous convictions with the Way of Jesus.

Over the centuries, my Celtic heritage experienced a white out. The colonial script erased all indigenous nuances into gross Black-or-White racial categories. My friend Rev. Nick Peterson, currently pursuing his Ph.D. in liturgics and ethics at Emory University, calls for a spiritual process of "de-Godding whiteness." It is the work of dismantling a whole world tirelessly built for white folks to thrive and be accommodated, to be worshipped and supreme. Meanwhile, Peterson laments, "Blackness stands as a Lucifer."

All the comforts and conveniences and cash advances of being white in American society function as "an invisible package of unearned assets" that white folks like me can cash in every day and practically everywhere.[209] Whiteness in the United States has always been exceptional. White is god. Supreme. On the throne.

Nick helpfully names that our unjust and oppressive society is built not on hate, but on supremacy. The problem is that most good, law-abiding white citizens continue to passively stay on the sidelines, saying and doing nothing to challenge the systems that oppress Black and Brown people. As long as the focus is on the KKK and neo-Nazis ("the bad guys"), then the white American majority can stay passively righteous and the real work to eradicate racism will remain undone.

Dr. King yearned for white folks to actively commit to the hard work of de-Godding whiteness. This is a constant practice of unlearning. In a back-and-forth text exchange during a particularly difficult season of grieving for me, Nick wrote:

White supremacy and patriarchy are definitely some demons to contend with and we all wrestle with various manifestations of them. They haven't been born overnight and their exorcisms will take a lifetime. We will leave maps and lexicons to help those who come after us.

Nick was simply seconding the motions that Spirit was

speaking through Lily. Embracing the long body is a spiritual marathon that requires some serious training. It will take a lifetime, but it always helps me to remind myself: I am not alone. We are all in this long process of recovery together.

31
Action

When the demon-possessed young boy was crying out and convulsing and foaming at the mouth, the disciples of Jesus wondered why they couldn't heal him. Jesus responded, "This kind can come out only through prayer" (Mark 9:29). The demons of race and gender have spent decades convulsing me. My own transfiguration will require a hell of a lot more than just knowing the right information. It's going to take a process of prayer, personal inventory and confession—and a beloved community of grace and accountability. I am deeply grateful for friends like Nick, Kim, Jim and Lily (and others)—a beloved community modeling an alternative to the colonial script.

My fear, guilt and fragility must be exorcised so that I can be freed up to do the real work. I'll never forget what Catherine Meeks told us at the Bartimaeus Institute during a Q and A session after her presentation on the history of lynching:

> White people need to learn how to have real conversations with other white people. Don't spend a second feeling guilty. It is a wasted emotion and it doesn't serve anybody. For those of us who have lived at the foot of oppression, the last thing we need is white guilt. It just takes up your energy. Don't choose to feel guilty. Choose to act.[210]

Eight months later and 3,000 miles north in Saskatoon, Sylvia

McAdam, the Lakota co-founder of Idle No More, a mass movement of indigenous resistance, told us the same thing:

> White people: no one is asking you to apologize for your ancestors. We are asking you to dismantle the systems they built and that you maintain. We have no use for your guilt. What we want from you is action.[211]

Dismantle the systems. No more justifying, finger-pointing, eye-rolling, apologizing or crying. Just action. Period.

Jyarland Daniels has helped me see that white folks, historically, will only work to eliminate white supremacy when it is in their own interest to do so. I met Jyarland one afternoon on the corner of Trumbull and Michigan Avenue in Detroit. She was the first one to the U-Haul that morning to help unload more than a thousand gallons of water to deliver to Flint. As it turns out, we graduated from the University of Kansas the same year. Rock Chalk Jayhawk.

One night, while we were walking to Sweetwater Tavern in downtown Detroit, we passed a half-dozen boisterous white women lip-syncing and dancing to Rob Base and DJ E-Z Rock. Alarm bells rang out in Jyarland's soul: "White people love Black culture. But do they love Black people?" This query goes far to explaining how I could grow up idolizing Black athletes like Michael Jordan while persistently quoting Black movie stars like Samuel L. Jackson, but still be painstakingly indifferent to policies plaguing black communities all over North America.

Jyarland reminded me recently that, in the lead-up to the 2016 Presidential election, the white governor of Virginia, a huge Hillary Clinton supporter, worked tirelessly to ensure that (mostly Black) ex-felons could get the right to vote—this after decades of Democratic Party support for mass incarceration of nonviolent offenders and felon disenfranchisement laws that crippled the Black community.

"So," Jyarland explained, "here is how this goes: we get rid of racist policies when white people see that their interests are impacted (or they are harmed) by racism—and not a moment before."

The good news is that it *is* in the self-interest of 99 percent of white people to work to end structural racism embedded in the American neoliberal framework. The concentration of wealth and power among the 1 percent is coupled with growing poverty and oppression for the other 99 percent. Black and Brown people are brutally overrepresented in the most despairing categories used to measure quality of life in the United States.[212]

Only when this system is overhauled can we all be free of bigotry in every form—the ongoing discrimination against women, queer folk, middle and lower classes, those who are too young or too old. Altruism is great (and most certainly "Christian"), but we must come to realize that racism (and every bigotry) works for the self-interest of only a tiny group of super-rich, Protestant, heterosexual, non-immigrant, White, Anglo-Saxon males.[213]

As it turns out, self-interest was the primary motivation for white leaders (like Abe Lincoln) in their work to end slavery in the 1860s and white leaders (like Lyndon Johnson) who promoted civil rights in the 1960s. Racism will not be eradicated unless people of faith and conscience actually engage people in power, demanding that every policy that cripples people of color be changed. This starts with convincing them that it is in *their* self-interest to do so. As King proclaimed over and over, this will only happen when the masses of good and sincere people speak up.

When it comes to matters of race, there are three main ways to unfollow Jesus: denial, projection and clinging to silent neutrality. These options separate the sheep from the goats. Those yearning for a "can't we all just get along" Jesus will not find him in the Bible. Jesus proclaimed "I came to bring fire to the earth" (Luke 12:49). He believed peace and unity could never come at the expense of justice.

Jesus declared that division is an inevitable response to honest truth-telling. "What I say to you in the dark, tell in the light," Jesus charged, "and what you hear whispered, proclaim from the housetops" (Matthew 10:27). Jesus' life was a lamentation about how power and violence and injustice works in our world—and what happens when a prophetic movement of whistleblowers refuses to cooperate with the status quo.

32
The Wondrous Exchange

Both the crucifixion of Jesus and the assassination of Rev. Dr. Martin Luther King Jr. provide explosive theological initiative going forward. As death threats piled up, King reflected openly on what his oncoming murder might mean. He viewed it as a kind of "redemption" payment to save the souls of his fair-skinned siblings—"the price I must pay to free my white brothers and sisters from the permanent death of the spirit." King viewed himself as a martyr for the cause.

The original Jesus followers, too, soul-searched for a deeper meaning of their leader's martyrdom. A few decades after the first Good Friday, Paul wrote:

> He indeed died for all, so that those who live might no longer live for themselves but for him who for their sake died and was raised (2 Corinthians 5:15).

And six verses later:

> For our sake he made him to be sin who knew no sin, so that in him we might become the justice of God (2 Corinthians 5:21).

Jesus' death prods his upwardly mobile followers to descend from their perches and exchange the colonial script for an all-out pursuit of justice. The 16th century German theologian Martin Luther (who King was named after) called this "the wondrous exchange." Our guilt is removed and our addictions are forgiven so that our lives can be fundamentally reshaped by a self-donating love for the most marginalized. Not to go to heaven when we die, but to bring heaven to earth right now.

Plain and simple, both the crucifixion of Jesus and the assassination of King call American Christians to *koinonia*. To solidarity. To conversion to the cause. To die to upward mobility and insularity. To commit our lives to tangibly loving our brothers and sisters of another color. Let us not be mistaken—the violent deaths of King and Jesus were *not* God's plan. The purpose of the actual death is not what is at stake. What matters here is the meaning derived in the wake of the tragedy of a martyred life.

The earliest followers of Jesus knew that he was killed by elites because what he said and did threatened their power. However, according to Walter Wink, the key questions were not about why, but *how*:

> How has God used this evil for good?
> How has God turned sin into salvation?
> How has God triumphed over the Powers through the cross?[214]

Evil, injustice, death and violence are never the will of the God of Steadfast Love. Never. But this God recycles it all, using these, often mysteriously, as substances for healing and growth. King believed that the Civil Rights Movement was more than just working for the rights of Black Americans. He believed it was about saving the soul of America. White supremacy itself, King noted, was "the Black man's burden and the white man's shame"—a burden in both life and death.

The death of Jesus (and King) does not mean the tab has been paid so believers can just "move on" with life. It frees up the faithful from guilt and shame so that they can actively pursue their own repentance and take steps toward a process of reconciliation—which is impossible without justice. To be born again is to usher in a new life shaped by *koinonia*.

*   *   *

W.E.B Dubois once proclaimed bluntly, "A nation's religion is its life and as such, white Christianity is a miserable failure."[215] Acknowledging the failure doesn't mean that white folks cower in guilt over complicity in structural racism or colonized versions of faith. White people of faith and conscience can confess it and follow the example of Frederick Douglass who consistently called for the abolition of slavery *and* the popular counterfeit Jesus of his day, "If Christianity were allowed to have a full and fair hearing, slavery would be abolished forever."[216] If the masses converted to a faith committed to authentic *koinonia*, the colonial script would be eradicated.

The real obstacle to ending racism is not the alt-right scripters and Confederate-flag-waving-Kid Rock-listening drifters. I'm learning not to waste my precious time and energy on those who will never change. "Don't throw your pearls to the pigs," Jesus implored, "If you do, they may trample them under their feet, and then turn and tear you to pieces" (Matthew 7:6). The problem, King said, is that "the good people" remain silent and complacent.

A faith committed to getting to the roots pledges solidarity with those neglected and demonized by the colonial script. The litmus test for anything that bears the name of Jesus is the willingness to unsilence the things that matter most. To be silent is to be unchristian and the faithful ought never fear saying it.

IX.
Stand

"It seems to be a fact of life that human beings cannot continue to do wrong without eventually looking for some thin rationalization to clothe an obvious wrong in the garments of righteousness."
Martin Luther King Jr.
April 27, 1965, UCLA

33
Our Own Two Feet

We gathered in a cabin on a cool summer night on the "tip of
the mitten" (as they say in Michigan), four hours north of
Detroit and forty days after the death of Daniel Berrigan. Bill
Wylie-Kellermann invited an intergenerational group from
among the original members and friends of the Detroit Peace
Community—so named by the holy rebels of Jonah House in
1980 during a week of civil disobedience at the Pentagon.

That evening's topic was the Catonsville Nine action of
1968, the mid-day, non-violent storming of the Catonsville,
Maryland, Vietnam-era draft board. They stole 378 draft files
and set them on fire with homemade napalm in the parking lot.
Then they waited in prayer and song for the police to show up.
It sparked hundreds of similar "politically informed exorcisms"
all over North America.[217]

Pastor Bill introduced the action by placing it in
historical context. Then we read *The Trial of the Catonsville
Nine*, a reworked transcript of the court proceedings, put to
poetry by Berrigan. A sample of the testimony:

> ...the world expects that Christians will speak out loud
> and clear, so that never a doubt, never the slightest
> doubt, could arise in the heart of the simplest man. The
> world expects that Christians will get away from
> abstractions, and confront the bloodstained face which
> history has taken on today.[218]

I was awestruck by the dedication of the Catonsville
Christians. The months leading up to their "hit and stay"
action were filled with prayer meetings, Bible studies and calls
of discernment—a "who's in, who's out" series of hand-raisings.
This brand of faith was covenantal, adventurous and daring. It

straddled the border of radical and bat-shit crazy.

The Catonsville Nine displayed a form of following Jesus that not only takes unjust, violent and oppressive realities seriously. They committed to transforming them. These disciples went far beyond connecting the dots and telling the truth. They stared down the very real possibility of spending years in federal prison.

Five decades after Dr. King proclaimed "the fierce urgency of now," there is a dire need for hundreds of contemporary Catonsvilles. Fortunately, there is still a network of Plowshares, Catholic Worker and similar "resistance communities" committed to keeping this disobedient fervor alive. These radical disciples, I am convinced, are motivated by a sincere altruism soaked through with rugged idealism. I am compelled by this work and want to support it and participate in it as much as I have the time, resources and energy to do it.

But here's the rub: The massive demands of this work and witness tend to pile up on the few who are fully committed to it. In this state of affairs, it is easy for these serious revolutionaries to forsake the personal in their all-out quest for political transformation. As I've participated in various community organizing circles, I've noticed that guilt and duty have a tendency of rearing their ugly heads.

Naturally, a subtle "shoulding" arises from a small movement tasked with an overwhelming number of issues to resist and rise above. The activist mentality tends to shun rest, relaxation, healing and "self-care" because, if poor and oppressed people do not have access to these, those with privilege shouldn't either. It turns burnout into a badge of honor. It refuses days off during illness and rejects healthy diet and exercise.

This lifestyle shortchanges sleep, schleps away the legitimacy of vacations, and often turns to various addictions to cope with heavy demands. Much of this leads to illness and disease, fatigue, social withdrawal, impatience and irritability, pessimism and joylessness.[219] In over-worked environments like these, relationships tend to be distant and/or strained. Brene Brown laments that these kinds of communities experience "common enemy intimacy." When all the attention and energy is aimed at "the bad guys," a real depth of connection rarely happens.[220]

In light of this, a drastic reorientation around inner work is needed. The Black poet Sonia Sanchez puts it plainly, "You can't have relationships with other people until you give birth to yourself." A lifestyle that honors the legacy of Rev. Dr. Martin Luther, Jr. is inherently committed to the tireless work of socio-economic and political restructuring. Yet more and more people of faith and conscience are waking up to the fact that we must make personal recovery a priority too: in our families, communities and organizations.

*   *   *

Back in the early 1970s, in the wake of King's assassination and the Catonsville action, Jim Douglass wrote a little book called *Resistance and Contemplation*. He urged followers of Jesus to take seriously both the political *and* the personal— what he called "the yin and the yang of the Movement."[221] In the second chapter, he excerpted highlights from the last lecture that Trappist monk Thomas Merton delivered in Bangkok, just hours before his death.

Merton told the story of Tibetan Buddhist monks being driven out of their homeland by Communist revolutionaries. Their whole world had been shattered. The elder monk tells the fretting younger prodigy, "From now on, Brother, everybody stands on his own feet." Desperate times call for connecting the dots and telling the truth.

Douglass, who, with his wife Shelley, established a "house of hospitality" in Birmingham, Alabama for folks in need of housing and long-term health care, seized on the spiritual metaphor of that historic moment:

> The people are drowning, or more exactly, they are
> being drowned by a system which submerges humanity
> beneath enormous power apparently controlled by a few
> but perhaps by no one. For the sake of everyone's
> humanity, a response is necessary. But to respond to the
> people and to resist the power of that system without a
> rock to stand on is simply to jump in the water and
> drown with the people.[222]

At the end of Jesus' famous "sermon on the mount," he tells his disciples that those who listen to his teachings and act on them are like the wise one who builds her house on the rock: "The rain fell, the floods came, and the winds blew and beat on that house, but it did not fall, because it had been founded on rock" (Matthew 7:25). The Apostle Paul attributed the rain and floods and winds to "principalities and powers" (Romans 8:38; Colossians 2:15), the forces always attempting to separate us from the steadfast love of the crucified God.

Over-spiritualized by Evangelicals as unseen angelic and demonic beings, the rich scholarship of theologians like William Stringfellow, Walter Wink and Bill Wylie-Kellermann has reclaimed "principalities and powers" as the systems and ideologies that organize our world. These are precisely what Michelle Alexander has named "a tightly networked system of laws, policies, customs, and institutions."[223] These demonic Powers have everything to do with the mechanisms and manifestations of the colonial script.[224]

All "principalities and powers"—families, corporations, churches, the economy, the criminal justice system, higher education, the transportation network, social media, capitalism, the military-industrial-complex—have an outward structure and inward spirituality. The Powers are intended to deliver more life to everyone and everything, both human and more-than-human. They are supposed to cultivate interdependency, mutual care and social cohesiveness.

However, the Powers inevitably become idols, shaped over time to serve themselves instead of serving the best interests of society at large. Decisions are made to keep institutions going—at all costs. The church and the university and the nuclear family often survive, each to the detriment of its members.

When the colonial script takes over, the interconnected Powers that weave the fabric of our lives strip us of our humanity and siphon the wonder and beauty that comes with life. They cultivate fear, greed, anxiety, resentment and despair. Not only do we need to get liberated from the Powers, but the Powers need to get liberated, too. This is the work of resistance and community organizing. However, people of faith and conscience who dare to transform the system will inevitably drown without the solid rock of spirituality.

Audre Lorde once wrote, "Caring for myself is not self-indulgence, it is self-preservation, and that is an act of political warfare."[225] And not just self-preservation. Societal restoration, too. Without a practice of rigorous personal moral inventory, everyone will unconsciously contribute to the dysfunctional and destructive cycles formed in our families, faith communities and workplaces.

This is not something we can expect anyone else to do for us. In fact, no one *can* do it for us. Earlier in his life, Merton wrote, "There can be no peace on earth without the kind of inner change that brings us back to our 'right mind.'"[226] What our faith communities need—what our families, neighborhoods and the nation itself need—are courageous people willing to travel the deep, dark, descending path of inner work—to reclaim "our right mind" from the colonial script. In the words of Douglass, "this Way is impossibly demanding and incredibly life-giving."[227] A real adventure wouldn't have it any other way.

34
Sarkos

The desperate need for inner work is deeply connected to one of the Apostle Paul's most important and misunderstood theological concepts: the Greek *sarkos*. Many English versions of the Bible translate it as "the flesh." The Evangelical Bible studies and churches I attended preferred "the sinful nature" (NIV). The theologian Walter Wink laments that these are perhaps the most unfortunate mistranslations in the English Bible.[228]

The translation of *sarkos* is critical because it is such a vital concept in the New Testament. In his letter to the little community bearing witness in the imperial capital, Paul writes, "To set the mind on the *sarkos* is death, but to set the mind on the Spirit is life and peace" (Romans 8:6). Spirituality is to confront the death that inevitably comes with *sarkos*. But what exactly is it?

My white Evangelical pastors taught me that "the sinful nature" is a life stained by original sin, forever confined to the imprisonment of human waywardness. The physical body was shunned, doomed by evil out-of-control desires, most notably sexual lust. Every young adolescent Evangelical male knows: It takes serious discipline, prayer and accountability partners to abstain from premarital sex and masturbation!

However, in the first book of their two-volume *Ambassadors of Reconciliation*, Elaine Enns and Ched Myers define *sarkos* as "the deeply-rooted, socially-conditioned worldview we inherit from our upbringing...the sum total of personal and political constructs and conventions that define what it means to be a member of a given culture."[229] *Sarkos* is the biblical term used to describe how humans become well-adjusted to the colonial script—in families, schools, social networks, jobs and everywhere else.

Unfortunately, *sarkos* shapes people in all sorts of dehumanizing ways. Just like everyone else, I have learned, from very early in life, how to fit in and play by the rules of the colonial script. And just like everyone else, I desperately seek love and trust in ways that counterfeit myself. I have my own strategies to cope with pain. These patterns carried me into adulthood, but they keep me from being present, centered and emotionally available.

In a conversation on a prairie highway about thirty kilometers north of Saskatoon, Canada, Ched Myers, predictably, got pedagogical. "When we become jaded or wounded," he explained, "one of three things happens":

1. We *blame* others and stay in denial, inflicting our pathologies on to everybody else.

2. We *burn out*, escaping into a myriad of unhealthy copings.

3. We *take responsibility*, committing to the challenging path of inner work.

In his mid-90's classic *Who Will Roll Away the Stone?: Discipleship Queries for First World Christians*, Myers introduced what he called "the discipline of dis-illusionment,"[230] the hard work of becoming empowered disciples in a context shaped by an imperial culture. We inevitably digest and replicate all the lies and illusions that the colonial script offers. The goal is to become dis-illusioned. This starts by identifying the lies and illusions and then taking serious steps to liberating ourselves so that we can live out a different way.

However, Ched deputizes readers to work out the details of this discipline in the diversity of their unique contexts. "It is far from clear exactly what it might consist of," he writes, "or how the process might be carried out in a popular fashion."[231] There is no formula. The ball is in our court.

*　　*　　*

For me, the discipline of dis-illusionment starts with a reorientation of what Jesus' death did to our sin. A week after his birth, Jesus' parents brought him to the Temple to dedicate him to the God of Steadfast Love. They adhered to the dictates of Jewish Law by sacrificing two doves at the altar (Luke 2:21-24). On the second day of Christmas, my true love gave to me: *two turtle doves.*

Hebrew Law stated that something sacred was required to find acceptance from God. A life for a life. However, after his torture and execution, Jesus' followers proclaimed that the cross of Jesus signified the end to all sacrifice. His death was the ultimate sacrifice. Once and for all. It finally became clear to these first followers of Jesus that the last thing this divinity wanted was bloodshed.

What the God of Steadfast Love *did* yearn for from humanity was a ruthless commitment to mercy. Instead of killing doves, God called for the protection and liberation of all life. This is part of what it means to say that Jesus died to save us from sin—the destructive patterns and copings that, all too easily, dehumanize us, and those we interact with.

Living into this radical mercy is a process that requires both confession and repentance. Confession, in beloved community, creates accountability. Transparency is contagious. Everyone can come out of hiding. Repentance signifies a real commitment to changing our patterns. It is signing on to growth and maturity.

In fact, this is one strand of Evangelical theology I'm sticking with. "Those who belong to Christ Jesus," Paul writes, "have crucified *sarkos* with its passions and desires" (Galatians 5:24). Our colonial scripted patterns need to be "nailed to the cross," as we used to say in my high school youth group. Only then can we be released from the guilt and shame that keep us locked in our old ways.

However, my ongoing tension with this Evangelical theology is the way that it is too-often preached as an eternal principle. It functions like a magic wand that God waves over someone. Say the simple prayer and we are forgiven. Forever. Voila! The problem is that we can pray the prayer once and for all, but, unless we cultivate a discipline of dis-illusionment, our default will continue to be the colonial script. That's not good news.

The brutal death of Jesus also exposed the way scapegoating and projecting operates in our world, both politically and personally.[232] We humans tend to do one of two things with our deep pain: blame or shame. I consistently do both. This is the problem with sin and the problem with doing nothing about it. It festers. Perhaps I'm forgiven, but the shaming and blaming continue. Either I take it all on or I project the pain on to others—usually on to those that are different than me (the "alien" other) or those closest to me (Lindsay). Irritability, rage and resentment spiral out of control.

Both shame and blame unnecessarily keep the cycle of pain going. The healthy, liberating move is to turn over our pain and destructive copings to the Crucified God. To nail it to the cross. This theology is transformative as long as confession and repentance remain vital aspects of the practice. Anything less is what German martyr Dietrich Bonhoeffer famously called "cheap grace."[233]

If Christians are those who, through their faithful allegiance, become slowly transformed into the image of Christ (Romans 8:29), then this means we actually become kinder, gentler, more honest, more open-hearted, full of integrity, more compassionate, more generous, humbler and more courageous. To live "according to the Spirit" (instead of "according to sarkos") is to be centered and emotionally available. It is to have FACES: to become Flexible, Adaptable, Coherent, Energetic and Stable.

The Apostle Paul challenged his Corinthian audience to a "mature" wisdom that refused to drift along with what was popular or powerful. He called this "the wisdom of the cross," contrasting it with the colonial script that was governed by "the rulers of this age who are passing away" (1 Corinthians 1:18-25; 2:6). In a recent interview, psychotherapist Francis Weller described maturity as a commitment "to carry grief in one hand and gratitude in the other and to be stretched large by them."[234] Grief and gratitude—the cross and resurrection—is the holy rhythm of a discipline of dis-illusionment.

My immature Evangelical faith tended to overemphasize gratitude. I was taught to thank God for my blessings and Jesus for his ultimate sacrifice. It inevitably led to denial about pain and suffering all around me and deep within me. As I slowly learn to grieve, my heart becomes fluid and soft, opening up space for compassion to arise. Dealing with grief means that we must grapple with our own deeply ingrained family myths. This doesn't equate to blaming our parents. Most parents did the best they could with what they were working with. After all, they too grew up in families that were far from perfect and in a world governed by the colonial script.

When it comes to assessing most of our families of origin, there is plenty to be grateful for. But our gratitude ought not lead to denial. The key step, according to Ched, is to intentionally grieve all the "ways we have been severed from our true selves."[235] My own commitment to a daily practice of naming both grief and gratitude is teaching me to stand on my own two feet—by being rooted in reality and connected to the God of Steadfast Love.[236]

35
Leaning Into My Truth

Living "according to the Spirit" will only become a reality if it goes beyond knowing correct information. The late rabbi and psychotherapist Edwin Friedman lamented this conundrum in the very first line of his classic *The Failure of Nerve*:

> The colossal misunderstanding of our time is the assumption that insight will work with people who are unmotivated to change.[237]

Rabbi Friedman, in his exhaustive work studying leadership in families, faith communities and organizations, concluded that the most important element for any leader is not proper technique to motivate others, but instead emotional presence. The ideal environment is one where the leader is centered, non-anxious, and can be both honest and emotionally connected.

The "well-differentiated leader" is a listener and open-hearted, but also can make decisions that might be unpopular with some people. She has a backbone. She says what she means and means what she says. Members of the team (or family or faith community) never have to worry about what is unsaid because the leader is straight-forward. Throughout the entire system, fear and anxiety diminish.

Rick Kidd, a marriage and family therapist and an important spiritual guide for Lindsay and me in our post-Evangelical journey, says that, as we seek to become "change agents" and "wounded healers," our ultimate task is learning to be free. Rick has taught us that one of the challenges of inner work is that when we commit to it, it is like we have been in a train wreck and we are at the bottom of the pile with our relatives, friends and co-workers. When we start working to get free, we inevitably move pieces around, bumping into those in our family systems and friend groups, most of whom just want to lie there and wait for someone else to save them. Most people most of the time do not (or cannot) commit to the hard work of getting free.

At the core of my own recovery, I'm working to address my strong tendency to seek value from outside of myself. My pattern has long been to find my identity in what I do and what other people think of me. Praise or criticism (or silence) from others tends to make me or break me. I put my best foot forward to put off an image of myself that I think others will admire. When I enter a room, I instinctually attempt to meet the expectations of others (or, at least, what I think their expectations are). All of this is automatic and unconscious.

These patterns, or copings, arise from pain lodged deep within me. I often feel alone, unknown and/or devalued. If I have tension or conflict with others, I am flooded with shame. I have learned that if other people have a problem with me (or anyone else), it is my responsibility to make repair. The shame I swim in leads me to over-function to make up for my own perceived unworthiness. I do not feel like I deserve to just be myself. I do not believe that I am enough.

Performance mode is exhausting though. Most of what I do is driven by duty and obligation. I am a classic conflict-avoider. I play nice and serve in ways to keep everything peaceable. I learned long ago to repress my feelings. After all, those feelings are just speed bumps on the road to achievement!

Eventually, I become easily irritated. I expect others to look out for my needs just as I'm vigilantly looking out for theirs. I get bitter and resentful. I go silent. I shut down emotionally. This almost always comes in the midst (or at the end) of a day where I work to get love and validation from others.

My daily discipline of dis-illusionment calls me, first and foremost, to name the truth. God is not just a head game.

The divine is closer to me than I am to myself and delights in me constantly. I am more than enough. Just because. These truths reflect the Source of my authentic identity—the God of Steadfast Love. Who I really am is not what I do or what others think of me. My healing is tied to a larger Story. Instead of living to fulfill the expectations of others, I embrace the identity of being an extension of who God is in the world. I am intimately intertwined with Steadfast Love itself.

None of this comes naturally. Like all soul work, it is challenging. My therapist exhorts me to lean into my truth instead of paying lip service to it. My true worth is not based on any merit based on achievement or the acclaim of others. This is a contemplative, mystical practice of every day life.

As I practice leaning into my truth, my challenge is to stay connected to myself and others, instead of distancing. To verbalize what I feel. To name my needs and ask for help. To breathe in my intrinsic belovedness. To let go of the need to constantly meet the expectations of others. It is a spirituality that confronts my self-sufficiency.

In my quest to live by the Spirit instead of the *sarkos*, I am intentionally pursuing what Weller calls "the primary satisfactions"—investing in deep friendships, spending time in nature and risking being vulnerable with people I trust.[238] Since the beginning of Advent 2014, I've begun every morning writing in a feelings journal. I'm learning to better identify the pain welling up in me.[239] I'm unlearning how I internalize these unrecognized emotions. Instead, I bring them up and out in ways that are healing. This has been a slow, but life-transforming process.

In order to stave off despair, my discipline of dis-illusionment is nurtured by spiritual practices not dissimilar to the daily Evangelical "quiet times" of my youth. Prayer is an opportunity to connect to Steadfast Love, to my real identity, to the loving Source that resides in everything. The goal is to "pray unceasingly" (1 Thessalonians 5:17) throughout the day.

I pause briefly and breathe deeply as I pivot from one action to the next. This decompresses time and centers me.[240]

My spiritual focus is on being in my body, staying rooted within. Like everybody else, most of the time I am stuck in my mind, unconsciously controlled by my thoughts and feelings, fears and desires. My painful messages guide me. On autopilot, I constantly pivot from private planning the future to feeling shame and regret over the past.

The goal, according to spiritual practitioner Eckhart Tolle, is to "go more deeply into the Now." There is an inner energy field of the body that accesses Steadfast Love, infinitely more intelligent than my mind running on the colonial script.[241] Something powerful happens when I notice and name the script in my head. And then breathe, let go and trust. My heart expands. I find my true identity deep within instead of outside of myself.

I am challenging myself to sit for 20-minute "mantra mindfulness" sessions. The focus is on clearing my mind and expanding my heart by focusing on one word or phrase. This mantra can come from a reading from a sacred text or, Benedictine monk John Main's preference, a consistent commitment to something like "Maranatha," the Aramaic word meaning "Come, Lord" that Paul writes at the end of his first letter to the Corinthians (1 Cor 16:22).[242]

As I mature, I'm not taking the highs and lows of either praise or criticism so seriously. I'm learning that busyness is not the badge of honor that the colonial script has trained me to think it is. I'm watching out for the times when I automatically say "yes" only out of duty and obligation. I'm setting limits. I can't do everything. I'm letting go of guilt and shame and setting boundaries.[243] As the poet nayirrah waheed writes, my "No" might make others angry, but it will make me free.[244]

I'm also learning how to surrender to being known and loved well. To give myself time for pleasure. To accept things I cannot control. To tolerate discomfort. I'm also reminding myself about others. When they are angry or disappointed with me, it (most often) is not really about me. Something I did or said triggered their own deep, unresolved pain or trauma. Sometimes people are actually relating with me, but usually they are working out their own issues through me. Knowing the difference between the two can be hard, but the ability to do this is a key marker of what Richard Rohr calls "the second half of life," the spiritual Promised Land.[245]

36

Every One of Us

In the last couple years of his life, Rev. Dr. Martin Luther King Jr. was constantly coping with the pain lodged deep within him. Like all our saints, he was not perfect. Far from it. He was sleeping around, drinking and smoking heavily to cope with a vicious depression. He was exhausted from work and travel. He was bitterly criticized by both his rivals and enemies. Instead of protecting him, the FBI was wiretapping and blackmailing him.

A discipleship of descent fueled by the life and teachings of King need not sweep his imperfections and addictions under the rug. A Black man growing up in Jim Crow South, King was deeply wounded by white supremacy and the terrorism it fueled. As a prophetic leader, he was targeted by white elites he spoke out against, but also by Black leadership who disagreed with his convictions and strategies. Like everyone else, he coped in ways that counterfeited himself and others. Perhaps he would have gone on his own deeper journey of recovery if he was not murdered at age thirty-nine (about the same age that I started my own journey).

Unfortunately, the colonial script stripped King of the opportunity for him to make his own transition into the second half of life. But the second half of life beckons me and everyone else honoring King's legacy. As I commit to a discipline of dis-illusionment, it is crucial that I consistently remind myself of the goal of this work. Gerald May, in his theological articulation of addiction and recovery, writes that we covenant to inner work "so that we can truly experience great unbounded love, endless creative energy and deep pervasive joy."[246] This is what is meant by "salvation" and "liberation" and "healing" and "recovery." This is, deep down, what every child of God yearns for.

What is at stake, in every coupleship and community, is the potential and capacity for intimacy. Imagine relationships that are safe and honest, where each person can be fully valued by being fully herself.[247] Intimacy is at the core of Jesus' call to wash one another's feet. At his final meal, he warns his disciples, "One of you will betray me" (John 13:21). Yet, none of the disciples have a clue who the betrayer was![248] This scene mirrors the kind of emotional bankruptcy that I've experienced in Sunday church services over and over again. There is singing and sermonizing, but before and after the formal gathering, talk stays on the surface. I rarely ever really know those seated in the pew next to me.

Intimacy in relationships is hard to come by. It is too easily blocked by dysfunctional dynamics—abuse, controlling and manipulating, caretaking, nagging, withdrawing, cutting-off and shutting-down, up/down relationships (a too-large power gap between two people) and addiction. These mechanisms come out to play when I am stuck in my pain without an exit strategy. They have hampered so many of my own relationships, one way or another.

May claims that everyone is "infused by the bondage of addiction and the hope of grace."[249] I am addicted to performance, to work, to ministry, to body image, to building my brand on Facebook. I cope with beer and exercise (an interesting combination) and a constant vision-casting tied to my identity (the illusion: The more I do, the more important I am). I spend far too much time trying to get likes and loves on social media. Addiction siphons the energy and desire for what is real: connecting to Steadfast Love and cultivating intimate relationships. Addiction holds me captive.

As Paul lamented in his letter to the Romans, "I am of the *sarkos,* sold into slavery under sin. I do not understand my own actions. For I do not do what I want, but I do the very thing I hate" (Romans 7:14-15). These are words from someone who, as recovering addicts testify, has hit rock bottom. He has finally admitted that his life is unmanageable. He has come to acceptance that he is powerless over his addiction and other people. Willpower will not work. The key step, May proposes, is detaching from the addiction, one day at a time. We have to go hungry and unsatisfied; we have to ache for something. It hurts.

Canadian medical doctor Gabor Mate proposes that another key step is to drop the self-hatred and shame. He stresses the need to cultivate a tenderness with ourselves, a compassionate curiosity with the one staring back at us in the mirror. Mate utilizes the acronym COAL: Curiosity, Openness, Acceptance, and Love.[250] This helps me learn to stop identifying with my pain. When I am triggered, I do not have to play out my old destructive patterns. When I do, I can step back, take a deep breath and tenderly explore why I did it again. Instead of shunning and shaming myself, I embrace curiosity and compassion as I seek to understand what is the deeper motivating factor.

I love what our friend and mentor Val Burris recently told Lindsay, "We can create a better world overnight, if we would just love ourselves enough." St. Francis called this "loving the leper within us," a spiritual practice of learning to handle our souls gently and tenderly so that we possess the space and energy to embrace everyone "outside" of us too.

Perhaps more than anything, I am learning to struggle

against powerful forces of denial. Far too often, facing the reality of injustice and oppression in socio-economic and political structures, in close relationships and in myself is simply too overwhelming and complicated. But this is the root of so much of what is dehumanizing me. As James Baldwin wrote, when we shut our eyes to reality—within us and all around us—we invite our own destruction.[251]

This intentional discipline of dis-illusionment must be cultivated over time. Progress, not perfection! Personal recovery has a long arc too. I know I need to commit massive amounts of time, energy and resources toward experimenting with what works for my own transformation.

*   *   *

With its focus on the individual and our own sinful struggles, Evangelical Christianity tends toward self-absorption, over-spiritualizing issues and widespread ignorance about the colonial script. However, with its penchant for the personal, the tradition of our youth paved the way for Lindsay and me to take recovery and healing seriously. Even though the vintage Evangelical "daily quiet times with God" are an easy target for mockery, they instilled in me a discipline of self-reflection and humility.

I remember singing Galatians 2:20-21 at midweek high school youth group meetings: "I have been crucified with Christ and it is no longer I who live, but Christ who lives in me and delivered himself up for me." Christian discipleship, from early on, challenged me to nail my ego to the cross and rise up with Jesus whose self-donating love became my model.

We would also belt out 2 Corinthians 12:9: "My grace is sufficient for you, for power is perfected in weakness." This theological potency grants me permission to come out of hiding, to take on a confessional mode and boldly name my weakness and pain and addiction so that I can experience grace and forgiveness and unearned belovedness. These shortcomings and afflictions are my "thorn in the flesh" (2 Corinthians 12:7b) that keeps me from becoming too entitled and self-sufficient and arrogant. All my faults and waywardness, unclothed with confession and compassion, keep me humble, centered and grounded.

Sometimes I am shocked at just how predatory I can be. My shame-driven workaholism, need to control and propensity to withdraw into resentment hold me back from the intimacy I crave. Unless I am in a consistent routine of taking my own inventory, I will inevitably project my pain and imperfections onto others. I will displace my self-loathing. This projection and scapegoating drown me spiritually and emotionally, spilling out onto those around me. I become a falcon on my perch, devouring those most dear to me. A painful cycle.

I find convenient political scapegoats too—Trump voters, Fox News watchers, Confederate flag wavers, Bible thumpers. I place them on the altar for slaughter. My friends gather around with delight. We bond over our shared disgust. Common enemy intimacy in action. We expend a whole lot of energy getting pissed off about the actions and attitudes of others we cannot control. In these conversations, we aren't changing the world. We aren't really bonding with each other either.[252]

True belonging, according to Brene Brown, comes when we display the courage to be transparent and vulnerable with each other. We risk sharing things about ourselves that have been covered by shame and self-hatred for decades. When we share our story with someone who can respond with empathy and acceptance, shame cannot survive.

As I work to stand on my own two feet, courageous soul friends have been vital. My marriage partnership with Lindsay has been the most powerful source of dis-illusionment. She feels deeply and lives in the moment. Lindsay is not only credentialed in family-systems therapy, she is anointed with a rare mind-heart-body congruency. She is passionate and honest, open-hearted and emotionally expressive. Most of all, she is thoroughly committed to her own personal and political liberation.

My relationship with Lindsay has opened me up to the spiritual power of what Audre Lorde calls "the erotic."[253] Not to be confused with sexuality (Lorde clarifies that it is the opposite of the pornographic), the erotic is the inner feeling and passion containing the core ingredients of a robust spirituality, which has too often been confused with the ascetic monk sitting alone in prayer 24/7 aspiring to feel nothing. In contrast, Lorde describes the erotic as the shared "physical, emotional, and psychic expressions of what is deepest and strongest and richest within each of us."[254]

With the support and nurture of beloved community, I am learning to verbalize my feelings, tapping into this passionate sense of joy, fearlessness, openness and energy that "heightens and sensitizes and strengthens all my experience."[255] Lorde rightly points out that most men value this depth of feeling enough to keep women around to exercise it in their service, but men fear the deep too much to examine the possibilities of it within themselves. I know this is true of myself and I am grateful for the precious role a few men play in my life who are summoning the courage to examine it within themselves.

Spiritual direction has been a gift, but therapy has been a game-changer. Having someone in my corner trained to get to the deep roots of my pain is deputizing me to stand on my own two feet. I also attend weekly Al-Anon meetings where I can share my own struggles with codependency and addiction and listen to the experience, strength, hope, pain and joy of others who have been cultivating their own discipline of dis-illusionment far longer than I have.

As I learn to stand on my own two feet, there is power in knowing that my struggle is shared. I am not an alien. The substance for authentic belonging is a spirituality rooted in knowing that we are all connected (even with our enemies!) by

Something that is far greater than ourselves. Something far below the surface in every living thing. Something constantly conspiring to teach us all more about what it means to live with the embrace of Steadfast Love.[256]

I am learning that both shame and blame are losing games. For everyone. When I commit to robust inner work, I find the substance, energy and resources to fend off the guilt and shame, the cynicism and narcissism, the denial and blame that inevitably comes with the territory.

It is clear to people of faith and conscience who take the legacy of Rev. Dr. Martin Luther King Jr. seriously that working to reconstruct socio-economic and political structures is vital. What seems less obvious is that a rigorous commitment to the restoration of our inner landscape is desperately needed too. Our souls have been paved over by the colonial script for too long. The institutions that are supposed to support us—the family, the church, non-profit organizations, the economy— have become unraveled. From now on, everybody stands on her own two feet. It starts with me. It ripples out from there. Only a well-choreographed discipline of dis-illusionment can keep us from drowning.

X.
Rise

"I have faith in the future because I know somehow that
although the arc of the moral universe is long
it bends toward justice."
Rev. Dr. Martin Luther King Jr.
April 27, 1965, UCLA

37
Revelation(s)

A few weeks into 2016, the Flint water crisis went viral. Tap water was poisoned with high levels of lead and bacteria. As complaints from residents came pouring in, city and state officials did nothing to change the situation. Just denial. For almost two whole years.

A month after the crisis made the headlines of every major newspaper in the world, Flint native and retired autoworker Claire McClinton drove sixty miles south to visit a group of us organizing for clean and affordable water in Detroit. These were Claire's opening remarks:

> We send you greetings from the occupied city of Flint. You can go to the gas station and get lead-free gas. You can go to the hardware store and get lead-free paint. Even a capitalist knows the dangers of lead. But we can't go to our sink and get lead-free water. I've got PTSD. In fact, everybody's got it if you care about humanity.

The disastrous decision to switch water sources was made by the full, unquestioned authority of a governor-appointed emergency manager who was appointed because of a $25 million accumulated deficit. In the decade leading up to this decision, the state government withheld $55 million in revenue sharing owed to Flint (all states redistribute a portion of sales tax revenue to local governments).[257] Flint, too, wasn't bankrupt. It was bankrupted.

The state government used Flint's sales tax revenue to plug holes in its own austerity budget, as taxes were slashed on the wealthy and corporations. There is also plenty of evidence that the decision to switch water sources in Flint was directly tied to campaign contributions from corporations seeking rich government contracts to build a new water pipeline to Lake Huron (in addition to fracking interests).[258]

A year after Claire visited us in Detroit, the state's Civil Rights Commission issued a scathing 135-page report naming "systemic racism" as a major factor in Flint's water contamination. Redlining, white flight to the suburbs, intergenerational poverty and "implicit bias" were all chronicled as contributing to the unnatural disaster.[259]

More than 50 percent of Michigan's Black residents have lived in cities governed by unelected and, most often, unresponsive, officials. Only 2 percent of white folks have had the same experience, even though there are many other financially struggling cities in Michigan that are majority white.[260]

Meanwhile, Michigan ranks last in the nation in transparency and accountability, as Governor Snyder signed multiple bills to conceal actions of the state government and shield the identity of the state's biggest political donors.[261] Fifty years after the Kerner Commission report, history has come full circle. White politicians still shrug off the fierce urgency of now.

And yet, Claire and her friends are the only reason that Flint's water crisis "made the news." They organized and recruited researchers from Virginia Tech to come test the safety of their water. They never gave up. As Claire boasts, "When they poisoned Flint, they poisoned the wrong ones." These grassroots leaders refused to accept the ending of the story that the powers scripted them into. They pulled off a miracle and the rest of the world came to believe.

*   *   *

Flint was an exposé. A *revelation*. Just like the final pages of the Christian Scriptures: The Book of Revelation. No "s" at the end. Most Christians mispronounce it. The real problem, though, is how they misinterpret it.

"Revelation" is the English translation of the Greek title *apokalypto*. The Apocalypse. The genre of apocalyptic literature, in the ancient world, utilized metaphor and hyperbole to "reveal" reality, to pull the curtain back on power. It was coded language—those on the margins were in on it. Those thriving in the mainstream were the butt of the joke.

Apocalyptic literature pierces through the veil of the colonial script to see reality more clearly. It strips away the denial and propaganda to expose suffering and injustice by taking the perspective of the poor and marginalized. It also infuses hope in a world as it should be by taking the perspective of a divine love that descends in solidarity with all who groan. Ched calls this the task of "apocalyptic double vision:" seeing the world as enslaved, but envisioning it liberated.[262]

So much of this is completely lost on those, like me, who grew up in an Evangelical faith mesmerized by Revelation as an end-times blueprint, retrofitting numbers and symbols to fit current events. Back in the '80's, I was taught that it was very likely that Communist Soviet Union was the Beast (Revelation 13) that would force us all to place a mark on our hand or forehead, and that we should be anticipating a False Prophet (Revelation 19:19-20) from the Democratic Party who would force the entire world to worship at his feet. Those of us who faithfully refused would live through the great tribulation, at least until we were raptured, leaving the world to burn in our salvific wake. This is what I learned from my junior high youth leaders in suburbia.

Written from the margins, however, the ancient roots of apocalyptic literature are anti-imperial. These scenarios were envisioned from places like the streets of Flint and Detroit, not the mega-churches of suburban Southern California. Revelation was written by one banished to exile, likely an indication that the author grew up with some semblance of privilege and then prophetically turned his back on the mainstream (those from lower classes, like Jesus, were beheaded or crucified).[263] John the Revelator descended like a dove.

The Book of Revelation, a challenging address to seven churches paralyzed by the colonial script, is a thoroughly stinging critique of power, wealth, comfort and the use of violence in service of greed. The beast and prophet were referring to Rome and Caesar during the first century. The great tribulation was what those followers of Jesus were suffering then—to exile, on crosses, in prisons and arenas. For them, it already was "the end times."

The spiritual power of Revelation is that every generation of disciples is called to "faithful resistance" (Revelation 1:9)—from beasts like power hungry Presidents and emergency managers, stripping human rights and shutting off water. If followers of Jesus since the fourth century read Revelation in ways that are more congruent with the original intent—if they got the timeless message—the history of Christianity would be dramatically different. If we grappled with "the prophetic" as a prodding to resist and recover, instead of as a foretelling of the future, we would have had access to a script that challenges and empowers instead of one fueled by fear and fantasy.

It is easy to miss the point when reading Revelation. Its message is more relevant than ever as the colonial script continues its vicious cycle. Fifty years ago, Dr. King lamented that Black Americans were being "crucified by conscientious blindness," linking that violent tribulation with the words of Jesus on the cross, "Forgive them, for they know not what they do." Today, more than ever before, mainstream America continues to be crucified by conscientious blindness.[264]

38
What the Hell?

Needless to say, the eye-opening reality on the ground in both Detroit and Flint has thrown my theology into a tailspin. After two decades of Evangelical visions of the afterlife, I had studied enough in seminary to discern a more complex understanding of heaven and hell. I found it absolutely crazy that millions of American Evangelical Christians would know for certain that Gandhi and billions of other kind, loving, wise and sincere people were in hell because they refused or neglected to "confess that Jesus is Lord."

However, through study and dialogue, I learned that all the hell passages in the Gospels were warning flags waved at the disciples of Jesus.[265] Not the unbelievers. Hell, in the Gospels, is actually "Gehenna," a smoldering trash heap outside Jerusalem (Mark 9:43; Matthew 5:22). It was a powerful metaphor for a life that resembles a landfill—the garbage of fear and anxiety and addiction and resentment piling up without recycling all the pain into newness of life.

My biblical study was intensified by my study of social analysis. I slowly learned why and how oppression operates in the world. I ruminated and lamented: How could all of these desperately poor non-Christians (in Latin America, in Africa, in Asia, in Detroit and Flint) be going to hell? They already are in hell—mostly as a result of American imperial policies endorsed by Evangelical Christians.

After seminary, I had concluded that Jesus was basically saying, "If you are going to live with bitterness and arrogance and hatred and violence, then you'll be living out a hellish existence. If you live in these ways, it's bad news for you and everyone who has to deal with you." It was both personal and present.

However, I also came to believe that hell represents the political realm too. It is the ugly result of structural sin—greed, injustice, oppression. It is the Kibera slum. It is poisoning Flint and shutting off Detroit. These places that I had visited literally looked like the smoldering trash heap of Gehenna. Hell, I came to believe, is not where unbelievers go when they die, but a very real situation for billions of people, right now. The dire consequences of a world running on the colonial script.

This is what my theology of hell boiled down to before we moved to Detroit. I still think it reflects much of the truth about reality, but it's simply not enough. It is too convenient and privileged. I can clearly recall that day when my soul got a notification that Hell 2.0 required another update. I was on the north end of Detroit, helping someone move, when a conversation organically arose among the half dozen of us filling up a U-Haul.

We put down the furniture and posted up on the porch for more than two hours. I listened to longtime Detroiters tell story after story about one politician after another, rearranging Detroit neighborhoods by pulling strings for their white suburban backers; one wealthy white billionaire after another, buying up buildings and sitting on the boards of corporations and foundations, making decisions about water shut-offs, school defunding and housing foreclosures. Big ballers and shot callers manufacturing even more misery for those on the margins.

That's when Monica Lewis-Patrick—fueled by the holy ghost and a cup of coffee sweetened with four sugar packets—let it all out:

> Either someone's going to jail or they better be going to hell!

Real justice demands accountability—what my white Evangelical fathers called "personal responsibility." How can powerful elites go unscathed despite all their manipulating, conniving, hoarding and propagandizing? Meanwhile, real people—millions and billions of them—lose homes, jobs, their health, their clean record, their water and their lives. Those living in the trenches of poverty and oppression know that hell's simply got to be real. Some way. Somehow. It is the only thing that can possibly be just.

On that afternoon, in that out-of-the-way neighborhood in Detroit, far away from my suburban perch, the shit got real for me. All of Jesus' teaching on fire and brimstone, on weeping and gnashing of teeth (Matthew 13:42), overwhelmed my soul. It sparked in me a righteous indignation. The biblical script was doing the deep work, echoing in the booming voice of a mother who lost her only son to gun violence:

> Listen! Your brother's blood is crying out to me from the ground (Genesis 4:10)!

Like Abel, the first victim of the colonial script and the father of all who have been scapegoated and disappeared, the blood of every precious mourning dove stalked and slaughtered on the way to economic growth and the American Dream (for a few) cries out to the God of the cross. Through Monica, Abel was "still speaking" (Hebrews 11:4).[266]

Monica's porch proclamation beckoned the voice of Jesus himself, assuring his oppressed disciples that there is One greater who will have the final say:

> Do not fear those who kill the body but cannot kill the soul; rather fear him who can destroy both soul and body in hell (Matthew 10:28).

God's wrath started simmering again that day, but it flipped my old Evangelical perspective on its head. Hell had nothing to do with refusing to believe. It had everything to do with refusing to care. The Lord Jesus himself prodded his own followers, using very harsh words, to stop living in ways that were dehumanizing and destructive—to themselves and others. Then he wept.

In one Gospel episode (Mark 2:23—3:6), Jesus is called out by religious and political elites for disrespecting the sacred Sabbath (the ancient version of the national anthem and Memorial Day). Jesus was permitting his disciples to feed themselves from the open fields. Then he healed a man with a crippled hand. He took a knee while everyone else remained standing.

What happens when hunger and hurt hold down hundreds of millions of Americans on the most holy day? Jesus calls the hierarchy into question. The plight of humanity is far more important than any holy tradition. It is a wonderful rule of life: Prioritize people before anything else—whether profits, projects or progress.

But then something controversial happened. Jesus showed his human side. He got angry (Mark 3:5).

At hunger and disease.
At the hoarding of food and healthcare.
At the rigidity of religious leaders.

Jesus is a model of what healthy anger looks like. Let it out. Grieve and heal. And whatever you do, don't let institutions bind you with injustice.

Jesus' prophetic fire is reflected in Rev. Jeremiah Wright, the Black pastor who President Obama disowned after his "God damn America!" sermon went viral. I heard Wright preach a sermon in Detroit on an episode from Luke's Gospel where he compared the seasonal hurricane pathway across the Atlantic with that of "the Middle Passage," the route shipping the enslaved from Africa to the Americas—same path. This is not mere coincidence. More like moral consequence. We are caught in a web of mutuality.

Jesus and Jeremiah Wright were no different from Rev.

Dr. Martin Luther King Jr., whose prepared sermon for the Sunday following his assassination was entitled "Why America May Go to Hell." King's "long arc" bending toward justice is where the God of Steadfast Love confronts the wealthy, powerful, falcon god of the mainstream. God's got justice and mercy in a slow cooker. Everybody's gonna get saved—eventually. Maybe the Catholic doctrine of purgatory represents the overtime needed by many of us in order to get the final touches on our redemption. Some of us require a longer arc than others.

There's intense mystery involved in this for me. I simply do not know how eternity plays itself out. I do, however, cling to a strong conviction about two things: (1) Hell is not an afterlife destination for people who don't "come to know Christ" in the way that American Evangelicals narrate it; and (2) Hell hasn't simply vanished into some sort of "love jacuzzi" as many liberal Christians imagine it. These two options just don't seem plausible from a divinity defined by Steadfast Love. Because the opposite of the God of Steadfast Love is not an angry God, but an apathetic God.

I confess: I'm afraid of anger. A vicious combination of white middle class suburbia and Evangelical Christianity trained me to repress my feelings. To be in control of my emotions. Yet, the typical rage of us white American males inevitably spills out—whenever our control and power is threatened.

However, anger—expressed in healthy ways—is *the* appropriate response to the poverty, abuse and oppression all around us. There are reasons why the world is so wretched. These reasons make emotionally mature people very irate. It leads them to work for transformation. To resist and rise above it.

I am slowly learning to tap into the prophetic rage of Jesus through icons like Monica and Claire and others, most of them Black and/or female. Their lives have been infused with a sacred sorrow that percolates from the simmering heat of constant oppression—treated as imposters, yet are true; as sorrowful, yet always rejoicing; as poor, yet making many rich; as having nothing, yet possessing everything (2 Corinthians 6:8-10). They pivot from truth telling to tenderness in fluid fashion. They fight fire with a different kind of fire, a "transphysics" that blends fierce love with raw truth.

The angry and loving God of the long arc is a divinity that refuses both violent retribution and inaction.[267] It is not a god of petty masculine rage who jealously longs for a stroked ego. It is a God who groans, with tears and mourning, for victims catching hell right now (Romans 8:22). The God of Steadfast Love incarnated in Jesus and King and Claire and Monica is passionate, filled with anger at any and every injustice, oppression and violence. This is now the only God I can possibly believe in.

39
Resurrection

A few decades after Jesus warned his disciples of the reality of hell, the Apostle Paul wrote to the faithful in Philippi, a little colony on the fringes of empire: "But our citizenship is in heaven, and it is from there that we are expecting a Savior, the Lord Jesus Christ" (Philippians 3:20). While Roman citizens in Philippi placed their faith in Caesar, their Lord and Savior, whose imperial forces would protect them from barbarians from the north, the Philippian Christians pledged allegiance to Jesus. Heaven, for Paul, was simply the anti-Rome. It was the divine anti-imperial force of love, compassion, justice and kindness incarnated in the body of a prophetic Jew who challenged the colonial script and its enforcers. Citizens of heaven pledged to carry out his legacy in their lifestyle.

However, the colonial script has convinced the American masses that when our physical bodies die, our souls are whisked away to an afterlife—heaven, hell or somewhere in between. This notion is soaked through with Greek dualism. That's a problem for those of us committed to reading the Bible carefully and critically. Jesus and Paul were Jewish. They conceived of a holistic world where body, spirit, mind and soul were interdependent and inseparable from each other. As Dr. King would say, "the interrelated structure of reality."

The rapture theology infused into my young Evangelical faith envisioned an End Times scenario when Jesus would triumphantly return to rescue us from the sin of the world. The rapture was trending in my generation due to the *Left Behind* series of books and movies that filled in the blanks of what the Bible assured us would soon happen:

> For the Lord himself, with a word of command,
> with the voice of an archangel and with the trumpet of
> God, will come down from heaven,
> and the dead in Christ will rise first.
> Then we who are alive, who are left,
> will be caught up together with them in the clouds
> to meet the Lord in the air (1 Thessalonians 4:16-17).

This is one of the most fanciful passages of the Bible. It was almost too much for my adolescent mind, conjuring images of mass disappearances—freeways suddenly littered with empty cars and football stadiums with fans flying into the heavens. Researching the historical context, though, has brought me back down to earth—literally.

Paul was playing off the Roman imperial concept of the *parousia*, the common belief, in many of the colonies of the first century, that the Lord Caesar would come and visit them soon. News of his official visitation would reach these Romans living in faraway imperial colonies (by trumpet proclamation!) and they would exit the gates of the city to meet the Lord Caesar on the road to accompany him back into the city.

Paul subversively envisioned a final redemption when Jesus returned and his followers would meet him in the sky and usher him *back to Mother Earth*. Jesus would bring justice and peace—"on earth as it is in heaven" as he taught his disciples to pray (Matthew 6:10).[268]

Paul placed his ultimate hope in *resurrection*, the "dead" rising up in our midst. This makes resurrection a contemporary experience that has everything to do with seen and unseen forces all around us. It means that our loved ones who have passed away are neither beyond our space/time reality "in heaven," nor are they just "in the ground." Those cherished mentors and heroes, who have gone on before us, are still present, helping or haunting us along the way.

Our ancestors are like Abel who "died, but through his faith he still speaks" (Hebrews 11:4b). They rise with us.

Rosa Parks: ¡*Presente*!
Dietrich Bonhoeffer: ¡*Presente*!
Martin Luther King: ¡*Presente*!
Dennis Airey: ¡*Presente*!

The late civil rights leader Vincent Harding described the magnitude of this spiritual force-field as "an ageless, pulsating membrane of light that is filled with the lives, hopes and beatific visions of all who have fought on, held on, loved well and gone on before us."[269] We are not alone.

By extending prayer to "calling on the Ancestors," we participate in the reality of resurrection—that "we are surrounded by so great a cloud of witnesses" wherever we find ourselves (Hebrews 12:1). As the Black folk poets would say, "Every shut eye ain't asleep, every goodbye ain't gone."[270] Those who have gone before us are with us—intimately, right now.

In the Hebrew Bible, God is described as One who has created and organized a world that carries the substance of our lives beyond the grave. In other words, the way our parents, grandparents and great-grandparents lived continues to play out in our lives:

> ...yet by no means clearing the guilty, but visiting the iniquity of the parents upon the children and the children's children, to the third and the fourth generation (Exodus 34:7; Numbers 14:18).

Many indigenous traditions are far better models of the intergenerational salvation story than anything claiming to be "Christian." These focus on "spiritual debt" instead of "original sin." It's not so much an individual's inherited stain of sin that needs to be whited out, but a passed-down pattern that needs to be worked out.

In this process, I am called to knowing those who came before me—not only those from my family and faith community, but also the indigenous who inhabited the land long before white folks settled it. For most of my life, these ancestors were virtually meaningless. I had barely known only two of my grandparents. They were dead before I made it to middle school. Besides, what did any of my forebears have to do with anything happening now? My Evangelical faith taught me that I would meet them in heaven someday—maybe.

The author and spiritual leader Martin Prechtel warns that cutting off from those who came before us leads to a life cursed either fighting our ancestors or riding the wave they started.[271] Prechtel was raised on a Pueblo Indian reservation in New Mexico and then spent several years living with the Tzutujil, a Mayan village in the mountains of Guatemala. He eventually had to flee north when Evangelical-funded militaries invaded and brutally murdered tens of thousands, including many of his own friends and family. He knows firsthand just how devastating the colonial script can be.

Prechtel homes in on the importance of grief. By this, he means a kind of intentionality of living that values eloquence, beauty and sacrifice.[272] Grief is an offering that matches the sentiments of the Apostle Paul, who challenged these disciples to "present their bodies as a living sacrifice, holy and acceptable to God," an act of worship that enabled them to be "transformed by the renewing of their minds" (Romans 12:1-2). Instead of a one-time event, grief is a lifelong sacrificial lifestyle of love and reverence for what came before and what will remain long after our life in its present form is finished.

This is all part of cultivating what Prechtel calls "the indigenous soul." Unfortunately, the ancient ways of grieving parents, grandparents and great-grandparents have mostly been erased. Instead, the colonial script counsels us to attend the funeral and then "try to move on." It is supposed to be a comfort that our loved ones are now "resting in a better place." Resurrection beckons us to something deeper than this. It assures us that our loved ones whisper to our souls, calling us to intentionally offer the world beauty—with work and worship, but also with play, parenting and politics.

40
The Point

A year after 9/11, Rick Warren began his Evangelical bestseller *The Purpose Driven Life* with a memorable line: *It's not about you*. True enough. Evangelicalism, at its best, preaches self-donating love, service and humility. A call to descend like a dove. The problem, however, is that the Christian tradition that has raised Warren up to the status of "the next Billy Graham" is fully rooted in the soil of me-centered questions about God and faith.

In fact, the first line of any Evangelical self-description details an individual relationship with God and a personal salvation in heaven. As Pastor Rick puts it, "You weren't put on earth to be remembered. You were put here to prepare for eternity."[273] This message has resonated with many. The updated paperback version boasts more than 32 million copies sold. It was what this message was missing, though, that sent Lindsay and me east seeking something more spiritually compelling.

In an Advent sermon delivered to a few dozen of us in Detroit, Jim Perkinson stretched and deepened Warren's message to cosmic proportions. Pastor Jim set himself to the task of decolonizing Jesus' Gospel warning tales about bridesmaids waiting for the groom and a master going on a journey, leaving the slaves behind to "keep watch" (Matthew 25:1-13). My Evangelical mind naturally conjured God as the groom and the master, one day returning to punish those who failed to get saved. Like a falcon swooping in from nowhere.

Perkinson, though, was taking his cues from biblical scholarship that refuses any sort of assumption that God is The Big Man On Campus.[274] The landlord, in the Gospels, is who he actually is in real life: a despot and oppressor—just like Detroit property hoarder Dan Gilbert turning downtown into a game of Monopoly and paying the janitors who work his buildings less than $10 an hour. The heroes and role models provided by the Gospel narratives, instead, are the fig tree and the enslaved— the more-than-human and those who have been made less-than-human by the colonial script (Mark 13:28-37).

In the end, the real hope is not in a Father who triumphantly comes back to save and punish. Salvation comes in the form of a Mother (Earth) who recycles and renews. She's got the whole world in Her hands. As Perkinson proclaimed, "It ain't finally about us."Like Pastor Rick. Only totally different. Not purpose-driven. More meaning-filled and mystery-infused. Not only in the future. But also right now.

Just five days earlier, on an unseasonably warm and windy November afternoon, Lindsay and I took my mom for a hike on Belle Isle, the 982-acre island in the middle of the Detroit River. It was long ago violently seized from the precious Huron, Odawa and Ojibwe peoples and then sold to some white dude for five barrels of rum and a belt of wampum.

After a hike through a forest of Fall colors, we sprinkled some of my dad's ashes under one of the majestic willow trees lurking across the chilly waters separating us from Canada. "Dust you are, and unto dust you shall return" (Genesis 3:19). Right there at the beginning of the Bible, the dust is displayed as the eternal destination of every living thing—back to our Mother. Dad is still speaking, in both spirit and soil. He's changed forms, just a breath away, whispering to our souls.[275]

The good news is that the Mother knows a story that counters the colonial script. She composts with consequences and coincidences. In the end, she will save the day, with all Her mechanisms and manifestations. The Bible, Perkinson assured us, contains traces of this indigenous wisdom, rising up like a little invasive mustard seed, always second-guessing the human-centered Greek philosophy that infuses the colonial script. Our undying hope is in the ultimate fact that we are not alone and it ain't finally about us.

*   *   *

When resurrection becomes more than a doctrine to believe in or a future event to await, it empowers us to reclaim what King called "the revolutionary spirit." It becomes an active power in our daily lives, a living Presence that can sustain us over and over again.

In 1980, before he was assassinated, the Catholic priest Oscar Romero boldly spoke out against the evil, violence and corruption of the U.S.-sponsored military dictatorship in El Salvador. He was asked if he feared that they would kill him. Romero responded, "If they kill me, I will rise again in the Salvadoran people." This is it! Resurrection as a Power and a Presence. The spirit of King Jesus and Rev. Dr. Martin Luther King Jr. animate and energize us—in word and deed. Right now.

With this mindset, resurrection becomes a spiritual

practice. It is a way of life fueled by "the same Spirit that raised Jesus from the dead" (Romans 8:11)—and King and Romero. Lynice Pinkard, the former pastor at First Congregational Church of Oakland and a board member of the Seminary of the Street, describes resurrection as abandoning the deadness of our lives and rising above life-limiting forces that plague us. It is a daily practice of "crossing over from self-interest to true solidarity."[276] In order to rise up, we are called to descend.

Resurrection is an invitation to follow the women of the Gospels who possess the courage and boldness to go all the way to the cross with Jesus, while all the male disciples scatter in fear. The women are the ones who find the tomb empty. The women are the ones who relay the resurrection message: that Jesus is going ahead of them, back to Galilee (Mark 16:7-8).

Galilee, Ched beautifully interprets, is the cue for the reader to go back to the beginning of the Gospel story. Going back to Galilee jump-starts Jesus' ministry. It announces an alternative way-of-life. It challenges the disciples to pledge allegiance to it. Follow the women back to the God of Steadfast Love, the God of the Second Chance. The subversive act of staring down death and despair is supported by the invitation to press the refresh button, to get recharged with wisdom, forgiveness, grace and hope.[277]

Galilee is the place of the poor and despised, all those that Salvadoran priest Jon Sobrino calls "the crucified people of the earth." Resurrection is the active hope that "crucifying realities do not have the last word."[278] At the end of the Gospel story, the focus is Galilee, not Golgotha where Jesus died. Our world, with all its pain and suffering, is viewed through the lens of resurrection.

*   *   *

There's still time to reverse course. Ongoing injustice and oppression, in every corner of the world, prod people of faith and conscience to become different kinds of *missionaries*. We bear *witness* to the horror of the colonial script, with all its intricacies. Then we work tirelessly to dismantle it. Most of all, in a world hijacked by emergency managers, we need to reimagine *evangelism*, the old Christian practice that Evangelicals are named after.

Instead of inviting "nonbelievers" to church so that they can get saved for eternal life and catering to the "felt needs" of friends and acquaintances pledging allegiance to the mainstream, this other way seeks to model a lifestyle committed, first and foremost, to alleviating the suffering of the marginalized. As King proclaimed to 11,000 in Memphis just hours before his violent death, "It's alright to talk about 'streets flowing with milk and honey,' but God has commanded us to be concerned about the slums down here, and his children who can't eat three square meals a day."[279] A commitment to naming just how catastrophic things become, in a world of denial, is to reject despair by inviting a thirsty world into a clear-eyed hope.

We need to get back to the basics, what the ancient Greeks called the *telos*—the "goal," or the whole "point," of life. The colonial script thrives as a default in a culture that lacks a coherent *telos*. What's the point of life? We aren't quite sure. We have simply become fragmented into dozens of disjointed sound-bites and mini-stories, many of them contradictory.[280]

Telos is the root of the final Greek word out of Jesus' mouth before he dies on the cross (*tetelestai*, John 19:30). "It is finished" is how it is translated by most English versions of the Bible. Evangelicals taught me that this meant the job was done—the sacrifice was offered so that the human race could finally be saved from their sins.

I interpret *tetelestai* as "The whole point of faith is revealed"—right here, up on the cross. The point of life is to cultivate love, defined by Jesus earlier in the Gospel as a willingness to lay down our lives for others (John 15:13-17). In the Gospel of John, this is clearly what the cross means. The colonial script has hoodwinked far too many of us into missing the point.

Rev. Dr. Martin Luther King Jr. described the love of Jesus as "the key that unlocks the door which leads to ultimate reality."[281] Love demands that every living thing, human and more-than-human, is essential. There is no hierarchy in the economy of the crucified God. No one is any better than anyone or anything else. No one is disposable. No one is supreme.

Back in the early 1970s, Black theologian James Cone started pushing back on the ways that white America sentimentalized the love of Jesus and King. Cone declared the kind of love articulated by the Gospels and embodied in the Civil Rights struggle as "militant." It demanded creative resistance and civil disobedience to confront the injustice and oppression that held down billions of people all over the globe.[282] Victims of the colonial script simply cannot be saved by the charitable band-aids of foundations and nonprofits. The roots of the devastation need to be tended to and transformed.

On many occasions, Dr. King pleaded for audiences to widen their concept of what love entails, extending the parable of the Good Samaritan beyond random acts of kindness "to see that the whole Jericho Road must be transformed." Real love isn't about just tossing our spare change to beggars. Real love calls us to change the system that produces beggars.[283]

In order for poverty and oppression to be alleviated in America, a fundamental shift must take place, going beyond addressing *symptoms* to transforming *systems*. This is the opposite of what Evangelicals taught me—that church folks ought to "stay out of politics" and create nonprofits like rescue missions and food pantries to care for those who lack jobs, healthcare and housing. Many of these organizations feature altar calls to get them saved before they are housed and fed.

After decades of participation and observation, I believe that Evangelicals continue to settle for charity and philanthropy work because (A) the results seem more immediate and rewarding, (B) it keeps them in a heroic position, and (C) they don't have to get their hands dirty with the messy, complex roots of poverty and oppression.[284] The problem is that this work does not actually work.

Charity is important, but it is not enough. We can deliver thirty gallons a week to victims of water shut-off. But the goal of the work is to get every tap turned back on. Only a drastic change in policy will save people from the dehumanizing toll of poverty. Real solutions are desperately needed: for housing, health, education, employment, transportation and much more.

Jesus changed the rules of the game, which was working only for an entitled few. "Something greater than the temple is here," Jesus proclaimed scandalously (Matthew 12:6). The point is not to preserve the institution at all costs. The point is the people, compassion, inclusivity, solidarity. Everything else will take care of itself. This is the *telos*, the end with which we must begin. Unfortunately, the professional religionists of Jesus' time, addicted to the "traditional" ways, didn't know how to play any other way.

The end may, or may not, be near. But the real end of life, the *telos*, is what we need to be striving for at this particular moment in history. This end is Steadfast Love—rising up out of deathliness, bringing heaven to earth, working for justice for all those catching hell. Justice, according to Dr. Cornel West, is what love looks like in public. Only with this kind of focus can we have faith in the future. If King was right, no matter how dire things get, the arc is long and it bends toward justice. But no matter how long it takes, justice is the goal.

Conclusion

"We will meet your physical force with soul force."
Rev. Dr. Martin Luther King Jr.
April 27, 1965, UCLA

40
Reality

Almost fifty years to the day of Rev. Dr. Martin Luther King Jr.'s "I Have A Dream" speech, Randy Woodley graciously invited Lindsay and me to join their community for their monthly "Jesus sweat" gathering. We were on the final leg of our 12,000-mile summer road trip scouting out compelling expressions of faith and conscience all over the continent. Randy, a Keetoowah Cherokee Indian descendent, ordained American Baptist pastor and a professor of faith and culture at George Fox University, lives on Eloheh Farm, twenty-five miles from Portland, Oregon, with his wife, Edith, and their four children. I met him a few months earlier on a trip to the Pacific Northwest with Ched. I was immediately struck, not only by his political and theological brilliance, but also his personal warmth and curiosity.

When he called it a "Jesus sweat," I was imagining a soothing and slightly more spiritual version of a sauna. However, we were only fifteen minutes into the ancient indigenous practice when I was pretty sure I was going to die of heat exhaustion. I hadn't felt this physically drained since I ran a ten-mile leg of the Boston Marathon up Heartbreak Hill in ninety-degree heat.[285]

In the midst of this newfound spiritual practice, I tried to remain calm with the blessed assurance that we were at Eloheh, a Cherokee term meaning "harmony, balance, well-being and abundance." In addition, I knew Randy was an elder I could trust. He had been facilitating sweats for the past quarter century from Oklahoma to Nevada to Alabama to Kentucky to Oregon, and not one white boy had ever died—yet.

Thirteen of us reverently filed into a lodge the size of an eight-person camping tent. We were white and indigenous, lesbian and straight, male, female and queer. It represented what Randy calls Jesus' "Community of Creation" (his

208

rendering of "the kingdom of God," the main topic of Jesus' teaching in the Gospels). It was a gathering void of hierarchy and brimming with a deep blend of openness and togetherness. Each and every one of us was a precious cracked vessel unable to contain the spilling out Spirit.

While I was lying on my back pouring water on my face, Randy's son, Young, explained that the focus of the Native American sweat is on confession and purgation. It was an invitation into vulnerability and forgiveness. A chance to release the pain and trauma weighing down our souls. This was a 500-year reminder of my complicity with the colonial script.

The lodge was completely dark. Heated by pouring water over lava rocks, it symbolized a mother's womb, where each participant has a born-again experience. Each "round" of the ceremony got hotter as we focused ourselves on prayer, song and open sharing around the circle. We spoke individually, counter-clockwise, concluding each prayer with a communal "aho," the Cherokee word for "amen." We emerged out of the refining heat into new life.

Jesus exhorted his disciples, "Whenever you pray, go into your closet and shut the door!" (Matthew 6:6). This "quiet time" was an important practice in my private, individualized Evangelical spirituality, but that afternoon when I overheated in the Mother God's womb at Eloheh Farm, it was a born again experience for me. I was baptized into a new understanding of the interdependent nature of reality.

The sweat formally introduced us to the beautiful Lakota concept of Mitákuye Oyás'in ("all are related"), a bold belief in a world infused with Spirit that connects everyone and everything. This is precisely what Dr. King was getting at when he preached, in what would be his final Christmas sermon, of the interrelatedness of everything:

> It really boils down to this: that all life is interrelated.
> We are all caught in an inescapable network of
> mutuality, tied into a single garment of destiny.
> Whatever affects one directly, affects all indirectly. We
> are made to live together because of the interrelated
> structure of reality.[286]

The divine design is holistic, not hierarchical. More like a band of doves than a lone falcon up on his perch. At Eloheh, I finally got the message loud and clear. The interrelated structure of reality—kept alive by Black and Brown voices for 500 years— was the key to descending like a dove. We either rise together or we fall together. America's greatness, though, has been constructed on a counterfeit reality.

A few counterfeit "great ones," Jesus warned, have become tyrants over the rest of us. But true greatness descends and decolonizes so that it gives life to the many. To be great, Jesus proclaimed, was to become baptized into a movement that challenges the colonial script. To drink from the cup of suffering, in solidarity with the dregs of life. To become a servant of all (Mark 10:35-45).

*   *   *

The mother's womb at Eloheh stoked a fire in my heart, fueled by the fact that harmony for a chosen few on the North American continent has always been built on the oppression of Black and Brown people. Most mainstream Christians in the United States attempt to disarm the dialogue with discourse over colorblindness. They say they've moved beyond race and that American society is post-racial. Many offer judgments about key differences in culture. The secrets to success, they say, is about work ethic, study habits, resiliency, obeying authority and staying clean and sober. They point to exceptional achievements like Obama and Oprah. They claim that everyone has the opportunity to be just like them.

A decolonizing faith confronts this spiritual conundrum with a combination of critical consciousness and compassion. Black and Brown people are disproportionally poor and in prison because this is how the colonial script has been written. The system is designed this way—for people of color to be confined to the reservation, the ghetto, the barrio, the cell. The interrelated structure of reality exposes the sham that opportunity and success is secured for the chosen few by silencing, disallowing, displacing and rendering powerless Black and Brown people. If I choose to remain silent, I stamp the status quo with my approval.

The system must be challenged and changed. It can be. Anything else is unconscionable. Fund education. End overseas military invasions. Mandate a living wage. Invest in health care. Create real jobs. Close prisons. Regulate the wealthy and powerful. Turn on the water. Action verbs are unavoidable.

The literal face of Jesus must be challenged and changed, too. The white Jesus in our picture Bibles and our stained glass windows dominates our imaginations. This is highly problematic. Jesus was not white. He was a Palestinian Jew. He had a darkened hue and kinky hair. For the past fifty years, Black and Brown theologians have offered this more historically accurate dark-skinned Jesus to infuse hope and worth into their communities of faith. White Christians, by and large, have dismissed it as either fiction or irrelevance. Reversing this trend can be a game changer.

The precious doves surviving on reservations, ghettos and barrios—all those that the colonial script has taught us to treat as second-class citizens—look far more like Jesus than I do. So I ponder: What if every time I read the Gospels or prayed "in Jesus' name" I was reminded of this? What if every time I talked to, or about, Black or Brown people, I was reminded of this?

In fact, Jesus is risen and alive in the faces of Black and

Brown Americans who are disproportionally represented among those called "the least of these." The most vulnerable are those Jesus most identified with: "I was naked and you gave me clothing, I was sick and you took care of me, I was in prison and you visited me" (Matthew 25:36).

In the economy of the God of Steadfast Love, every life matters. However, in the economy governed by the colonial script, some lives matter far more than others. This is not just "back then." It is right now too. To hashtag #BlackLivesMatter or proclaim that "God privileges the poor" is not reverse racism. It is the road forward.

The capitalization of Black and Brown bestows upon Blackness and Brownness a sacred quality that the colonial script has attempted to vanquish for 500 years. It subversively questions the supremacy of whiteness. It is the focus and framework of the Jesus kind of love that "covers over a multitude of sins" (1 Peter 4:8). Anything less leaves the disinherited in a ditch on the drive to dignity.

The giant triplets of racism, militarism and extreme poverty continue to dominate the competition, but this is a long season and it's not a spectator sport. To win, accomplices are desperately needed to join the action and to recruit others to the team as well. Unfortunately, what is actually happening on the court is getting more and more difficult to discern.

42
A Marginalized Endeavor

During the twentieth anniversary commemoration of Martin Luther King's "I Have a Dream" speech, civil rights activist Elena Rocha proclaimed, "If Martin Luther King could get up from the grave he would see that he'd have to start raising hell all over again."[287] Behold, the undomesticated and unsanitized Martin Luther King! And Jesus, too! The messages of Dr. King and Jesus of Nazareth have been hijacked and domesticated by a powerful and privileged religious establishment with a large white and wealthy following. Jesus and King have been falconized and mainstreamed—marinated in the colonial script, spiritualized in the heart and futurized in heaven.

If the whole future of America really does depend on the impact and influence of Dr. King, then society is wading through some deep shit without a shepherd. Meanwhile, lounging in the penthouse of the tower he named after himself, the President of the United States boasts of "alternative facts." We live in a context of distractions, distortions, addictions and blatant lies. This, however, is nothing new.

King addressed the difference between "facts" and "truth" on that warm April afternoon at UCLA in 1965. "A fact is merely the absence of contradiction," King explained, "but the truth is the presence of coherence." It's easy to state facts, but still be disconnected from the ultimate truth. What would King think now in an era when basic facts are not even required for what qualifies as public dialogue?

Today, most white Americans most of the time dismiss facts about who Jesus was, what the Bible really "says," who Rev. Dr. Martin Luther King Jr. was and what he really thought about the fundamental principles and policies behind what so many white Americans mean when they harmonize about "Making America Great Again." The "again" at the end of that last line is terrible news because it takes us back to some point in history when "greatness" was built, even more than it is today, by sacrificing the lives and livelihoods of Native and Black Americans, women, immigrants, residents of the global South, gays and lesbians and other scapegoated or neglected peoples.

From page one of this book, though, I have hoped to outrun both denial and despair. This isn't about tearing down a tradition, but about being *apocalyptic* in the truest sense of its Greek roots: an experiment in revealing and unveiling. Indeed, I've simply wanted to expose a post-Evangelical audience to alternative ways of following Jesus. To conjure more compelling visions of what it means to be human. To cultivate a clear-eyed hope that resists every form of denial and despair.

*   *   *

Hope hollered my name one afternoon while I was biking home on Michigan Avenue in thick summer humidity. It was Ann, a fellow We The People of Detroit volunteer. I hadn't seen her in months, since that winter day at the office when she held out her hand and prophesied, "These lemon drops will make your sweet tooth go sit in a corner and put on a dunce cap." Swimming in a society double-teaming her with denial and despair, Ann defiantly practiced resurrection.

Drenched in sweat, I hopped off my bike ready for more of Ann's vintage storytelling. She was transferring buses back home after a frustrating morning at the doctor's office in Southwest Detroit. "They talking about 'pain management,'" she lamented and then continued, "I don't want my pain managed. I want it obliterated!"

This descending dove, precious icon of Jesus, wasn't just taking personal inventory. She was proclaiming truth in parable, layer upon layer upon layer of depth pouring out into possibility. Because the colonial script thrives on keeping the masses in situations just barely managing to survive, people of faith and conscience must confront systems built on pain and oppression and violence, groaning for one thing: the utter obliteration of the colonial script.

Ann's testimony reminded me of the Gospel episode that came right after Jesus had twice multiplied loaves and fishes. Once again, the disciples forgot to pack lunch for their boat journey to the other side of the lake! Jesus then warned them of "the leaven of the Pharisees and Herod." The dense disciples spiraled in shame, convinced he was passive-aggressively referring to the bread they left on the kitchen table. Jesus was digging deeper, though. He was speaking in parable, warning of the devious ways that the colonial script was working through the dough kneading their community together (Mark 8:14-21). They were just managing the pain, barely keeping their heads above water.

The day after Ann's humid sidewalk sermon, I took my exercise routine indoors. I packed up my white privilege and walked right through the lobby and into the fitness center of the Doubletree Hotel in downtown Detroit. I hopped on the elliptical and, what I did next, no one should *ever* try at home. I grabbed the TV remote and changed the channel to Fox News.

One middle-aged white man was interviewing another middle-aged white man, the chief executive of a Pennsylvania coal company that had just reopened a mine after President Trump announced that he was deregulating the industry. The multimillionaire CEO with an MBA from the University of Texas triumphantly declared, "The war on coal is over!"

At the conclusion of the conversation, he was asked about his employees and their opinions of the President. He still had his game face on:

> We try to stay away from the day-to-day outrage, the day-to-day hysteria that the mainstream media generates. We just keep our head down, stimulate the economy and help lower the cost for consumers.[288]

We live in what the indigenous poet Paula Gunn Allen called a "time when living has become survival."[289] We are scripted to keep our head down and stimulate the economy and then figure out how to manage the pain on our own. A discipleship of descent aims for a kind of revolution of values that can transform the surviving into thriving. This will only come through the discipline and dignity of what King called "soul force."

Following the subversive spirituality of Jesus and Gandhi,

Dr. King ushered in a wakeup call. Soul force is not only a nonviolent strategy, but a whole nonviolent way of being that has nothing whatsoever to do with passivity or avoiding conflict. Just the opposite. It is a dramatic call to keep our heads up and pay attention to all the ways that "stimulating the economy" is directly connected to the suffering of the masses. We cannot connect the dots and tell the truth with our heads down in stimulation mode.

Descending like a dove is betting everything on King's unwavering hope "that unarmed truth and unconditional love will have the final say in reality." Doves like Ann, time and time again, have revealed to me the power of a renegade soul force, infusing courageous acts that come from a compassionate and critical consciousness. The only way we are going "to make America what it ought to be" is to stop giving air-time and attention to the falcons. And then organize ourselves.

*   *   *

In the early 20th century, the ultimate connect-the-dots-and-tell-the-truth journalist was Upton Sinclair. He reportedly told audiences, "It is difficult to get a man to understand something when his salary depends upon his not understanding it." The paycheck pulls a lot of weight. In 1957, Dr. King asked Billy Graham to reconsider an upcoming event where he was sharing a stage with the intensely segregationist governor of Texas. Graham, ever-walking the political tightrope, rejected the request.[290] After all, what would Bible Belt supporters think if he took such a "political stand?"

In 2017, the famous Evangelical author, professor and pastor Eugene Peterson practically broke the internet when he told an interviewer that he would officiate a same-sex wedding. Two days later he retracted his comments after Lifeway, the largest Christian retail chain in the U.S., threatened to pull his books from their shelves.[291] Little has changed with white

Evangelical leadership over the past century. Salaries and social status trump soul force. American Christianity has paid a heavy price for it.

I started paying my own heavy price in my late twenties. I was a bi-vocational, tent-making minister like the Apostle Paul (Acts 18:1-3; 2 Thessalonians 3:8), working sixty to eighty hours a week as the athletic director at a large public high school and as an associate pastor at a local Evangelical church plant. I spent my long days patiently pivoting between hyper-vigilant parents lamenting over-bearing coaches failing to meet playing time expectations and hyper-competitive coaches lamenting over-whelming parents and the under-whelming work ethic of their children. At night, I would fellowship with young professionals prioritizing their relationship with the Lord while trying figure out how to pay the mortgage.

The singer/songwriter Lauryn Hill is one year younger than me. When she was 23, she released her first and only record *The Miseducation of Lauryn Hill.* She won five Grammys. Since then, she's been on a spiritual journey. At a recent concert, she arrived late and people complained that she was selfish. Hill responded, "I gave you all of my twenties." This is very much how I feel about my relationship with Evangelical Christianity during my first decade of adulthood. *I gave you all of my twenties.* By 30, I was exhausted and jaded.[292]

Then I started reading liberation theology. I stepped down from pastoral ministry, scaled down my work commitments and spent $40,000 on a seminary education. I am forever grateful to the high school principal who convinced me to stay on as a part-time teacher so I could keep my health care and pay for rent. Eventually, we moved to Detroit where our theology was rearranged even more by realities of race, gender, sexuality and economics.

I cannot take credit for where the Spirit has led me. Spirit, in the New Testament Greek, is a feminine noun (*pneuma*) meaning "wind" or "breath." She has blown me and Lindsay down this road, nurturing us and challenging us through people we've met, places we've seen and books we've read. She has spoken powerfully through the doves who have descended upon us: through Aida's journey north to the U.S.; through Weldon Nisly's peace pilgrimage to Iraq; through Jennifer's testimony at the Colville Indian Reservation; through Pastor Bill's water department direct action; through happy hour conversations with Jim Perkinson; through afternoons of door-to-door canvassing in northwest Detroit with Val, Monica and Debra; through the writings and lifestyles of countless spiritual sojourners.

The ancestors have been at work, too. They woo and warn in ways that are truly mysterious. I carry their wounds and waywardness with me. These continue to be a secret source of spiritual wisdom. Unlike my Celtic mothers, I struggle to comprehend most of this soul whispering. But I believe in a resurrection that is ongoing, not just a day in the distant future. All of creation is groaning, yet it is almost impossible to hear over the rancor of the colonial script.

In both life and death, Spirit has spoken through my quiet, inquisitive father. He faithfully served as a deacon at his small fundamentalist Bible church for the last three decades of his life. But while the white men at his church busied themselves echoing Fox News sound bites about "death panels" and everything else threatening their way of life, Dad refused to buy it. I doubt he ever openly confronted any of their forwarded emails and post-Bible study rants. However, Dad could spot fake news long before it became a projectile weapon of the White House.

When he wasn't watching ESPN Sports Center or Jimmy Fallon, Dad was tuning in to Book TV and CSPAN. During the last year of his life, he read seventy-six works of fiction and created a spreadsheet ranking them on a 5.0 scale (only one book received a Dennis Airey 5.0, while six received a

4.9). He truly delighted in different perspectives. It is a gift he keeps on giving to me. He paved the way, granting me permission, as that old Rilke poem prophesied, to "go far out into the world."

I am not one who has been burned by the church. The Evangelical churches, Bible studies and ministries that introduced me to Jesus privileged my voice and catered to my felt needs. Yet all this could not keep me in the fold. I have never had an issue with God and Jesus and faith and fellowship and church and prayer and gospel and heaven and even hell. The problem for me has always been how these have continually been interpreted, defined and utilized to legitimize a mainstream lifestyle advocated by the colonial script. Different from Dad, Evangelical Christianity is a movement that rarely makes room for difference. This is a lamentable diversion from the original path of Jesus.

43
Perspective

Jesus' original disciples called themselves "the Way" (Acts 9:2). My Evangelical pastors and teachers taught me that this meant we knew the way to heaven—the *only* Way. And it was our responsibility to share with others how they, too, could get there. They quoted Jesus prolifically, "I am the Way, the Truth and the Life. No one comes to the Father, but through me" (John 14:6). The Way to heaven was why Jesus was born and why he died. His resurrection proved that this one and only Way was legitimate—a triumphant falcon flying up out of the grave to lead the righteous few to the heavenly promised land.

What was almost always left out of the Evangelical formula was Jesus' life and teaching. Between the original Christmas and Easter, an entire thirty-three years was swept to the sidelines! However, Jesus was far more human and far more Hebrew than my Evangelical leaders ever gave him credit for. Jews like Jesus and the Apostle Paul comprehended religion and faith holistically. It was a spiritual *path* (from the Greek *ho odos*) that affected every aspect of life.

Jesus' path descended like a dove. He fasted in the wilderness, emptying himself of the social, economic and political enticements of power and legacy (Luke 4:1-13). This was also the path of Paul, who held on to massive prestige as a Pharisee before his conversion to the Way (Philippians 3:4-6). Rev. Dr. Martin Luther King Jr., too, could have stayed silent and pursued a comfortable career as a middle-class Black preacher. He put his reputation on the line, spoke hard-to-stomach truths and boycotted the colonial script. All three paid the ultimate price for connecting the dots and telling the truth.

The path of descent backtracks even further. The Hebrew Bible detailed a prophetic lineage of downward mobility. Abraham was called to leave the wealth and comfort of his home in Ur and enter into a nomadic wilderness covenant of listening and learning (Genesis 12-15). Moses grew up in Pharoah's palace, but had to flee after his justice-fueled rage killed an oppressor. He lived for forty years in the wilderness tending his father-in-law's flock before he returned to deliver God's emancipation proclamation (Exodus 2-3). The prophet Isaiah had a full-frontal faith, decolonizing his sackcloth and his sandals. He walked barefoot and naked for three years to expose the colonial script (Isaiah 20:1-6).

When the earliest Christians called themselves "the Way" (in Greek, *ho odos*), they understood it as a continuation of the long, winding path of the Hebrew prophets. It was a challenging way of life they covenanted themselves to. "The gate is narrow," Jesus taught, "and the road (*ho odos*) is hard that leads to life, and there are few who find it" (Matthew 7:14). Contrary to the Evangelical interpretation that only a chosen few would be going to heaven, Jesus was lamenting that most would remain immersed in the wide, well-traveled path of the colonial script.

When Jesus met the blind man Bartimaeus in Mark's Gospel, he was sitting on the side of the road (*ho odos*). Jesus asked what he needed. Bartimaeus went for the jugular. "Let me see again" (Mark 10:51). After Jesus healed him, the Gospel account attests, "Immediately he regained his sight and followed him *on the way*" (*ho odos*, Mark 10:52). Bartimaeus is the vintage Jesus follower who, after coming to awareness, stops sitting on the sidelines and joins him on the path of descent.

At the end of Luke's Gospel, Jesus joins two sad and scared disciples "on the road" (*ho odos*, Luke 24:32) in their post-Good Friday descent down Mt. Zion to an obscure little village called Emmaus. Strangely, the disciples didn't recognize Jesus, but their hearts burned as he asked curious questions and then animated a prophetic Bible study. These disciples are reminders that on the spiritual path of descent, we are not alone. People of the Way are challenged, encouraged and inspired by the Spirit of the risen Jesus, always mysteriously with us.

The words of the Emmaus disciples color the core of my spirituality: "Were not our hearts burning within us while he was talking to us on the road, while he was opening the Scriptures to us?" (Luke 24:32). I sense this divine burning sensation at the deepest core of who I am when, like this ancient couple on the road to Emmaus, I pursue the challenging path intersecting intimacy, community and justice.

Jesus' Way of descent is not a problem to be solved. It is not about nailing down correct doctrine in my head. Authentic spirituality is being attuned to what is percolating deep in my heart. It is a steady, lifelong migration from the ego to the soul. When I make this move in a disciplined fashion, I gain access to massive reserves of love, wisdom and discernment.

Like the original members of the Way of Jesus, I am committed to a spiritual path that places ultimate trust in an intimate animating life force that is passionately committed to love and justice, contrary to the ancient Greek gods who were indifferent and ambivalent about human suffering. Jesus assured the crowds, a brutally colonized and oppressed people, that their lives mattered as much as anyone else because the God of Steadfast Love was a nurturing parental figure who knew the number of hairs on the head of every one of them. This God was determined to clothe and care for them, just as this God clothed and cared for the birds and wildflowers and everything else there is (Matthew 6:25-33). This is the good news that starts us on the path of the challenging Way.

*   *   *

I offer no proof that my interpretation of Jesus' Way is on the correct path, let alone absolutely true. All I have are my own experiences, observations and stories, both historic and contemporary, of saints daring to live it out. Like the first disciples, I simply "cannot stop speaking about what I've seen and heard" (Acts 4:20). I'm not so interested in converting others to "Christianity," but in the conversion of Christianity itself—toward what is more authentic to the original version.

Jesus' Way of descent is not an *absolutist* faith. That is: It does not claim to have a monopoly on the truth. There are plenty of others (both inside and outside the Christian tradition) who have brilliant perspectives on what is true, right and beautiful.

Jesus' Way of descent is not a *universalist* faith. That is: It does not flow from a conviction that all paths lead back to the same Source. Today, within Christianity alone, there are more than 22,000 diverse denominational voices attempting to describe Jesus. When we listen to just a few of these, we know full well they can't possibly be talking about the same guy.

Jesus' Way of descent is not a *relativistic* faith. That is: It does not tolerate and bestow equal airtime to all truth claims. Too many of these are destructive, dehumanizing, banal or bogus. Our lives do not have time for this free-for-all open mic.

Jesus' Way of descent is a thoroughly *perspectivist* faith. That is: It adamantly proclaims that every child of God comes at life from unique experiences, and that this colors how we view God, the world and everything else there is. Our differing perspectives on what matters most make it imperative that we own and name the factors that might skew our judgments and tunnel our visions. John Goldingay, one of my favorite professors in seminary, once told our class: "10 percent of the things I believe are wrong. The only problem is I don't know which 10 percent." I know I desperately need to listen and learn from others. This is hard and humble work.[293]

The Jesus tradition is my pivot foot. It grounds my spirituality. It centers me. I keep coming back to it over and over and over again—daily, hourly. It is my mother tongue. I continue to find the old Bible stories both familiar and layered with spiritual depth. These are ancient reminders that the world is enchanted. There is something that keeps composting what is dark and deathly into newness of life.

Jesus beckoned followers to take on his easy yoke, promising rest for the weary and burdened. He also prodded them to take up the cross and stand up to all the imperial shenanigans of his context. Jesus taught that the main ingredient of the source of life was Steadfast Love, passed along to every created thing. If absolutely nothing can separate us from this mighty force, then it changes everything.

But I do need more than just Jesus for this journey. Nigerian author and spiritual practitioner Bayo Akomolafe writes, "The world is too preposterous to be decided in one neat framework."[294] I attend 12-step al-anon meetings. I go to therapy. I learn from the wisdom of the Enneagram. I participate in a weekly *lectio divina* Bible study. I marinate in the truth and beauty of poetry and fiction, especially from women and Black and Brown voices. I am immersed in ethno-autobiography work, emphasizing a powerful spiritual connection to my ancestors and the natural world. I am committed to studying the ways that race, gender, class and sexuality counterfeit me.

This collection of diverse traditions and practices sharpens my spiritual sightlines. They complement each other. Together, they open my eyes to see Jesus and the world and my own waywardness clearer. They help me make sense of something that is wider and higher and deeper and longer than my own mini-dramas.

This kind of multifaceted perspectivism calls me to humility and constant transformation. My spiritual journey necessitates a beloved community of sojourners, especially those from "the other side." These bear witness to personal experiences of the violence and oppression spurred on by the colonial script. As icons of Jesus, they open my heart and heal my blind spots, of which I have many.

A perspectivist faith has given me permission to step away from the powerful trance of dualism. The colonial script binds us with binaries. It claims we must be either Republican or Democrat, Catholic or Protestant, Conservative or Liberal, Capitalist or Communist. Our imaginations are confined by this either/or conformity.

Abundant life, though, transcends paper or plastic. The best option is usually "neither." So I'm boycotting the binary. I'm mustering the curiosity and courage to make my exodus out of "traditional" boxes. I'm bringing my own bags.

But just because I'm neither Republican nor Democrat doesn't mean that I'm not political. And just because I'm neither Catholic nor Protestant doesn't mean that I'm not a Christian. And just because I am "neither" doesn't mean that I'm indifferent, cynical, apathetic or relativistic.

The bridge to "neither" is part of the "radical restructuring" that King called my dad's generation to. I'm learning that it requires concrete convictions fortified over time by prayer, study, experience and dialogue. These are the tools that build a better world—one where austerity and white supremacy are water under the bridge.

I've also learned (over and over again) that just because I'm "post-Evangelical" doesn't mean that I inhabit a fundamentalism-free zone. These "isms" creep in quickly— pacifism, anti-imperialism, antiracism, my precious vegetarianism. All of these can quickly shape-shift into language-policing judgmentalism. All fundamentalisms, though, work like an ideological game of Jenga—you pull out one little time-hardened belief and the triumphant tower comes crumbling down. Foundations constructed on unquestioned certainty are landscaped in fear. None of us has all our shit together.

I'm learning that faith, like everything else in life, ought to mature and deepen as I grow older. I'm in my fourth decade of pledging allegiance to Jesus. And yet, I've learned that white Evangelicals do not have the monopoly on hypocrisy and incongruity. Far from it. These are always within me and ever before me. And I keep learning that, in the midst of this painful reality, laughter is a vital spiritual practice.

44
Circling Back to the Beginning

We had just arrived back in Detroit, two weeks after my Dad's sudden death overtime in California. Matthew, the soup kitchen guest with long, curly, flaming red hair, warmly embraced me at the front door of the St. Peter's Peace and Justice Hive. He announced to a nearby audience of about a half-dozen that I'm the type of guy most at home in a nudist colony. I wasn't really sure what he meant, but I felt the love because he proclaimed it with a huge smile, nodding massive approval. He was still living in a makeshift yurt on the side of the church, twenty yards from Michigan Avenue.

Surprisingly, Matthew wasn't in church the next Sunday. But Thurman was. Right after Pastor Bill concluded his homily with a tender "Amen," Thurman keeled over sideways on the pew and launched into the first of two back-to-back seizures. The first to his aid were Janet and Cindy, a married couple in their 50's who, about a decade ago, adopted a whole family of children, including Samantha (aka, "Sami"), a teenager with Down Syndrome, who frequently came to church repping a One Direction t-shirt.

Sami was whimpering a blend of compassion and despair, standing right next to Gail, the Detroit native and university professor with a Ph.D. in philosophy. Back in the 1970's, when Gail was a teenager, she hightailed it to northern California with some friends and, on the drive out west, memorized T.S. Eliot's epic poem "The Love Song of J. Alfred Prufrock." She would regularly perform it on the street for tourists to earn income. I believe her story because she recited it from memory around the bonfire at the church retreat two months earlier.

After Thurman was revived and resting comfortably, we gathered around the healing circle. This was always when I felt like the real church service began. We were no longer passively listening or mechanically reciting. We were participating. It was unscripted, raw, messy, vulnerable and intimate. We anointed each other's foreheads with oil. We blessed each other with words of encouragement and peace. We smiled and hugged. Sometimes we cried.

But Sami wasn't just a participant in this beloved practice. She was a professional. She gushed Steadfast Love, tenaciously bear-hugging every member of the congregation, no matter how uncomfortable or awkward they felt. Black or white, sober or drunk, young professional or veteran activist, clear-minded or mentally ill—Sami showed no hint of partiality.

Gospel singer Ange Smith closed the service with the Black spiritual "Wade in the Water," long ago utilized by Harriet Tubman as a signal to runaway slaves to find refuge in a nearby body of water so that the dogs of slave catchers couldn't sniff them out. Per tradition, Sami pounded the tambourine and grooved us out of the service with a liturgical dance that would make just about anyone blush. She had to ignore the glares from Janet so she could plead innocence after incorporating well-timed booty shakes and pelvic thrusts.

No matter how muddled my heart had previously been, these holy antics at the conclusion of every service at St. Peter's Episcopal Church in Detroit would inevitably percolate something deep inside of me. In the midst of my ongoing journey of decolonization, I've drawn strength from the holy mischief of Samantha, the dancing dove of Detroit.

*   *   *

Surprisingly, Samantha's Sunday stunts shimmer with the ancient script. Take it back now y'all. On the day when God parted the Red Sea so that the Israelites could walk right out of empire on dry ground, the prophetess whipped out her tambourine and got funky with something real smooth (Exodus 15). Miriam celebrated because the God of Steadfast Love was just about to make Israel great again. The way to real greatness, though, went by way of the wilderness. For forty years.

My own wilderness journey keeps calling me back to the beginning. Although, I have distanced from the Evangelicalism of my adolescence, some elements of this old-school faith are arising into newness of life. On a recent Wednesday morning, while sipping a quadruple espresso at my favorite coffee house in Ann Arbor, I clicked on YouTube to sample the latest popular white Evangelical worship songs. Whether it was the caffeine or the Spirit, I was deeply drawn to one song that riffed on "the overwhelming, never-ending, reckless love of God," a Higher Power who never gives up coming after me, no matter where I've gone or what I've done.

Unfortunately, since walking away from the Evangelical movement, I've distanced from claiming an emotional, intimate connection with the God of Steadfast Love. My impulse was to join post-Evangelical jokes about singing love songs to Jesus and dismiss it, along with the Republican platform it had been strategically packaged with. However, my personal relationship with God is undergoing a reintegrating renaissance.

I am both comforted and challenged by the fact that it was a deeply personal connection with Jesus that changed Dr. King's life one night after he arrived home late from a long day of meetings with organizers of the Montgomery bus boycott in early 1956. The phone rang and the voice on the other end made death threats. His fear and exhaustion drove him to prayer:

> The words I spoke to God that midnight are still vivid in my memory. "I am here taking a stand for what I believe is right. But now I am afraid. The people are looking to me for leadership, and if I stand before them without strength and courage, they too will falter. I am at the end of my powers. I have nothing left. I've come to the point where I can't face it alone."

> At that moment, I experienced the presence of the Divine as I had never experienced God before. It seemed as though I could hear the quiet assurance of an inner voice saying: "Stand up for justice, stand up for truth; and God will be at your side forever." Almost at once my fears began to go. My uncertainty disappeared. I was ready to face anything.[295]

For the rest of his life, King told audiences that Jesus himself spoke to him that night in Montgomery. Three days later, his house was bombed. He recalled later:

> Strangely enough, I accepted the word of the bombing calmly. My religious experience a few nights before had given me the strength to face it.

King had the presence of spirit to calm and comfort and inspire the angry crowd that gathered at his house later on:

> A night that seemed destined to end in unleashed chaos came to a close in a majestic group demonstration of nonviolence.[296]

What he called "the quiet assurance of an inner voice" sustained his leadership, averting an uprising that would have been devastating at that juncture of the Montgomery bus boycott.

*　　*　　*

Today, I continue to suffer allergic reactions to the masculine falcon God, conjured as distant, authoritarian, disappointed, angry, retributive, demanding and controlling, expecting the weary and burdened to pull themselves up by their own bootstraps. I shiver with shame. I start catastrophizing. Because in these moments, I am convinced that I'm never quite good enough. However, for reasons not entirely known, instead of quickly disposing of Divinity, I've joined in the long journey of decolonizing Her.

God is Steadfast Love. A Power that is present everywhere in the universe, deep in every human heart.

Steadfast Love is a force greater than the sum of its parts. She conspires to move everything closer to justice and truth and intimacy and beauty and reconciliation. She's always there—closer than we are to ourselves. She mysteriously breaks through our pain and suffering and comes out the other side in newness of life. She pleads with us to never let our pain define us. We are beckoned to trust the process.

Yet, Steadfast Love is cultivated and passed along through discipline. I keep hearing the call to rescue "personal responsibility" from those who have used it to demonize the poor and oppressed. Love whispers to us to stay awake, to repent, to pray, to actively serve and share, to seek the interests of others, to reject attitudes of indifference, apathy and cynicism.

For now, the fullness of my humanity depends on whether I side with Steadfast Love in the ordinary, mundane, day-to-day activities of my life. Or not. Love is, as King proclaimed, the key that unlocks the door to the universe. And so, I attempt to organize my life so that I am aligned with this force that will have the final say in reality. Steadfast Love will win, somehow, someway.

Love doesn't sit on the throne. She surrounds us like a mist. I can feel Her. When I stop worrying and grasping. When I trust. When I let go. When I surrender and accept what is. There is no need to fear. It is never over. The Spirit is not limited by a shot clock. There's always more.

I wait for Steadfast Love to conspire. I know deep down that I have cosmic companionship. And I know this truth, not by proving it with formula or argument or data, but by feeling it in the still, silent moments of my life. I experience it over and over again. My heart burns.

Steadfast Love does not coerce. She compels. In the breeze and on our breath and through bold action. There is humility and tenderness. There is patience and kindness. There is fierce advocacy for what is right and fair and dignifying. There is beauty and delight. There is strength, hope, pain and joy. There is God.

Ultimately, divinity is defined by militant love. This animating life force is tender and nurturing and compels people of faith and conscience to do whatever it takes to make sure those on the margins are given full dignity. Above all else, this Ancient One is just—which means that the Universe takes sides in the struggles of history. And so will I.

ACKNOWLEDGEMENTS

Writing a book is a marathon of gut checks. By this, I mean, a long series of triggers that consistently tap into my own deep pain of feeling devalued, alone and unknown. In short, the whole process—from organizing to writing to editing to publishing to promoting—has conspired with my shadows by shouting, "This is a really stupid idea!"

I am deeply grateful for the cloud of witnesses carrying me. My cloud includes the unseen whispering ones who have gone ahead yet remain mysteriously present: Dad. Mike. Grandma Billie. Rev. Dr. Martin Luther King Jr. Many more.

I burst with thanksgiving for a multitude of others:

For Lindsay whose vintage verbal processing offered acute, deep and flavorful insights throughout this long exodus and wilderness journey. Her head and heart are imprinted on every page of this book. I cannot even fathom this adventure without her.

For Sue and Nancy whose love and support have been unconditional even as our life has become increasingly unconventional.

For Ched Myers and Elaine Enns who received us for who we were: desperately-seeking post-Evangelical pilgrims. In early 2016, Ched met my doubts and skepticism over this book project with "I would love to see you do it."

For all those who offered hospitality and writing space along the way: Marcia and Clancy Dunigan on the Puget

Sound, The Clyde Rice Place on the Clackamas River, Solveig and Peter Nilsen-Goodin on the Willamette River, Greg and Casey Lamont on the Deschutes River, Sue Airey and Nancy Lamont on old Trabuco Creek, St. Peter's Peace and Justice Hive on the Detroit River, RoosRoast Coffee House on the Huron River, and Jeannette Ban and Lola West on the Ventura River.

For Michael Smith, mostly for cherished friendship, but also for all the points and miles generously donated; and for loaning us the Prius for 75 days and 12,000 miles during the summer of 2013.

For Tim Nafziger, Chris Dollar and Joyce Hollyday who read entire early versions of the manuscript and seasoned praise with pointed, constructive criticism.

For Kati Bennett who helped edit the manuscript between block periods, tutorials and long into the night.

For Casey Lamont who crafted a beautiful book cover. Check out her art and design at www.myfairletters.com.

For Tim Wasemiller who advised me on a marketing plan and gifted me with advertising credits.

For Nora Miller who copy edited the final manuscript.

For all those who read chapters and offered valuable insights: Michael Smith, Craig and Julie Landino, Greg and Casey Lamont, Marcia Dunigan, Ched Myers, Sara Jo and Steve Craw, Hayden and Hannah Coplen, Kristen and Sam Orr, Kyle Mitchell, Courtney Rutenbar, Tom Ressler, Melanie Magee, C. John Hildebrand, Gavin Fabian and, of course, Lindsay Airey.

Acknowledgements

For the invigorating reading community in Pasadena
organized by Rev. Josh Lopez-Reyes. Deep encouragement
flowed from these: Josh and Grecia Lopez-Reyes, Sue Hur,
Shady Hakim, Joe Roos and Lindsay Airey.

For the ten members (now twelve) of the Manna and Mercy
House, a beloved community sharing experience, strength,
hope, pain and joy—one day at a time.

For all those, starting in 2014, who have generously
contributed financially to empower our vocation of soul-
accompaniment.

For the staff and faculty of Capistrano Valley High School,
the city on a hill that taught me, coached me, encouraged
me, supported me, SIOPed me and sent me.

For Dale and Stacy Fredrickson who started us on our
exodus out of Evangelical categories by communicating with
salt and pepper shakers at Panera Bread Company.

For Charles Cha who deepened my social analysis and
stimulated reflection on our adolescent Evangelical
adventures.

For Daniel Smith-Christopher (Loyola Marymount
University, Fall 1992), Francisco Marmolejo (Irvine Valley
College, Spring 1994) and Bill Tuttle (University of Kansas
(Spring and Fall 1995) who each planted radical seeds in
my adolescent Evangelical mind. The arc of my own moral
universe is long, but it bends towards justice.

For DiAnne Schultz, Terry Hargrave and Rick Kidd, three
wounded healers leading me to freedom.

For the People's Water Board Coalition—women-led,

women-sustained and women-maintained—who has never asked for free water. Just clean and affordable water. They won't stop until they get it for everyone.

For Sister Marianne, Father Tom, Brother Luke, Uncle Jeff, Grandpa Byron, Dr. Darrell and all the volunteers at Manna Meal soup kitchen in Detroit.

For Jyarland Daniels whose friendship, brilliant play-by-play banter and on-the-fly social analysis have kept us afloat.

For Lydia Wylie-Kellermann and Erinn Fahey who midwifed our move, encouraged this project and continue to partner in the work of RadicalDiscipleship.Net.

For the *lectio divina* circle sharing what shimmers every Wednesday in Southwest Detroit.

For Jim Perkinson and Lily Mendoza who compelled us with the story of Detroit...and then gave us the tour!

For Bill Wylie-Kellermann, Denise Griebler and the quirky radical disciples of St. Peter's Episcopal Church in Corktown for receiving Lindsay and me with open arms.

For Lydia Wylie-Kellermann (*On The Edge*), Sheldon Good (*The Mennonite*), Aiden Enns (*Geez*), Julie Poulter (*Sojourners*), Elizabeth Palmer (*The Christian Century*) and Jamie Pitts (*Anabaptist Witness*) for reading my work and believing in it enough to put it out there.

For Monica Lewis-Patrick, Debra Taylor, Val Burris, Ebony McClellan, Aurora Harris, Christine Griffith and Tangela Harris who baptized us into the struggle while canvassing a Detroit neighborhood in Fall 2014. Our souls haven't been the same since.

For Nick Peterson whose vigilant texts kept reminding me that my worth is not a reflection of how much I can be Superman for others as much as it mirrors that I was made to know love, to be loved and to give love.

For Peter Nilsen-Goodin who, on the Oregon Coast, anointed me with almond butter and dark chocolate, assuring me, "You are enough!"

For the bountiful gift of my nephews: Riley, Mason and one more on the way. Your passion, joy, curiosity and sensitivity to justice model the way forward (Luke 18:16).

For Lily Mendoza who charged into our conversation from the back room to say, "You need to self-publish!"

NEXT STEPS?

It is my deepest desire to dialogue with others about what it might mean to be a Christian in this context where the colonial script coerces and constrains. If your faith community or friend network is interested in a book reading followed by a time of open sharing, email me at tommyairey@gmail.com. I envision these intimate circles in living rooms, church basements, coffee houses or tap rooms. More than anything, Lindsay and I are interested in listening to stories from post-Evangelical pilgrims and brainstorming how it is that we can experiment more faithfully and effectively with spaces that resist and rise above the colonial script.

NOTES

[1] Martin Luther King Jr. speech delivered on April 27, 1965, at University of California at Los Angeles. https://www.youtube.com/watch?v=ny6qP0rb_Ag

[2] Cornel West, *The Radical King* (Boston: Beacon Press, 2016), x.

[3] James McClendon, *Systematic Theology, Volume II: Doctrine* (Nashville: Abingdon Press, 1994), 44.

[4] Pew Research Center's latest statistics on religion in the United States is best accessed on their website: http://www.pewforum.org/2012/10/09/nones-on-the-rise/

[5] Martin Luther King Jr., *Why We Can't Wait* (New York: New American Library: Harper & Row, 1964), 54.

[6] Cornel West, *Democracy Matters* (New York: Penguin, 2004).

[7] Bill Wylie-Kellermann, *Seasons of Faith and Conscience: Kairos, Confesson, Liturgy* (Maryknoll, NY: Orbis, 1991).

[8] Martin Luther King Jr., "Beyond Vietnam." Delivered to Riverside Church, New York City, April 4, 1967.

[9] For important scholarship on "the Powers" in the Bible, see works by William Stringfellow, Walter Wink and Bill Wylie Kellermann.

[10] Kimberlé Williams Crenshaw, a professor at UCLA Law, is widely credited with coining the term and defining the concept of "intersectionality" in the 1980s.

[11] bell hooks, "Understanding Patriarchy," http://imaginenoborders.org/pdf/zines/UnderstandingPatriarchy.pdf

[12] adrienne maree brown, *Emergent Strategy* (Berkeley: AK Press, 2017), 47-48.

[13] The Seminary of the Street in Oakland (CA) has experimented with a 12-step process of Recovery from Dominant Culture: www.seminaryofthestreet.org.

[14] Mary Oliver, "Mysteries, Yes," *Evidence* (Boston: Beacon Press, 2009), 62.

[15] Brian Blount, *Then The Whisper Put on Flesh* (Nashville: Abingdon Press, 2001), 119.

[16] Walter Brueggemann, *Texts Under Negotiation: The Bible*

and *Postmodern Imagination* (Minneapolis: Augsburg Press, 1993), 62-63.

[17] Kelly Brown-Douglas, *Stand Your Ground: Black Bodies and the Justice of God* (Maryknoll, NY: Orbis, 2015), 148.

[18] Frederick Douglass, *Narrative of the Life of Frederick Douglass: An American Slave* (Dover Publications, 1995), 123.

[19] The Hebrew word for "Steadfast Love" is *hesed*. It pops up sixty-six times in the Hebrew Bible.

[20] Ibid.

[21] A public dialogue facilitated by Ched Myers with Jennifer Henry and Pam Brubaker at the Bartimaeus Cooperative Ministries Kinsler Institute in February 2016.

[22] Neil Elliot, *The Arrogance of Nations* (Minneapolis: Fortress Press, 2008), 7.

[23] This is found in many of King's sermons and speeches, including Selma 1965. He is actually quoting an 1853 sermon from Unitarian minister and abolitionist Theodore Parker.

[24] Kelly Brown-Douglas, *Stand Your Ground: Black Bodies and the Justice of God* (Maryknoll, NY: Orbis, 2015), 210.

[25] Francis Weller, "To and From the Soul's Hall." *Utne Reader*, Fall 2016.

[26] Rainer Maria Rilke, "Sometimes A Man Stands Up" translated by Robert Bly in *The Soul is Here for Its Own Joy* (Hopewell, NJ: The Ecco Press, 1995).

[27] Bayo Akomolafe, *These Wilds Beyond Our Fences* (Berkeley, CA: North Atlantic Books, 2017), 212.

[28] James Perkinson, *Messianism Against Christology: Resistance Movements, Folk Art, Empire* (New York: Palgrave, 2013), 29.

[29] Rick Founds, "Lord, I Lift Your Name On High," Universal Music - Brentwood Benson Publishing, 1989.

[30] Leon Olguin, "White as Snow," Maranatha Praise, Inc.\Sound Truth Publishing, 1990.

[31] Rich Mullins, "Awesome God," Universal Music - Brentwood Benson Publishing, 1988.

[32] 2010 census data: https://www.census.gov/2010census/

[33] "Robertson Letter Attacks Feminists" in *New York Times*, August 26, 1992. http://www.nytimes.com/1992/08/26/us/robertson-letter-

attacks-feminists.html

[34] Borg, Marcus. *The Heart of Christianity: Rediscovering a Life of Faith* (San Francisco: Harper Collins, 2004).

[35] David Bebbington, *Evangelicalism in Modern Britain: A History from the 1730s to 1980s* (Unwin Hyman, 1989).

[36] Darren Paul Shearer, *In You God Trusts* (Xulon Press, 2009), 165.

[37] George Marsden, *Fundamentalism and American Culture: The Shaping of Twentieth Century Evangelicalism, 1870-1925* (Oxford University Press, 1982), 233.

[38] Ibid.

[39] Steven P. Miller, *Billy Graham and the Rise of the Republican South* (University of Penn Press, 2009), 95.

[40] A.C. Green, *Victory* (Lake Mary, FL: Creation House Publishing, 1994), 9.

[41] Rufus Burrow Jr., *A Child Shall Lead Them: Martin Luther King Jr., Young People, and the Movement* (Minneapolis: Fortress Press, 2014).

[42] Martin Luther King Jr., speech at Cobo Hall in Detroit, June 23, 1963. http://kingencyclopedia.stanford.edu/encyclopedia/documentsentry/doc_speech_at_the_great_march_on_detroit.1.html

[43] Michael Eric Dyson, *April 4, 1968: Martin Luther King's Death and How It Changed America*, (New York: Basic Civitas Books, 2008), 19.

[44] Ibid, 22.

[45] Cornel West and Christa Buschendorf, *Black Prophetic Fire* (Boston: Beacon Press, 2014), 68.

[46] Martin Luther King Jr., speech delivered at University of California, Los Angeles, April 27, 1965.

[47] Ibid.

[48] Parker Palmer, *A Hidden Wholeness: The Journey Towards An Undivided Life* (San Francisco: John Wiley and Sons, 2004).

[49] Mark Noll, *The Scandal of the Evangelical Mind* (Grand Rapids: Eerdmans, 1994).

[50] James Cone, *A Black Theology of Liberation* (Maryknoll, NY: Orbis, 1970), 141.

[51] N.T. Wright, *The New Testament and the People of God* (Minneapolis: Fortress Press, 1992).

[52] For more on the concept of "visionary organizing," see the work of Grace Lee Boggs. Grace Lee Boggs, *The Next American Revolution* (Berkeley, CA: University of California Press, 2011).

[53] James Perkinson, *Messianism Against Christology: Resistance Movements, Folk Art, Empire* (New York: Palgrave, 2013), xxix.

[54] Ched Myers, *Binding The Strong Man* (Maryknoll, NY: Orbis, 1988), 11. Listen to Rob Bell interview Ched Myers on his Robcast (May 2017): https://robbell.podbean.com/e/ched-myers/. Also, listen to Ched and his partner Elaine Enns on their own semi-monthly podcast here: https://www.bcm-net.org/resources/podcasts

[55] Ched Myers and Matt Colwell, *Our God Is Undocumented: Biblical Faith and Immigrant Justice* (Maryknoll, NY: Orbis, 2012).

[56] Ibid, 12-13.

[57] Pew Research study, February 2017. http://www.people-press.org/2017/02/16/2-views-of-trumps-executive-order-on-travel-restrictions/

[58] Martin Luther King Jr., speech at Gross Pointe High School, March 14, 1968. http://www.gphistorical.org/mlk/

[59] Jeanne Theoharis, *A More Beautiful and Terrible History: The Uses and Misuses of Civil Rights History* (Boston: Beacon Press, 2018), 178.

[60] Jyarland Daniels, "When Networking Goes Wrong: The Trouble With 'Come Meet A Black Person,'" November 15, 2017. http://www.harrietspeaks.com/blog/2017/11/15/when-networking-goes-wrong-the-trouble-with-come-meet-a-black-person

[61] Ched Myers, *Binding The Strong Man* (Maryknoll, NY: Orbis, 1988). *Binding* is a thick, scholarly text. I highly recommend Ched's popular version *"Say to This Mountain:" Mark's Story of Discipleship* (Maryknoll, NY: Orbis, 1996).

[62] For starters, check out Walter Wink's "Homosexuality and the Bible" online here: http://www.godweb.org/wink.htm

[63] Richard Rothstein, *The Color of Law: The Forgotten History of How Our Government Segregated America* (New York: Liverlight, 2017).

[64] Ched Myers, *The Biblical Vision of Sabbath Economics* (Washington D.C.: Tell The Word, 2001).

[65] James Perkinson, *Political Spirituality in an Age of Eco-Apocalypse* (New York: Palgrave, 2015), 45. This section drew heavily upon Chapter Two: "Cain's Offering and Abel's Cry: Reading Sabbath Jubilee at the Crossroads of Farming and Foraging."

[66] Martin Luther King Jr., "I've Been to the Mountaintop," speech at Mason Temple, Memphis, TN, April 3, 1968. http://www.americanrhetoric.com/speeches/mlkivebeentothemountaintop.htm

[67] Ched Myers, *Binding The Strong Man* (Maryknoll, NY: Orbis, 1988). See also *"Say to This Mountain:" Mark's Story of Discipleship* (Maryknoll, NY: Orbis, 1996). This section was greatly influenced by Myers and Jim Perkinson. See also Daniel Erlander's beautiful book for children and adults *Manna and Mercy: A Brief History of God's Unfolding Promise to Mend the Entire Universe* at mannaandmercy.org.

[68] Martin Luther King Jr., *The Atlantic Monthly*, August 1963, "The Negro Is Your Brother," Volume 212, pp 78-88.

[69] Ibid, xvi.

[70] Brene Brown, *Braving the Wilderness: The Quest for True Belonging and the Courage to Stand Alone* (New York: Random House, 2017), 32-34.

[71] James Perkinson, "Theology and the City: Learning to Cry, Struggling to See" in *Cross Currents*, Spring 2001, Vol. 51, No 1. http://www.crosscurrents.org/perkinson0151.htm

[72] Richard Rohr, *Dancing Standing Still: Healing the World from a Place of Prayer* (Mahwah, NJ: Paulist Press, 2014), 48, 52-53.

[73] Howard Thurman, *Jesus and the Disinherited* (Nashville, TN: Abingdon Press, 1949).

[74] For more on Christian Peacemaker Teams, see www.cpt.org.

[75] For more, see Weldon's "Neighbors in Iraq" on TheMennonite.org (May 1, 2010): https://themennonite.org/feature/neighbors-iraq/

[76] Cornel West. *Democracy Matters*, (New York: Penguin, 2005), 151.

[77] Adrienne Pine, "Gospel Crusade, Inc. and Friends," *Jacobin*

Magazine, Spring 2017, 105-107. See also "U.S. Concedes Contras Linked to Drugs, But Denies Leadership Involved." *Associated Press*, April 17, 1986.

[78] Oliver North, "Fox News Sunday with Chris Wallace," May 20, 2018. http://www.foxnews.com/transcript/2018/05/20/oliver-north-on-nras-response-to-texas-school-shooting-sen-lindsey-graham-on-status-trump-kim-summit.html

[79] Sara Diamond, *Spiritual Warfare: The Politics of the Christian Right* (Boston: South End Press, 1989).

[80] Deb Preusch and Tom Barry, *The Soft War: The Uses and Abuses of US Economic Aid in Central America* (New York: Grove Press, 1988).

[81] Sara Diamond, *Spiritual Warfare: The Politics of the Christian Right* (Boston: South End Press, 1989).

[82] Ibid.

[83] Lauren Frances Turek, "To Support a "Brother in Christ: Evangelical Groups and U.S.-Guatemalan Relations during the Ríos Montt Regime." *Diplomatic History* (2015) 39 (4): 689-719.

[84] William Appleman Williams, *Empire as a Way of Life* (Oxford University Press, 1980).

[85] Lily Mendoza, "Healing Colonial Trauma: EA as Decolonizing Practice," public talk delivered at the Graduate Center, University of Pretoria, August 16, 2016.

[86] Blaine Harden, "The Grand Coulee: Savior for Whites, Disaster for Indians." http://aliciapatterson.org/stories/grand-coulee-savior-whites-disaster-indians

[87] Sherman Alexie, *You Don't Have to Say You Love Me* (New York: Little, Brown and Company, 2017), 132-133.

[88] Martin Luther King Jr., "Remaining Awake Through a Great Revolution," delivered at the National Cathedral, Washington, D.C., on March 31, 1968.

[89] Ben Norton, "U.S. Paid P.R. Firm $540 million to Make Fake al-Qaida Videos in Iraq Propaganda Program," October 3, 2016. http://www.salon.com/2016/10/03/u-s-paid-p-r-firm-540-million-to-make-fake-al-qaida-videos-in-iraq-propaganda-program/?utm_source=facebook&utm_medium=socialflow

[90] Tim De Chant, "Income Inequality in the Roman Empire," December 16, 2011. https://persquaremile.com/2011/12/16/income-inequality-in-the-

roman-empire/

[91] Paul Ortiz, *An African-American and Latinx History of the United States* (Boston: Beacon Press, 2018), 164.

[92] John Perkins, *Confessions of an Economic Hit Man* (New York: Penguin, 2004).

[93] George Monbiot, "The Ideology at the Root of all our Problems," *The Guardian*, April 15, 2016.

[94] Cornel West, *The Radical King* (Boston: Beacon Press, 2016), 247.

[95] Facundo Alvaredo, Lucas Chancel, Thomas Piketty, Emmanuel Saez and Gabriel Zucman, "Inequality is Not Inevitable—But the U.S. 'Experiment' is a Recipe for Divergence," *The Guardian*, December 14, 2017. See *The World Inequality Report 2018:* http://wir2018.wid.world.

[96] Matthew Stewart, "The 9.9% is the New American Aristocracy," *The Atlantic*, June 2018. https://www.theatlantic.com/magazine/archive/2018/06/the-birth-of-a-new-american-aristocracy/559130/

[97] Obery Hendricks, "The Uncompromising Anti-Capitalism of Martin Luther King Jr.," *Huffington Post*, January 20, 2014. http://www.huffingtonpost.com/obery-m-hendricks-jr-phd/the-uncompromising-anti-capitalism-of-martin-luther-king-jr_b_4629609.html

[98] The Souls of Poor Folk: A Preliminary Report by the Institute of Policy Studies (December 2017): https://poorpeoplescampaign.org/wp-content/uploads/2017/12/PPC-Report-Draft-1.pdf

[99] Krister Stendahl, *Paul Among Jews and Gentiles* (Minneapolis: Fortress Press, 1975).

[100] Ibid.

[101] Brian Blount, *When The Whisper Put on Flesh: New Testament Ethics in an African-American Context* (Minneapolis: Abingdon Press, 2001),122.

[102] Neil Elliott, *The Arrogance of the Nations* (Minneapolis: Fortess Press, 2008.), 72-77. The Greek *dikaiosyne tou thou* usually translated "the righteousness of God."

[103] John Dominic Crossan, *God and Empire: Jesus Against Rome, Then and Now* (New York: Harper-Collins, 2007). Crossan writes that fear and trembling, for followers of Jesus,

comes from a lifestyle of courageous resistance to "the normalcy of civilization"—what I call "the colonial script."

[104] Marcus Borg and John Dominic Crossan, *The Last Week: What the Gospels Really Teach About Jesus' Final Days in Jerusalem* (San Francisco: Harper Collins, 2006).

[105] Walter Wink, *Engaging the Powers* (Minneapolis: Fortress Press, 1992).

[106] Elaine Enns and Ched Myers, *Ambassadors of Reconciliation, Volume I* (Maryknoll, NY: Orbis, 2009).

[107] James Cone, *The Cross and the Lynching Tree* (Maryknoll, NY: Orbis, 2011).

[108] Mark Lewis Taylor, *The Executed God: The Way of the Cross in Lockdown America* (Minneapolis: Augsburg Fortress, 2001), 269.

[109] Ibid.

[110] See the work of Equal Justice Initiative (www.eji.org). EJI released a report "Lynching in America: Confronting the Legacy of Racial Terror" (Third Edition): https://lynchinginamerica.eji.org/report/

[111] Ched Myers, *Who Will Roll Away the Stone* (Maryknoll, NY: Orbis, 1994).

[112] James Perkinson, *Messianism Against Christology: Resistance Movements, Folk Art, Empire* (New York: Palgrave, 2013).

[113] Rufus Burrow Jr., *A Child Shall Lead Them: Martin Luther King Jr., Young People, and the Movement* (Minneapolis: Fortress Press, 2014).

[114] Martin Luther King Jr., *The Atlantic Monthly*, August 1963, "The Negro Is Your Brother," Volume 212, pp 78-88.

[115] Jeanne Theoharis, *The Rebellious Life of Mrs. Rosa Parks* (Boston: Beacon Press, 2013).

[116] Charles Euchner, *Nobody Turn Me Around: A People's History of the 1963 March on Washington* (Boston: Beacon Press, 2011).

[117] Daniel Berrigan, "An Open Letter to the Kampus Krusade," *The Rag*, November 23, 1970.

[118] Amy Goodman, *Democracy Now!: Twenty Years Covering the Movements Changing America* (New York: Simon and Schuster, 2017), 319.

[119] www.rosemarieberger.com

[120] See the documentary *The Trial of the St. Patrick's Four* (2006). http://www.imdb.com/title/tt1095510/

[121] David Leonhardt, Kevin Quealy and Justin Wolfers, "1.5 Million Mission Black Men," *The New York Times*, April 20, 2015.

[122] Michelle Alexander, *The New Jim Crow: Mass Incarceration in the Age of Colorblindness* (New York: The New Press, 2010).

[123] Ibram Kendi, *Stamped From the Beginning* (New York: Nation Books, 2016), 435-438.

[124] Chris Hedges, "The New Slave Revolt," *Common Dreams*, October 11, 2016. http://www.commondreams.org/views/2016/10/11/new-slave-revolt

[125] Michelle Alexander, *The New Jim Crow: Mass Incarceration in the Age of Colorblindness* (New York: The New Press, 2010).

[126] James Perkinson, "Unsettling the Strait: On Listening to Watershed Haints and Living Relatives in Detroit," *On the Edge*, Fall 2015.

[127] Martin Luther King, "Beyond Vietnam," April 4, 1967, Riverside Church, New York City, NY

[128] Ibid.

[129] Michelle Alexander, *The New Jim Crow: Mass Incarceration in the Age of Colorblindness* (New York: The New Press, 2010).

[130] Howard Zinn, *Violence: The Crisis of American Confidence* (1972).

[131] Willie Jennings, "Becoming the Common: Why I Got Arrested in North Carolina," ReligionDispatches.org, June 18, 2013. http://religiondispatches.org/becoming-the-common-why-i-got-arrested-in-north-carolina/

[132] Daniel Berrigan, "An Open Letter to the Kampus Krusade," *The Rag*, November 23, 1970.

[133] www.poorpeoplescampaign.org

[134] Brian Terrell, "Dorothy Day's 'Filthy, Rotten System' Likely Wasn't Hers At All," *National Catholic Reporter*, April 16, 2012. https://www.ncronline.org/news/people/dorothy-days-filthy-rotten-system-likely-wasnt-hers-all

[135] Michelle Alexander, *The New Jim Crow: Mass Incarceration*

in the Age of Colorblindness (New York: The New Press, 2010). See also the earlier work of Loic Waquant, "Deadly Symbiosis: When Ghetto and Prison Meet and Mesh," *Punishment & Society* (London: SAGE Publications, 2001).

[136] Dan Baum, "Legalize It All," *Harper's Magazine*, April 2016. https://harpers.org/archive/2016/04/legalize-it-all/

[137] See the full report on the We The People of Detroit website: https://wethepeopleofdetroit.com/communityresearch/water/; See also, Dana Kornberg, "The Structural Origins of Territorial Stigma: Water and Racial Politics in Metropolitan Detroit, 1950s-2010s," *International Journal of Urban and Regional Research* (Urban Research Publications Limited, 2016).

[138] Ibid.

[139] Report of the National Advisory Commission on Civil Disorders, released February 29, 1968. https://www.ncjrs.gov/pdffiles1/Digitization/8073NCJRS.pdf

[140] Ibid.

[141] Stewart Burns, *To The Mountaintop: Martin Luther King Jr.'s Sacred Mission to Save America: 1955-1968* (San Francisco: Harper Collins, 204), 404-405.

[142] David Smith, "Half Century of Civil Rights Gains Have Stalled or Reversed, Report Finds," *The Guardian*, February 27, 2018.

[143] Martin Luther King Jr. speech delivered on August 28, 1963, Washington D.C. http://www.americanrhetoric.com/speeches/mlkihaveadream.htm

[144] Martin Luther King Jr. speech delivered on September 12, 1962, New York City. https://www.youtube.com/watch?v=k7t35qDYHgc

[145] This clear, simple choice between "community" and "development" was first described to me by Jim Perkinson during a beer tasting on the third-floor of St. Peter's Episcopal Church during the summer of 2015.

[146] adrienne marie brown, *Octavia's Brood: Science Fiction Stories from Social Justice Movements* (AK Press, 2015), 26.

[147] Jennifer Dixon, "Detroiter Sues, Says His Lifelong Home Demolished in Ambush Style Eviction," *Detroit Free Press*, June 18, 2017.

[148] Barbara Reynolds, "I Am Acting in the Name of Martin Luther King," *Chicago Tribune*, January 11, 1976.

[149] MSNBC, "Lean Forward," November 27, 2014. https://www.youtube.com/watch?v=ZIK7aNd80DM

[150] Audre Lorde, "Poetry is not a Luxury," *Sister Outsider* (Freedom, CA: The Crossing Press, 1984), 37.

[151] Ibid.

[152] Kelly Brown-Douglas, *The Black Christ* (Maryknoll, NY: Orbis, 1994), 108-109.

[153] Julianne Hing, "New Report Details Barriers to Black Girls' Success," Colorlines.com, September 25, 2014. http://www.colorlines.com/articles/new-report-details-barriers-black-girls-success

[154] Kali Halloway, "African-American Women Now Top the List of Most-Educated Group in the Country," alternet.org, June 2, 2016. http://www.alternet.org/gender/black-women-most-educated-people-america

[155] Ibram Kendi, *Stamped From the Beginning* (New York: Nation Books, 2016), 439.

[156] Audre Lorde, "Eye to Eye," *Sister Outsider* (Freedom, CA: The Crossing Press, 1984), 146.

[157] Martin Luther King Jr., "I've Been To The Mountaintop," April 3, 1968, Mason Temple, Memphis, TN.

[158] Alice Walker, *Anything We Love Can Be Saved: A Writer's Activism* (New York: Ballantine Books, 1997), 4.

[159] Ibid, 14.

[160] http://www.doctrineofdiscovery.org

[161] Emma Brockes, "Chimamanda Ngozi Adichie: 'Can people please stop telling me feminism is hot?'" *The Guardian*, March 4, 2017. https://www.theguardian.com/books/2017/mar/04/chimamanda-ngozi-adichie-stop-telling-me-feminism-hot

[162] For more, listen to the interview Krista Tippett conducted with Alexander at https://onbeing.org/programs/michelle-alexander-who-we-want-to-become-beyond-the-new-jim-crow/

[163] See Nancy Buirski's documentary *The Rape of Recy Taylor*. http://deadline.com/2017/11/the-rape-of-recy-taylor-documentary-nancy-buirski-the-orchard-1202213408/

[164] Jeanne Theoharis, *A More Beautiful and Terrible History:*

The Uses and Misuses of Civil Rights History (Boston: Beacon Press, 2018), 177-179.

[165] *Double Jeopardy: To Be Black and Female* is the title of a pamphlet written by Frances Beal in 1969.

[166] bell hooks, "Understanding Patriarchy," ImagineNoBorders.org. http://imaginenoborders.org/pdf/zines/UnderstandingPatriarchy.pdf

[167] Jeanne Theoharis, *A More Beautiful and Terrible History: The Uses and Misuses of Civil Rights History* (Boston: Beacon Press, 2018), 155-160.

[168] Ibid, 161-165.

[169] Barbara Ransby, *Ella Baker and The Black Freedom Movement* (University of North Carolina Press, 2003), 129.

[170] Cornel West and Christa Buschendorf, *Black Prophetic Fire* (Boston: Beacon Press, 2014), 96.

[171] bell hooks, *The Will To Change: Men, Masculinity and Love* (New York: Atria Books, 2004).

[172] Thanks to my friend Tim Nafziger for passing along the work of former soldier-turned-pacifist Stan Goff (*Borderline: Reflections on War, Sex and Church*) who builds on the scholarship David J.A. Clines. Tim wrote a wonderful essay for *The Mennonite* reviewing Goff's work and reflecting on his own experience of what it means to be a man growing up in U.S. culture: https://themennonite.org/mennonites-can-learn-jesus-delta-force-veteran/

[173] Kelly Brown-Douglas, *The Black Christ* (Maryknoll, NY: Orbis, 1994), 113-117.

[174] Riane Eisler, *The Chalice and The Blade: Our History, Our Future* (San Francisco: Harper Collins, 1988).

[175] Chimamanda Ngozi Adichie, *We Should All Be Feminists* (New York: Penguin Random House, 2014). Ted Talk: https://www.youtube.com/watch?v=hg3umXU_qWc

[176] For more, see Jyarland's blog at www.harrietspeaks.org.

[177] See the Combahee River Collective Statement (1977) available online at http://circuitous.org/scraps/combahee.html.

[178] Dolores Williams, *Sisters in the Wilderness: The Challenge of Womanist God-Talk* (Maryknoll, NY: Orbis, 1993), 205.

[179] Toi Marie Smith, Facebook post, July 29, 2017. Check out

her writing at www.toimarie.com.

[180] "What The (Bleep) Happened to Hip-Hop" was a 2015 collaboration between Shamako Noble, the Executive Director of Hip Hop Congress, and Move To Amend, a grassroots organization working to amend the Constitution to "end corporate rule and legalize democracy." See www.movetoamend.org.

[181] James McClendon, *Doctrine: Systematic Theology, Volume II* (Nashville: Abingdon Press, 1994).

[182] George Marsden, *Fundamentalism and American Culture: The Shaping of Twentieth Century Evangelicalism, 1870-1925* (Oxford University Press, 1982),

[183] Cornel West and Christa Buschendorf, *Black Prophetic Fire* (Boston: Beacon Press, 2014), 76.

[184] Arundhati Roy, "Capitalism: A Ghost Story," *Outlook India*, March 26, 2012. http://www.outlookindia.com/magazine/story/capitalism-a-ghost-story/280234

[185]

https://reaganlibrary.archives.gov/archives/speeches/1986/1188 6a.htm

[186] Justin Gomer and Scott Petrella, "Reagan Used MLK Day to Undermine Racial Justice," *Boston Review*, January 15, 2017.

[187] Jeanne Theoharis, *A More Beautiful and Terrible History: The Uses and Misuses of Civil Rights History* (Boston: Beacon Press, 2018), 178.

[188] http://www.huffingtonpost.com/marlo-thomas/the-fierce-urgency-of-now_1_b_3805600.html

[189] Neal Conan, "The Story of King's Beyond Vietnam Speech," National Public Radio, March 30, 2010. https://www.npr.org/templates/story/story.php?storyId=125355 148

[190] Jeanne Theoharis, *A More Beautiful and Terrible History: The Uses and Misuses of Civil Rights History* (Boston: Beacon Press, 2018), ix-x.

[191] Ched Myers, *Binding The Strong Man* (Maryknoll, NY: Orbis, 1988), p.11.

[192] Ignacio Ellacuría and Jon Sobrino *Systematic Theology: Perspectives from Liberation Theology* (New York: Orbis

Books, 1993).

[193] Jon Sobrino, *The Principle of Mercy: Taking the Crucified People from the Cross* (Maryknoll, NY: Orbis, 1994).

[194] Kelly Brown-Douglas, *Stand Your Ground: Black Bodies and the Justice of God* (Maryknoll, NY: Orbis, 2015), 190-196.

[195] Paul Ortiz, *An African-American and Latinx History of the United States* (Boston: Beacon Press, 2018), 12.

[196] Martin Luther King Jr., "Remaining Awake Through a Great Revolution," March 31, 1968, Washington D.C., sermon at the National Cathedral.

[197] Ta-Nehisi Coates, "My President Was Black," *The Atlantic Magazine*, January/February 2017. https://www.theatlantic.com/magazine/archive/2017/01/my-president-was-black/508793/

[198] Amy Traub, *The Asset Value of Whiteness: Understanding the Racial Wealth Gap* (Demos.org, 2017). http://www.demos.org/sites/default/files/publications/Asset%20 Value%20of%20Whiteness.pdf

[199] Peter Coy, "The Real Reason Whites are Richer than Blacks," *Bloomberg*, February 8, 2017. https://www.bloomberg.com/news/articles/2017-02-08/the-big-reason-whites-are-richer-than-blacks-in-america

[200] Jeanne Theoharis, *A More Beautiful and Terrible History: The Uses and Misuses of Civil Rights History* (Boston: Beacon Press, 2018), xiii.

[201] Michael Eric Dyson, *I May Not Get There With You: The True Martin Luther King Jr.* (New York: Simon and Schuster, 2000), 29.

[202] Michelle Alexander, *The New Jim Crow* (New York: The New Press), 244.

[203] Mark Leviton, "Dangerous Love," *The Sun Magazine*, Issue 466. http://thesunmagazine.org/issues/466/dangerous_love?page=3

[204] James Perkinson, "Unsettling Whiteness: Refocusing Christian Theology on Its Own Indigenous Roots," *Wrongs to Rights: How Churches Can Engage the U.N. Declaration on the Rights of Indigenous Peoples* (Mennonite Church Canada, 2016).

[205] Ibid.

206 Kim Redigan, "The Violence of White Silence: As Sick As Our Secrets," a reflection given at First Unitarian-Universalist Church, Detroit, Nov. 27, 2016. https://radicaldiscipleship.net/2016/12/22/the-violence-of-white-silence-as-sick-as-our-secrets/

207 Lily Mendoza, "Healing Historical Trauma: Ethnoautobiography as Decolonizing Practice" (Transcript of public talk delivered at the Graduate Center, University of Pretoria, August 16, 2016).

208 Ibid.

209 Joshua Rothman, "The Origins of Privilege," *The New Yorker*, May 12, 2014.

210 For more, see Catherine's book *Living Into God's Dream: Dismantling Racism in America* (New York: Morehouse Publishing, 2016).

211 For more, see www.idlenomore.ca

212 Keeanga-Yamahtta Taylor. *How We Get Free: Black Feminism and the Combahee River Collective* (Chicago: Haymarket Books, 2017), 12.

213 Ibram Kendi, *Stamped From the Beginning* (New York: Nation Books, 2016), 503-511.

214 Walter Wink, *Engaging the Powers* (Minneapolis: Fortress Press, 1992), 314.

215 W. E. Burghardt Du Bois, *The Journal of Race Development,* Vol. 7, No. 4 (Apr., 1917), pp. 434-447.

216 D.H. Dilbeck, *Frederick Douglass: American Prophet* (Chapel Hill: UNC Press, 2018), 66.

217 Bill Wylie-Kellermann, *Principalities in Particular* (Minneapolis: Fortress Press, 2017), 41. "A politically informed

exorcism" was what theologian William Stringfellow called the Catonsville action.

218218 Daniel Berrigan, *The Trial of the Catonsville Nine* (University of Fordham Press, 2004). http://ada.evergreen.edu/~arunc/texts/catonsvilleEdited.pdf

219 Michael Bader, "When Progressive Leaders Burn Out, We All Lose," *Psychology Today*, February 19, 2012.

220 Brene Brown, *Braving the Wilderness: The Quest for True Belonging and the Courage to Stand Alone* (New York: Random

House, 2017).

[221] James Douglass, *Resistance and Contemplation: The Way of Liberation* (Garden City, NY: Doubleday and Company, 1972), 46.

[222] Ibid., 55.

[223] Michelle Alexander, *The New Jim Crow: Mass Incarceration in the Age of Colorblindness* (New York: The New Press, 2010).

[224] William Stringfellow, *Essential Writings* (Maryknoll, NY: Orbis, 2013); Walter Wink, *Engaging the Powers* (Minneapolis: Fortress Press, 1992); Bill Wylie-Kellermann, *Principalities in Particular* (Minneapolis: Fortress Press, 2017).

[225] Jordan Kisner, "The Politics of Conspicuous Displays of Self-Care," *The New Yorker*, March 14, 2017.

[226] Thomas Merton, *Gandhi on Non-Violence* (New Directions Publishing, 1964), 31.

[227] James Douglass, *Resistance and Contemplation: The Way of Liberation* (Garden City, NY: Doubleday and Company, 1972), 5.

[228] Walter Wink, *Engaging the Powers* (Minneapolis: Fortress Press, 1992), 61-63.

[229] Elaine Enns and Ched Myers, *Ambassadors of Reconciliation, Volume I* (Maryknoll, NY: Orbis, 2011).

[230] Ched Myers, *Who Will Roll Away The Stone: Discipleship Queries for First World Christians* (Maryknoll, NY: Orbis, 1994), 100-108.

[231] Ibid.

[232] Rene Girard, *The Scapegoat* (Baltimore: Johns Hopkins Press, 1989).

[233] Dietrich Bonhoeffer, *The Cost of Discipleship* (New York: Touchstone, 1995).

[234] Tim McKee, "The Geography of Sorrow: Francis Weller on Navigating Our Losses," *The Sun Magazine*, October 2015. http://thesunmagazine.org/issues/478/the_geography_of_sorrow

[235] Ched Myers, *Who Will Roll Away The Stone: Discipleship Queries for First World Christians* (Maryknoll, NY: Orbis, 1994).

[236] This rhythm of naming grief and gratitude is the daily Ignatian practice of Examen. For more, check out the wonderful book *Sleeping With Bread* (1995) by Dennis, Sheila

and Matthew Linn.

[237] Edwin Friedman, *Failure of Nerve: Leadership in the Age of the Quick Fix* (Seabury Press, 1999), 1.

[238] Tim McKee, "The Geography of Sorrow," *The Sun Magazine* October 2015. http://thesunmagazine.org/issues/478/the_geography_of_sorrow

[239] Walter Wink, *Just Jesus: My Struggle to Become Human* (Image Books, 2012).

[240] David Steindl-Rast, *Gratefulness, The Heart of Prayer: An Approach to Life in Fullness* (Ramsey, NJ: Paulist Press, 1984).

[241] Eckhart Tolle, *The Power of Now: A Guide to Spiritual Enlightenment* (Novato, CA: New World Press, 1999), 112-119.

[242] John Main, *The Present Christ: Further Steps in Meditation* (New York: The Crossroad Publishing Company, 1986).

[243] Melodie Beattie, *The Language of Letting Go* (Center City, MN: Hazelden, 1990).

[244] Nayirrah Waheed, *Salt* (self-published, 2013), 133.

[245] Richard Rohr, *Falling Upward: Spirituality for the Two Halves of Life* (San Francisco: Jossey-Bass, 2011).

[246] Gerald May, *Addiction and Grace: Love and Spirituality in the Healing of Addictions* (New York: HarperCollins, 1988).

[247] Ibid.

[248] Wes Howard-Brook, "John's Gospel Call to be Reborn of God," in *The New Testament—Introducing the Way of Discipleship*, ed Wes Howard-Brook and Sharon Ringe (Maryknoll, NY: Orbis, 2002), 94. See also Wes' *Becoming Children of God: John's Gospel and Radical Discipleship* (Maryknoll, NY: Orbis, 1994).

[249] Gerald May, *Addiction and Grace: Love and Spirituality in the Healing of Addictions* (New York: HarperCollins, 1988).

[250] Gabor Mate, *In the Realm of Hungry Ghosts: Close Encounters with Addiction* (Berkeley: North Atlantic Books, 2008).

[251] James Baldwin, *Notes of a Native Son* (Boston: Beacon Press, 1955), 174.

[252] Brene Brown, *Braving the Wilderness: The Quest for True Belonging and the Courage to Stand Alone* (New York: Random House, 2017).

[253] Audre Lorde, "Uses of the Erotic: The Erotic as Power,"

Sister Outsider (Freedom, CA: The Crossing Press, 1984), 53-59.

[254] Ibid, 56.

[255] Ibid, 57.

[256] Brene Brown, *Braving the Wilderness: The Quest for True Belonging and the Courage to Stand Alone* (New York: Random House, 2017).

[257] Anna Clark, *The Poisoned City: Flint's Water and the American Urban Tragedy* (New York: Metropolitan Books, 2018).

[258] Curt Guyette, "A Deep Dive into the Source of Flint's Water Crisis," *Detroit Metro Times*, April 19, 2017.

[259] Michael Gerstein, "Snyder Commission: Racism Played Role in Flint Crisis," *The Detroit News*, February 17, 2017. http://www.detroitnews.com/story/news/michigan/flint-water-crisis/2017/02/17/flint-report/98058024/

[260] Anna Clark, *The Poisoned City: Flint's Water and the American Urban Tragedy* (New York: Metropolitan Books, 2018).

[261] Ibid.

[262] Ched Myers, "The Rich Man and Lazarus: Warning Tale and Interpretive Key to Luke," RadicalDiscipleship.net, September 22, 2016. https://radicaldiscipleship.net/2016/09/22/the-rich-man-and-lazarus-warning-tale-and-interpretive-key-to-luke/

[263] Wes Howard-Brook, *The New Testament—Introducing the Way of Discipleship* (Maryknoll, NY: Orbis, 2002), 192-193.

[264] Martin Luther King Jr., *Strength to Love* (Philadelphia: Fortress Press, 1963), 45-48.

[265] James McClendon, *Systematic Theology, Volume II: Doctrine* (Nashville, TN: Abingdon Press, 1994).

[266] James Perkinson, *Messianism Against Christology: Resistance Movements, Folk Art, Empire* (New York: Palgrave, 2013), 28-37.

[267] Elaine Enns and Ched Myers, *The Ambassadors of Reconciliation, Volume I* (Maryknoll, NY: Orbis, 2009).

[268] N.T. Wright, *Jesus and the Victory of God* (Philadelphia: Fortress Press, 1996).

[269] Vincent Harding, *There is a River: The Black Struggle For Freedom in America* (Orlando: Harcourt Brace, 1981).

[270] Elizabeth Alexander, *The Light of the World: A Memoir* (New York: Grand Central Publishing, 2016). See Alexander's April 2013 speech " 'Don't Forget to Feed the Loas:' Near Ancestry in Contemporary Black Arts" at Princeton University: http://aas.princeton.edu/event/toni-morrison-lectures-by-professor-elizabeth-alexander/

[271] Derrick Jensen, "Saving the Indigenous Soul: An Interview with Martin Prechtel," *The Sun Magazine*, April 2001. http://thesunmagazine.org/issues/304/saving_the_indigenous_s oul

[272] Martin Prechtel, *The Smell of Rain on Dust: Grief and Praise* (Berkeley: North Atlantic Books, 2015).

[273] Rick Warren, *The Purpose Driven Life* (Grand Rapids: Zondervan, 2002).

[274] William Herzog, *Parables as Subversive Speech* (Louisville, KY: Westminister/John Knox Press, 1994).

[275] See Bayo Akomolafe, *These Wilds Beyond Our Fences* (Berkeley, CA: North Atlantic Books, 2017), 12-26.

[276] Mark Leviton, "Dangerous Love: Rev. Lynice Pinkard On the Revolutionary Act of Living the Gospels," *The Sun Magazine*, October 2014. http://thesunmagazine.org/issues/466/dangerous_love?page=3

[277] Ched Myers, *Binding the Strong Man: A Political Reading of Mark's Story of Jesus* (Maryknoll, NY: Orbis, 1988).

[278] Kelly Brown-Douglas, *Stand Your Ground: Black Bodies and The Justice of God* (Maryknoll, NY: Orbis, 2015), 188.

[279] Martin Luther King Jr., "I've Seen the Promised Land" Mason Temple Church (Memphis, Tennessee), April 3, 1968.

[280] Jonathan Wilson, *Living Faithfully in a Fragmented World: Lessons for the Church from MacIntyre's "After Virtue"* (Harrisburg, PA: Trinity Press, 1997).

[281] Martin Luther King Jr., "Beyond Vietnam" speech delivered to Riverside Church, New York City, April 4, 1967. http://kingencyclopedia.stanford.edu/encyclopedia/documentsen try/doc_beyond_vietnam/

[282] James Cone, *Martin and Malcolm and America: A Dream or a Nightmare* (Maryknoll, NY: Orbis Books, 1991).

[283] Martin Luther King Jr., "Beyond Vietnam" speech delivered to Riverside Church, New York City, April 4, 1967. http://kingencyclopedia.stanford.edu/encyclopedia/documentsentry/doc_beyond_vietnam/

[284] Rev. Nick Peterson has been a vital conversation partner on this issue.

[285] I never came close to qualifying for Boston. But in 2012, I joined an intimate relay to illegally substitute for my injured and pregnant sister-in-law, Kristen. I legitimated it, though, because she qualified eight months earlier to honor her father who was struck down by pancreatic cancer.

[286] Martin Luther King Jr., "A Christmas Sermon on Peace" December 24, 1967, Ebenezer Baptist Church, Atlanta, GA.

[287] Charles Mohr, "Marchers Exhorted to Go After 'Deferred Dreams,'" *New York Times*, August 28, 1988.

[288] "Pennsylvania Coal Company To Open Second Mine Since Trump Took Office," Fox News, August 20, 2017. http://www.foxnews.com/politics/2017/08/20/pennsylvania-coal-company-to-open-second-mine-since-trump-took-office.html

[289] Lorraine Anderson, *Sisters of the Earth: Woman's Prose and Poetry About Nature* (New York: Vintage Books, 2003), 392.

[290] Frances Fitzgerald, *The Evangelicals: The Struggle to Shape America* (New York: Simon and Schuster, 2017), 203-204.

[291] Jonathan Merritt, "Eugene Peterson On Changing His Mind About Same-Sex Issues and Marriage," Religion News Service, July 13, 2017. http://religionnews.com/2017/07/12/eugene-peterson-on-changing-his-mind-about-same-sex-issues-and-marriage/

[292] Kameelah Janan Rasheed, "Stakes Is High—And Black Lives Are Worthy of Elaboration," June 7, 2014. http://gawker.com/stakes-is-high-and-black-lives-are-worthy-of-elaboratio-1587471910

[293] James McClendon, *Systematic Theology, Volume III: Witness* (Nashville: Abingdon Press, 2000).

[294] Bayo Akomolafe, *These Wilds Beyond Our Fences* (Berkeley, CA: North Atlantic Books, 2017), 250.

[295] Rufus Burrow, *Martin Luther King and the Theology of Resistance* (Jefferson, NC: McFarland and Co., 2014), 82.

[296] Ibid.

Notes

90200800R00168

Made in the USA
Middletown, DE
20 September 2018